More Praise for *New Trading Dimensions*

"Bill is one of the truly brilliant educators in the field of trading. In this new book, he gives the novice as well as the professional trader new insights into the true workings of the stock, bond, and commodity markets. The book should be in the trading arsenal of every trader who wishes to find a unique approach to the markets."

George A. Fontanills
Author, *The Options Course*
President, Global Investment Management Corp.
and Pinnacle Investments of America, Inc.

"I have known Bill Williams for over eight years and have watched his approach to trading Chaos develop through those years. I believe he has an approach that ANY trader would be wise to investigate. Bill has the uncanny ability to make the complex simple by 'breaking it down' into digestible pieces, allowing the 'mouse' (the average trading student) to eat the 'elephant' (the chaos theory) one bite at a time."

Joe Krutsinger
CTA and Author of *The Trading Systems Toolkit*
and *Trading Systems: Secrets of the Masters*

"Bill Williams is one of the most creative innovators in the commod-
ty trading arena. He has taught me, as well as thousands of his stu-
ents, a great deal about trading commodities, and I have always
und his material to be consistent, readable, and easy to understand.
w Trading Dimensions is no exception. It is a vital work which
rits everyone's attention."

Ted Tesser
Certified Public Accountant
President, Waterside Financial Services, Inc.
Author, *Trader's Tax Survival Guide*

NEW TRADING DIMENSIONS

WILEY TRADING ADVANTAGE

Trading without Fear / Richard W. Arms, Jr.
Neural Network: Time Series Forecasting of Financial Markets / E. Michael Azoff
Option Market Making / Alan J. Baird
Money Management Strategies for Futures Traders / Nauzer J. Balsara
Genetic Algorithms and Investment Strategies / Richard Bauer
Seasonality: Systems, Strategies & Signals / Jacob Bernstein
Managed Futures: An Investor's Guide / Beverly Chandler
Beyond Technical Analysis / Tushar Chande
The New Technical Trader / Tushar Chande and Stanley S. Kroll
Trading on the Edge / Guido J. Deboeck
Trading the Plan / Robert Deel
The New Science of Technical Analysis / Thomas R. DeMark
Point and Figure Charting / Thomas J. Dorsey
Trading for a Living / Dr. Alexander Elder
Study Guide for Trading for a Living / Dr. Alexander Elder
The Day Trader's Manual / William F. Eng
The Options Course: High Profit & Low Stress Trading Methods / George A. Fontanills
The Options Workbook / George A. Fontanills
Analyzing and Forecasting Futures Prices / Anthony F. Herbst
Technical Analysis of the Options Markets / Richard Hexton
Pattern, Price & Time: Using Gann Theory in Trading Systems / James A. Hyerczyk
Profits from Natural Resources: How to Make Big Money Investing in Energy, Food & Metals / Roland A. Jansen
New Commodity Trading Systems & Methods / Perry Kaufman
Understanding Options / Robert Kolb
The Intuitive Trader / Robert Koppel
McMillan on Options / Lawrence G. McMillan
Trading on Expectations / Brendan Moynihan
Intermarket Technical Analysis / John J. Murphy
Forecasting Financial Markets, 3rd Edition / Mark J. Powers and Mark G. Castelino
Neural Networks in the Capital Markets / Paul Refenes
Cybernetic Trading Strategies / Murray A. Ruggiero, Jr.
The Option Advisor: Wealth-Building Techniques Using Equity and Index Options / Bernie G. Schaeffer
Gaming the Market / Ronald B. Shelton
Option Strategies, 2nd Edition / Courtney Smith
Trader Vic II: Principles of Professional Speculation / Victor Sperandeo
Campaign Trading / John Sweeney
The Trader's Tax Survival Guide, Revised / Ted Tesser
The Mathematics of Money Management / Ralph Vince
Portfolio Management Formulas / Ralph Vince
The New Money Management: A Framework for Asset Allocation / Ralph Vince
Trading Applications of Japanese Candlestick Charting / Gary Wagner and Brad Matheny
Trading Chaos: Applying Expert Techniques to Maximize Your Profits / Bill Williams
New Trading Dimensions: How to Profit from Chaos in Stocks, Bonds, and Commodities / Bill Williams

NEW TRADING DIMENSIONS

How to Profit from Chaos in Stocks, Bonds, and Commodities

BILL WILLIAMS, PhD

JOHN WILEY & SONS, INC.

New York • Chichester • Weinheim • Brisbane • Singapore • Toronto

The NFA requires us to state that, "HYPOTHETICAL OR SIMULATED PERFORMANCE RESULTS HAVE CERTAIN INHERENT LIMITATIONS. UNLIKE AN ACTUAL PERFORMANCE RECORD, SIMULATED RESULTS DO NOT REPRESENT ACTUAL TRADING. ALSO, SINCE THE TRADES HAVE NOT ACTUALLY BEEN EXECUTED, THE RESULTS MAY HAVE UNDER-OR-OVER COMPENSATED FOR THE IMPACT, IF ANY, OF CERTAIN MARKET FACTORS, SUCH AS LACK OF LIQUIDITY. SIMULATED TRADING PROGRAMS IN GENERAL ARE ALSO SUBJECT TO THE FACT THAT THEY ARE DESIGNED WITH THE BENEFIT OF HINDSIGHT. NO REPRESENTATION IS BEING MADE THAT ANY ACCOUNT WILL OR IS LIKELY TO ACHIEVE PROFITS OR LOSSES SIMILAR TO THOSE SHOWN."

This book is printed on acid-free paper. ♾

Published by John Wiley & Sons, Inc.

Published simultaneously in Canada.

Library of Congress Cataloging-in-Publication Data:

Williams, Bill, 1932–
New trading dimensions : how to profit from chaos in stocks, bonds, and commodities / Bill Williams.
p. cm–(Wiley trading advantage)
Includes index.
ISBN 0-471-29541-8 (cloth : alk. paper)
1. Futures. 2. Stocks. 3. Bonds. 4. Commodity futures.
I. Title. II. Series.
HG6024.A3W536 1998
332.63′2–dc21 98-3765

Printed in the United States of America.

10 9 8 7 6 5 4 3

This work is dedicated to a young professional trader
who will someday soon become world famous for her
efforts and skills:
Justine Gregory-Williams
who is not only a great trader and a brilliant teacher,
but who is also my youngest daughter.
Justine constructed many of the illustrations used in this book.

ACKNOWLEDGMENTS

One of the greatest of all joys in succeeding at any endeavor is the chance to share that success with others. When those others then contribute to your further success—it just doesn't get much better.

I would like to thank some people who are very special to me. They are special not only because of what they have done but, even more, because of what they mean to me. This book would have never been possible without the unselfish sacrifices made by the entire staff at the Profitunity Trading Group.

I cannot begin to cover all the people who have made direct contributions to my life and the success of our company. Ours has been a most blessed existence due to the encouragement and enlightenment given to us by our colleagues and our friends in this business. Thanks: To Commodity Quote Graphics, who, through the years, continued to increase their support of our ideas and made them available on their software. To Tim Slater, who sent me around the world and sponsored my work that others might profit from it. To Thom Hartle, editor of *Technical Analysis of Stocks and Commodities* magazine, for resonating with our ideas and generating nuances from them. To Ron Michaelson and Blake Conover, for their unswerving support in making this material available to a wider audience than would otherwise have received it. To Joel Robbins, who published our first fledgling efforts of sharing. To Rick Boerke and Mike Boren, who have to be the best two brokers in the world. To Chris Myers, who supported this work decades ago when we once gave a workshop and only two people attended and who now is responsible for and takes the financial risk involved in getting information to the public. To Pamela van Geissen, my editor, who absolutely proves that dynamite comes in small packages. Again, to all of you who have attended my private tutorials, thanks for your thanks—you have made my life better than I ever dreamed it could be.

My thanks also to Georgina Perez, who brightens our lives every day.

It is an indescribable pleasure to be able to work with these people and share not only our days and our ambitions but also our deep love and caring for each other. It is difficult for me to imagine a better or more desirable life. I thank you all.

My first book was dedicated to my wife, who not only stood by me in the good times but was also able to make the bad times fun. Thanks again, Ellen; I love you more every day!

And last, and never to be left out of my gratitude and affection, are all of you who have studied with us and shared our life and our home in the private tutorials. My fondest wish is that my contribution to your life might someday match what you have already given to mine. I will never forget you for making that old saying—"When you teach, you learn twice"—so true for me.

CONTENTS

INTRODUCTION

WOULD YOU LIKE TO KNOW WHAT I KNOW ABOUT YOU?

How presumptuous can I get? What do I know about you? Quite a lot, actually. I have been actively trading and working with traders for over 40 years. During that time, I have conducted workshops for over 25,000 traders. In private tutorials here in our trading room, I have trained over 700 individuals to become successful speculators. From that experience, this is what I know about you:

1. You are in the top 10 percent, intelligence wise, of the entire population. That's where new and inquiring speculators can be found. This field attracts open-minded, adventurous, ambitious, and highly intelligent people. Because I know that about you, let me thank you here and now for the honor you are giving me by reading this book. That is not all I know about you. There is more.
2. You have already been successful in some form of business and/or profession. It is extremely rare for someone just out of high school or college to be seriously interested in a life of speculation. You have already proven yourself in some way, and now you are looking for a better, more profitable, more rewarding endeavor that can enrich your life not only with money but with experience, adventure, and satisfaction. Again, I am pleased that someone with your talent and background is visiting my material. But wait, there is still more I know about you.

3. You have been successful in accumulating excess capital that you are considering risking in the markets. I assume this is true because I know of no brokers who would open an account on a Visa or Mastercard. So, welcome, my new friend, to potentially the most profitable, fun-filled, and fascinating adventure of your life.

Those are just some of your outstanding qualities. I am sure there are many more. One of the purposes of this book is to help you get in touch with those qualities and use them for fun and profit in the markets. There is at least one more thing that I know about you:

If the answers you have been seeking
could be found in the places
you have been looking,
you would not be reading this.

So let me congratulate you on more than your membership in an elite group who have the three qualifications above. Even though you haven't found the answers you have been seeking, let me welcome you. My job in this material is to make "the" answers become "your" answers.

WHY WE LOSE IN THE MARKETS: OUR HYPNOTIC TRANCE

From over 40 years of experience in active and successful trading, I can anticipate some of the first questions you want to ask:

1. What do I have to do to win consistently?
2. Why do I lose?

The most likely problem is that you are lost. *You are using the wrong logic maps.* You are using what you have been taught to use or what has worked for you in the past in business and/or a profession. But now, despite all your efforts, background, and intelligence, you are losing. What you are really searching for is a kind of Holy Grail. You have come to the right place! There is a Holy Grail and I am more than happy to share it with you. It is simple and easy, and you only have to remember five simple words:

Want what the market wants.

There it is—one of the key answers you have been searching for. Can it be that simple and easy? Sure! It is the number one commandment of trading, and if you abide by it you will never have to seek help elsewhere. But therein lies the problem; in fact, there are two separate problems:

1. How can I know what the market wants?
2. How can I convince myself to want what the market wants?

The first answer is much easier than the second. This book answers both questions.

HOW TO READ/STUDY THIS MATERIAL

If you are in a great hurry, have considerable trading experience, and are unwilling to muddle through the philosophy behind this approach, you might want to skip the early part of this book, go directly to Chapter Three, and begin learning this profit-producing strategy.

If (and I hope this is true) you are a person who wants to know as much as possible about everything you do, I suggest you read through this book from beginning to end before taking any action. Then I suggest that you reread it slowly and thoughtfully, taking notes on those parts that seem to apply specifically to you. You will find that each time you go over a particular section, you will learn something different. Not because it was hidden on the first read; rather, it is different because you are different. The old saw, "When the student is ready, the teacher will come," is absolutely true. The teacher in this case is not me but the universe.

Einstein was once asked: "What is the most important question we could ever ask?" He replied: "The most important question you could ever ask is: 'Is the universe a friendly place?'" Think about that. Is the market a friendly place for you? It should be; it can be. This book will take you through it step by step. It will take you out of the losing trance you might be in and introduce you to a number of trance-ending experiences. You will find these experiences simple and enlightening.

OUR PLAN OF ACTION

This material is organized to begin with a basic overview of the market and of how a speculator's life can be. This is followed by a rather basic explanation of the new Science of Chaos and how it affects your everyday life and your ventures in the market. Next, we will spend six chapters on what the market is attempting to communicate about itself. Finally, we will sum up with more material on how *we* can change to become best friends with the market and enjoy our game of trading. We will also explore how to make this material easier to trade through new and advanced software and our own Investor's Dream™ software, which does three things:

1. Takes the errors out of analysis (eliminates mistakes).
2. Points out all the opportunities.
3. Makes your job doable in minutes each day.

For this material to be meaningful to you, you need to know where I am coming from and what my basic assumptions are. If you were to ask me to state some of the most important concepts I have acquired in 40+ years of active trading, I would answer that the most basic assumption is that what we all trade in the markets has little to do with price and time.

We all trade our basic belief systems.

That's right, I mean *all* of us. Whether we are trading extremely small amounts, pension plan funds, bank funds, corporations, institutional funds, or countries, we all trade our own belief systems. From our point of view, the markets are not economic, fundamental, technical, or mechanical—the markets are *behavioral*. The markets are composites of all the different traders with all their different time frames, different backgrounds, different amounts of capital, and very different goals. That's why, on some days, the markets appear very human and have temper tantrums, get confused, become moody, and are wide awake, while on other days they are napping most of the time. We can make some interesting analogies between individual behavior (yours and mine) and that of the market.

THE BASIC BUSINESS OF THE MARKET

The basic mission of the market is to *communicate*—to communicate your desires to the market, and to communicate back to you, and to the world, whether those desires produce a profit or a loss for you. There are three underlying principles of individual communication that you need to understand in order to really see what the market is doing below the surface. These principles not only apply to the market; they also reflect our personal everyday communications. These three principles are:

1. *Ninety percent of everything that you hear is lies.* As an individual, what comes out of your mouth is usually not what is going on in your "twin-hemispheric necktop" computer. You modify your communications according to your expectations of the receivers. The same is true with the market. Ninety percent of what you hear and/or read about the market is not true, in the sense that it does not accurately describe the underlying behavior of the market.
2. *You cannot lie.* At first, this may seem a contradiction to the first principle, but we are talking in terms of total human communication. Whenever you tell less than the truth, there are physiological changes that happen in your body: tremors, a slight tilt of the head, an unconscious raising of an eyebrow, and so on. That is the principle of the polygraph (lie detector). It taps into some of these nonverbal channels, and if they don't match the verbal channels, your statement or answer to a question is considered a lie. The market acts the same. It always tells the truth and it is usually on some nonobvious channel.
3. *You can only talk about yourself.* If I say "This room is warm," that is not a statement about the room; it is a statement about the status of my nervous system at this moment. This is true in the market also: the market can only talk about itself. When we begin to understand the underlying structure of the market and its language, our actions in the market get much more accurate, precise, and profitable.

The basic makeup of the market is quite similar to your own makeup. As you begin to understand one better, you automagically understand the other better. That's why trading with the proper attitude is probably the most efficient learning and growth experience you could have.

HOW THIS BOOK IS ORGANIZED

I have included in this material what I have learned in decades of trading, in teaching tens of thousands of traders in workshops, and, more specifically, in interacting with the 700+ people who have studied privately in our own trading room. I have seen many persons turn their lives completely around for the better. I have seen many move up to a lifestyle that they never thought would be possible for them. I have seen marital relationships get better when trading improves. I have also seen some failures and have spent a great deal of time trying to understand why some succeed so spectacularly while others can't seem to match that performance.

I have used all that I have learned in eliminating the superficial and unproductive parts and have concentrated on only those techniques that have proven their worth in a variety of national and international commodity and stock markets.

Here is a brief map of the journey you and I will take together in this book.

Chapter One is a further introduction to this business of speculation and the essential elements you need in order to understand why the markets do what they do.

Chapter Two is a practical (not too technical) explanation of the Science of Chaos and how to view it in your everyday life and speculation.

Chapter Three begins our own proprietary methods of analyzing and taking profits from the markets. We call it the Alligator.

Chapter Four explains and demonstrates our first trading dimension, the fractal.

Chapter Five explains and demonstrates our second trading dimension—the Awesome Oscillator. This is comparable to reading tomorrow's *Wall Street Journal.*

Chapter Six explains and demonstrates our third trading dimension—the Momentum Accelerator/Decelerator. This is comparable to reading the day after tomorrow's *Wall Street Journal.*

Chapter Seven explains and demonstrates trading in "the Zone"—how to maximize your return on investment (ROI) once you have positioned yourself correctly in the market.

Chapter Eight explains and demonstrates trading the Balance Line between the Strange Attractors.

Chapter Nine explains and demonstrates how to take profits and when to get out of trades.

Chapter Ten is a review of all signals (with examples and practice pages) to make sure you understand this approach before putting your money on it.

Chapter Eleven returns to the psychology of trading and how to use speculation to enhance your entire life, not just your activity in the markets.

I will also give you access, on the Internet, to our proprietary software, which automagically ferrets out all of the five dimensional signals and lets you practice bar by bar on your own. I will make sure you understand our latest developments.

So, once again, welcome to your next wonderfully enlightening and profitable journey of learning more about who you are and what this world is all about.

NEW TRADING DIMENSIONS

1

BLASTING OFF

In the market:
honesty Is power,
simplicity Is energy,
and innocence Is ability.

You are standing in the airport terminal of Your Life, and the jet plane departing for the 21st century is about to take off. You must make a choice: Do you remain in the terminal, eating the stale vending-machine food of outmoded thinking? Or do you get on the plane and soar into the stratosphere of trading computerization, swept along by the jet stream of evolving technology? Do you enjoy the in-flight snack of virtually unlimited information access, secure in the knowledge that when you encounter the inevitable turbulence of rapid market fluctuations, you are holding, in this book, the "automatic pilot" of expert advice and guidance?

That is the vision of tomorrow that I am offering you. Let's explore together this amazing new cyberworld of science and trading. If you don't know about these latest advances in science and trading, have no fear. I'm not going to bombard you with technical gobbledygook. I'm going to present you with simple, practical, well-organized, easy-to-understand information and guidance. If you are ready to travel to places you have never been before, let's queue up.

Our goal in this chapter is to understand how our personal biases determine whether we become consistent winners or chronic losers. If you are a type A++ trader, you may be tempted to go directly to Chapter Three and begin to use our energetic and trading dimensions immediately. Instead, I recommend that you study this material from the beginning. I believe that understanding the underlying structure of trading is imperative if you hope to reach your potential in trading for profits. Let's begin our journey of understanding by looking at one of the most important underlying aspects of all markets—and, actually, of any endeavor we select.

CONTENT VERSUS PROCESS

Suppose that you are a space traveler. You have just landed from a faraway planet, and you find yourself in a room where a chess set has been arranged on a table. You want to understand exactly what is going on in this strange Earth. You examine the chess pieces individually and notice that there are several different shapes and sizes. You want to really understand, so you do an "electron analysis" of each individual piece. You know the exact location, size, and makeup of each piece. You thoroughly understand the makeup and the content of the entire set. But unless and until you understand the *process* of playing chess, you will never understand the game and its significance will be lost on you.

In over four decades of observing traders and trading, I have come to the conclusion that most traders approach the market with the same orientation as our fictitious space traveler. Both are primarily concerned with content as opposed to process. Our space traveler will never understand the game of chess until he observes two people playing and competing against each other. This is not necessarily bad; it just doesn't have a great payoff. We traders do it with each other when we ask:

- How much did you make this month?
- Did you go long the gold?
- What kind of car do you drive?
- Will you show me your P&L statements?
- Can you give me someone who is using your approach profitably?
- Did you know that this market is heavily oversold?

All the above examples center on content rather than process. Both my scientific background and my experience in trading have convinced me that the primary difference between winners and losers is whether they focus on content or process.

ENDING YOUR STRUGGLE AND DANCING WITH THE MARKET

Most guys had this happen in high school. You ask a pretty girl to go to a dance and she accepts. Now you are in trouble! You fear you will make a fool of yourself dancing and not only will she never speak to you again, but she will tell all the other girls in the school that you are a klutz. You practice with your little sister and your cousin before the date. When you get to the dance, you are determined to make the dancing work. *You try hard* to be a better dancer than you really are (you are content-oriented). But because you try so hard, you end up stepping all over your partner's feet. Your life is ruined; you were never meant to be anything but an other-handed klutz.

If you could have only relaxed and become a bit more process-oriented, you could have pulled your partner close to you, she could have felt your movements, and you both would have appeared to be dancing with some skill. The key to dancing well—and profiting in the market—is an ability to relax and simply go with the flow. That is what this book is about—*getting with the process;* letting go and going with the flow.

This material will defuse much of the miseducation of modern technical analysis and demonstrate the way the market really works and how to profit from that knowledge. When *Trading Chaos*[1] was written several years ago, our goal was to take 80 percent out of a trend move. We wanted to get in on the bottom 10 percent and get out on the top 10 percent of the price movement. In the intervening years, we have sharpened both our research and our strategy. Today, our goal is not to take 80 percent from a trend move but to take 300–500 percent of the trend move. Previously, if there was a 200-point move in a commodity or stock, we were well satisfied with 160 points in our pocket. Now our achievable goal is to bank 600 to 1,000 points on that same move. Unbelievable? Not after you have read this book and seen the results in your own trading.

[1] Williams, Bill M. *Trading Chaos—Applying Expert Techniques to Maximize Your Profits*. New York: John Wiley & Sons, 1995.

THE MARKET *VERSUS* ME OR THE MARKET *AND* ME

The average trader feels that trading the markets is a highly stressful occupation. Below are some actual questions we have received from active traders:

- How can I both enjoy trading and make profits trading the markets?
- Why am I so addicted to doing this when there are so many disappointments (losses)?
- How can I keep serenity inside myself and my loved ones while living in this turbulent world of the markets?
- How can I stop worrying so much in such a threatening atmosphere?
- Why do so many traders/investors lose money so consistently?
- How can I distinguish among all the hucksters who are hawking their wares as being *the* answer, when none of them seems to last even a couple of years?
- Why does my broker give me such bad advice?
- Why do all the newsletters I read boast of such enviable track records, but when I start trading them, they lose money?

Even when we are winning, there is an undercurrent of fear that the next trade will probably be a loser. We exhaust ourselves as we try to control the present and the future while our minds futilely search for ways to recreate the past.

We yearn to trade while being more relaxed, calmer, more in control, and excited about trading. To most traders, the possibility of that kind of life seems like a long-lost dream. The joy of trading is gone, and our life is filled with stress. We have tried all the hotlines, newsletters, psychobabble, books, and private sessions. Our love of the market is wearing thin. Something is very wrong. But what is it?

We often blame government action, bad information, surprising crop and corporate reports, and other vagaries of the market. But these are not the real causes of our distress and our constant struggle with the market. The answer lies at a deeper level.

After much research and personal experience, I have come to the conclusion that those who approach trading with serenity rather than struggle—those who have looked beyond the confusion and mastered the art of "dancing with the market"—are consistent winners.

Dancing with the market
is moving with
the flow of the market—
up, down, or sideways—
with a feeling of harmony,
trust, gratitude,
and yes, even love.

To really dance well and enjoy the process of dancing, you must let yourself be moved by the music rather than follow any preplanned agenda. In other words, the dance floor (market) must become a friendly place. *Friendly* here means comfort, relaxed enjoyment, and a place where *you* feel friendly.

Remember Einstein's most important question: Is the universe a friendly place? I want to assure you, based on not only my personal experience but the experience of over 700 people whom I have privately trained to become independent speculators, the market *is* a friendly place. Any unfriendliness always comes from us, not from the market.

We often hear phrases like "The market stopped me out." The market never in all its history stopped any trader out. We all do it to ourselves. Win or lose, it is always our own fault. That is because no one trades the market; we all trade our own personal belief system. Remember the Jimmy Buffett song "Margaritaville," where the singer concludes that no one should blame a woman; his problem is his own damned fault. Well, he was right.

Those of you who have worked with me and are familiar with my work know that what I say comes largely from my own experience. I have had much help and advice from other traders and from researchers using modern technical tools, but the actual implementation of this research is a very personal matter. We are going to look closely at how we create our own internal struggle, which goes on whether we are winning or losing. My 40 years of research and trading experience have produced what I think is the most successful approach to trading available today. Recently, I was offered a seven-figure amount if I did *NOT* show this material to other traders. That money is a mere pittance compared to what is possible using these techniques.

I have come a long way on this issue of dancing with the market, and I am amazed at how obvious it all becomes once a person starts experiencing the reality of this approach to trading. I am reminded of an ancient Buddhist saying: "The road is smooth; why do you throw rocks before you?"

We all do this in the market. All of us, at times, throw rocks before us, and it is difficult to dance on rocks and come out pain-free. So let's begin by clearing the debris and making way for a more profitable, peaceful, joyful, and abundant trading life.

RISING ABOVE THE CLOUDS OF DOUBT

To say that trading is simple, easy, and profitable is incredulous to most traders and absolutely absurd to others. Almost all traders experience a great deal of doubt. In this section, we are going to look at ways to rise above the clouds of doubt. This will ultimately happen only after enough experience in using my trading techniques to prove their overall profitability. The key to rising above doubt is to again realize what game we are playing. The game is *trading our own belief systems.* If we want to change our results, we must change our beliefs.

Beliefs are what we "know" to be true. We almost never question our deep beliefs, but that is exactly what a losing trader must do: question personal beliefs not only about the market but, even more, about themselves. Very few traders know *why* they trade, much less *how* they trade. We all can spout our superficial reasons: to make money fast, to enjoy competing with other traders, to gain the prestige of being able to say "I am a trader," and so on. In your last trade, did you lose because you couldn't see the market going the other way, or because of a deep, unexamined belief that you shouldn't get rich that easily? If the latter, it's time to free yourself from some old beliefs.

RELEASING THE OLD BELIEFS

Your next task is to release, get rid of, or, at the very least, become aware of these beliefs. The best method is to examine the difference between process and content. Classical sciences have always tended to deal with content. "My head, it hurts" is an example of how the classical sciences divide everything into three parts:

1. The observer.
2. The thing being observed.
3. The process of observing.

Modern sciences (relativity, quantum physics, and the Science of Chaos) do not create or condone this separation. A quantum scientist would report, "I am in the process of headaching myself"—a much more accurate description. Modern science does not believe there is any such thing as nouns. Everything is energy and all energy is process. Buckminster Fuller titled his autobiography *I Am A Verb.*

This distinction between process and content will become very important to our proficiency at dealing with the market. In general, we are educated to be goal-directed, making *what isn't* more important than *what is.* We make lists of our goals, plan them out, and then neglect the present and live, in our head, in the future.

The problem with living in the land of goals rather than the land of now is that when we center our attention on the future, we cannot concentrate on or even accurately observe what is happening now.

We can't dance well while thinking about how we are dancing. We can't trade well when we're planning what we are going to do (trade) tomorrow. Living in the now is a necessity to good trading. Living in the now is another way of saying: Pay attention to process rather than future goals or desires. One way of living in the now is to make sure that all our observations (or as many as possible) are based on "grounded versus ungrounded" assessments. Again, this is not an economic, fundamental, technical, or mechanical approach. It is a *behavioral* approach using only market-generated information.

GROUNDED VERSUS UNGROUNDED ASSESSMENTS

All of our decisions are based on our personal assessments of what is going on, whether we are traders in the market or shoppers in the supermarket. A grounded assessment is an assessment that can be agreed on by a hypothetical jury of our peers. Anything else is an ungrounded assessment. For example, you see your friend is wearing a shirt. The statement "He has on a shirt" is a grounded assessment. We all agree on that fact (provided, of course, that he actually does have on a shirt). If you say, "He has on a *nice* shirt," you have rocketed yourself into the land of ungroundedness where truth cannot be determined by observation.

Almost everything that we say or hear about the market falls into the ungrounded world. Ungrounded assessments create never-never-land market analyses. Here are some examples of ungrounded market assessments.

- The market is topping out.
- The market is oversold (or overbought).
- We are in a third wave.
- This is a short covering rally.
- One should never take more than a $500 loss.
- Never risk over 2 percent of your total equity on one trade.
- The seasonal activity will take this market higher.

All of these statements are totally ungrounded assessments and do not, in any accurate way, describe the market or market behavior. Ungrounded assessments create chronic losers. If you are a losing trader, I can assure you that one of the principal causes is that you are making decisions based on ungrounded assessments. Grounded assessments are real, verifiable, unambiguous, and accurate, and they come directly from the market itself. The material and indicators in Chapters Three through Ten include only grounded market-generated assessments.

Basically, all of our observations (assessments) go through a part of the brain (the reticular activating system, or RAS), which acts as an analyzer and gives us only the information that passes our filters (what we want to hear). In no way does it give us a true take on reality or on what is really out there. A camera does not have an RAS to filter its incoming information. It just records what is present in a certain vibratory octave. It will take a picture of a yellow vehicle with black writing on it, and that is what you get. We, however, identify the yellow vehicle as a school bus and immediately all of our prejudices and preconceived notions jump to the forefront rather than seeing what is actually there. We think about slowing down, not passing, and watching carefully for small children. Our actions are not based on grounded assessments but on our history (belief system) with that particular concept.

It is said that generals always fight the previous war rather than the one they are in. We traders generally trade our last mistake rather than what is happening in the current market. In other words, we set up our own prejudices based on past experiences, and any incoming information will be filtered to make sure that it does not contradict our belief systems. If reality does conflict with our belief systems, we will deny reality and distort incoming information to keep our unquestioned beliefs intact. No wonder we perform so miserably in the market even though we may have been extremely successful in other professions or businesses. In the market, you either confront reality or you create losses.

If we want to climb off this ladder to distress, we must confront what is really going on in the market rather than our ideas about it. I will briefly review here what is going on. I refer the reader to my previous book for a more complete description.

The primary purpose of the market is to find *immediately* the *exact price* where there is an:

Equal disagreement on value
and
an agreement on price

The last time you bought a car, you and the dealer or person you bought it from had to agree on a price. Before the price could be fixed, you had to negotiate a disagreement on value. Without a disagreement on value, there is no market. You wanted the car more than you wanted the money you were ready to spend to purchase it. The person you bought it from wanted your money more than the car. All free market transactions must have these two elements. When they are present, you have created a commodity or stock market.

When someone tells you the market is "oversold," it simply means that the market went lower than the person *thought* it would. It says nothing about the market. I respect the analysts' right to use this or any other term, but there just isn't any such condition as oversold or overbought. The primary function of any market or exchange is to make sure that this condition does not exist, even for a second. Whenever you read that there is a 60 percent bullishness in bonds, it only means all the bears haven't been surveyed. If the market were 50.01 percent bullish, the price would have already gone up. Here is the truest statement I can make about the market:

The market is where it is
because that is where it is
supposed to be, and
it is supposed to be there
because that is where it is.

Think about this for a moment. Once you grasp this concept, you will:

1. Know more about the market than 95 percent of those who have money invested in it.
2. You will have started down a yellow brick road to more profits.

The market is where it is because, at this point in time, this is its fair value simply because you have an equal number of contracts buying and selling at that price.

Don't get me wrong: I'm not trying to convince you of anything. I don't have even a thimbleful of missionary blood in my veins. If you really believe there is such a thing as bullish/bearish consensus and/or oversold/overbought conditions, be my guest. Would you also like a spare tooth to put under your pillow tonight for the tooth fairy? It is time to get serious or get ripped off.

"The market is . . ." definition above is a true, brief, and accurate description of what is happening every time a commodity or a share of stock is sold or bought. We don't need all the millions of ungrounded assessments (opinions) floating around. In our private tutorials, we strongly suggest that there is no need to seek out any source for information other than the market-generated information. Reading the *Wall Street Journal, Barron's,* or *Investors Daily;* subscribing to advisers' newsletters or hotlines; or tuning in to financial TV or radio is more destructive to your financial health than smoking is destructive to your physical health.

MAKING MONEY SPECULATING IS SIMPLE; CHANGING YOUR BELIEF SYSTEM IS NOT NECESSARILY EASY

Making money is simple *IF* you understand the underlying structure. It is also simple because the market is a master teacher. It will always tell you exactly what to do and when to do it. If you mess up, it will tell you exactly where you went wrong and what you should have done instead. As one of the greatest teachers in the world, the market is always willing to be there for you and to show you exactly how to act. That, in fact, is what this book is about: understanding the language of the market and its instructions about what to do. The book will make it so easy that a computer will be able to communicate with you about the market's grounded assessments.

TO TUNE IN TO THE MARKET ITSELF, YOU MUST RELAX YOUR PERSONAL GOALS

Despite what all the "do it better" gurus are saying, we diminish the present any time we set goals. In the market, things sometimes work out the way we want them to, but sometimes they don't. We don't enjoy our preparation for trading the market if we are worried about losing. We don't enjoy the miracle of our children's growth if we worry about how they will turn out. We don't enjoy maturing if we are worrying about what malady will take us from this life. We lose the freedom to soar that comes from enjoying the vast riches that life and the market are offering us in the here and now.

In trading, if you set your heart on a certain trade result, you enter into a state of rigidity. On the other hand, if you set your heart free, you enter a state of flow. The question then is: How can you trade without setting goals? The answer is: Set as many goals as you want. Then do the necessary preparation, and work to bring that goal to fruition. When you are satisfied that you have done the most appropriate trade for that moment, LET GO OF THE OUTCOME. Years ago, I traded with a very bright trader who was decades past the normal retirement age. After observing my trading for a while, he said, "Bill, if you were a farmer, you would go broke on your first crop." When I asked him why, he replied, "If you were a farmer and farmed like you trade, you would plant corn and then come back every day and dig up the seeds to see how they were doing. Once you decide and put on a trade, let it grow, mature, and ripen. Don't keep digging up the seeds." He was exactly right. I learned a great deal from that mature trader.

One of the most important lessons I can teach you is how to monitor your trading minute-by-minute in the market. It is really quite simple. When you look at the current chart and you know your present positions, ask yourself this simple question:

Do I care which way the market moves?

If you care, you are addicted. If you honestly don't care, you are trading well and you *want what the market wants.* Any time you care, you are wanting what *you* want—not what the market wants. The market is neutral. It doesn't know or even care what you want.

As traders, we are simply not capable of knowing what the market is going to do, nor can we see the grand possibilities that the market will offer us tomorrow. Sometimes, losses can be turned into great assets if we learn from our experience. In that situation, we gain either profits or learning, and both can be wins.

Tomorrow's market is not just unknown, it is *unknowable.* Traders are simply not capable of knowing what the market is going to do or what grand possibilities the market will offer tomorrow.

Probably the most *inappropriate* question we can ask at the end of a trading day is: "Did we make money today?" From our point of view, that is basically irrelevant. The only appropriate question at the end of a trading day is: "Were we in tune with the market?" There will be days when you will be in tune with the market and *lose* money, but if you stay in tune, the market will bless you greatly.

There is no such thing as a bad trader.
There is only a well trained or a badly trained trader.

THE PROCESS OF TRANSFORMATION FROM LOSING TO WINNING

This book is basically for traders who can't win for losing and for winning traders who want to improve their efficiency at winning. It is not for those individuals who have no interest in working through their power trips in relation to themselves, other people, and the market. If you are not willing to *allow* sweeping changes to occur in your life as a result of this material, you should not attempt the techniques described herein.

Every trader is responsible for his or her own behavior. Part of maturation is the ability to draw the "honesty cards" about oneself to the forefront of awareness, in order to decide on a course of action. The consequences of immature judgment or of toying with trading can include psychosis, aggravation of neuroses, acceleration of disease processes, and suicide. On the other side, an awakening into certain states of consciousness can bestow gifts of such value that they are beyond price—and I do not mean only monetary profits.

The markets themselves are the most accurate and brilliant psychological mirrors in the world today. Trading can be the most naked and efficient psychotherapeutic growth program in which one could engage, if approached with an appropriate attitude.

Here is a statement that many traders will hoot at: Making profits is not the most important reason for trading. Read well—I did not say *unimportant,* I said *not the most important.* To us, the primary reason for trading is the most important reason for doing anything: TO FIND OUT WHO YOU ARE. That perspective makes all the difference.

The intention of this book is not to please. Its purpose is to tilt you from the limited possibilities for experience that you now have. The material is offered to those who are ready to begin an awakening process—those who know at the deepest level of their awareness that they are ready for a change. Your desire to change your unfulfilling life and unsuccessful trading patterns into a state of consciousness is vital to your success.

In this chapter, I want to deliver a truly believable message from a true believer in your trading and investing success. As you know, there are basically two kinds of traders: the successful ones, and everyone else.

Michelangelo once pointed out that there are two ways of creating a statue. The first way is to create a statue from a piece of material. The second and more masterful way is to see that the statue *is already inside* the material, and sculpting is merely a process of getting rid of the material that does not belong there. Another equally famous philosopher pointed out that there are two ways of becoming enlightened: (1) by building on your good qualities and (2) by eliminating what doesn't belong.

Robert Frost wrote, "Two roads diverged in a wood, and I—I took the one less traveled by, and that has made all the difference."[2] In this book, we are going to take a journey on a road less traveled by eliminating much that isn't true about trading. We are going to unravel some tangled ideas and win for a change. I want to share with you our truth about trading.

Let me hasten to add that I am not much enamored by the concept of TRUTH. Actually I have very little interest in *The TRUTH.* I am much more interested in *lies that work* than I am in The TRUTH. The

[2] Palgrave, F. T. *The Golden Treasury of the Best Poems.* New York: New American Library, 1961.

reason is: Truth (with a capital T) doesn't last. In fact, it seems to change with each generation. Truth once was that the world was flat. All of the intelligent people in the world agreed on that "fact." Mapmakers made a good living by believing that Truth. Truth once was that Zeus ruled the world from a mountaintop in Greece. Truth once was that bleeding was a cure for many ills; check with our first President about that Truth. It cost him his life. And let me state here that some of the Truth you know about the market today is costing you your financial life. Let's look at the Truth of the current situation.

If you are attempting to categorize this material, you would most likely classify it as an *unpopular trading guide* because it contradicts what I call the *popular guides* to trading success. Any popular guide to trading will tell you exactly what you want to hear. That's why the guides are popular. They have titles like *Big Bucks—No Risk!* They are worth their selling price because the publisher always promises:

An easy to understand,
proven system
for turning little or no initial
investment capital into a fortune,
in virtually no time whatsoever.

Wouldn't it be great if we really could make a fortune like this without working? Well, we can't. These things could never be right. Be real; if we are raking in all that money, who is going to supply the losers? Who is going to lose all that money to us? And if it really works that well, why doesn't the publisher of *Big Bucks—No Risk* take its publishing budget and put the money to work in the markets? There, "with little effort and absolutely no risk," it can make vastly more money than by publishing a competitive book that has skinny profit margins. The only sure thing about popular guides is that you are going to lose your money following their advice.

If the popular guides tell you what you want to hear (so they can sell you books) and we tell you what is actually true about trading, then this must be an unpopular guide to trading. The Truth is that a limited number of talented, rational people who know what they are doing can beat the market consistently. This is not just a game, it is life. And one of the primary purposes of the business of speculation is to make money.

These are turbulent times. Past generations were not as turbulent. Remember when real estate was a fortune-building safe haven? Bonds were safe as the government. Savings and Loans were safe depositories, and heaven knows there could never be a problem with Insurance companies. If you chose to hold cash, it could never make you poor.

As a hardworking trader/investor, you probably know about seminars, tutorials, books, systems, hotlines, and so on, that are supposedly designed to give you an edge in the markets. Maybe you have even attended a few, and perhaps you feel guilty about the ones you did not attend. Tell me, have you ever known anyone—and I mean *anyone*—who has gone to a weekend seminar as a losing trader and, from something learned there, has become a consistent winner? I have spoken to over 25,000 traders, and I have yet to find the first one. Nor did I go from losing to winning by attending workshops. Does that mean that they are useless or not worth the money? No, not at all. Workshops are great places for getting ideas but are simply no good at changing behavior, which is the topic of our discussion here. If you change your beliefs, you will change your results.

Let me ask you two questions. (1) If I gave you $10,000 and a ticket to Las Vegas and asked you to go there and lose that $10,000, do you *honestly feel* that you could do that for me? (2) What if I gave you the same money and ticket and asked you to go there and double my money? These are quite serious questions. If you really understand why you answered both of them the way you did, you are very close to understanding why you are not a more consistent winner. Let me throw a different concept at you. Whichever way you answered the questions and whatever you did when you got to Las Vegas, you would be successful. In answer to the first question, you would be a successful loser because you did exactly what you expected to do. You were successful at losing. You were a winner at losing, and there is no difference in being a winner at losing and a winner at winning. You get whatever you set up for yourself. Trading is a self-discovery process and a very personal experience.

To make money in the markets consistently, you must know what your job is. Let me tell you the most important words you will ever hear about speculation and trading.

Speculators get paid for buying what nobody wants when nobody wants it and selling what everybody wants when everybody wants it.

While we are at it, here are a few things that speculators never get paid for: fundamental analysis, technical analysis, overbought/

oversold analysis, Elliott Wave analysis, Gann analysis, cycle analysis, pattern analysis, oscillators, relative strength, econometric models, seasonal analysis, profile analysis, value analysis, sunspots, star positions, and a dozen other vogues, fads, and fantasies, except to the extent that they happen, by luck or design, to cause their proponent to demand the supply or supply the demand.

MORE NOTES ON SPECULATION AND LIFE

Here is the key. Trading is a game that you set up and agree to. You only have two choices about *how* you will get to where you are going. The first is an unconscious method; your mind will create your reality from your pictures of the past. And you know that it is most ready and willing to do that. In fact, that is one of the main functions of your brain's left hemisphere. But this part of your brain can only *duplicate* earlier situations—IT CANNOT CREATE. In fact, your mind cannot accept the notion of creation or the notion of disappearance.

Your only other option is to become conscious of your notions. A *notion* is another word for *noticing.* When you notice something (or get a notion), you give it your attention. When you begin to *notice how you are noticing,* you fall into AWARENESS. When you start becoming aware, you will be out there on the razor's edge of choice and always willing to make one. You will become aware that what you see on your brain screen is much more important than what you see on the monitor screen.

The market can become your own tree to sit under until you reach enlightenment. Enlightenment in this case is seeing the market for what it really is. So let's repeat:

**The market is nothing but agreement on price
and disagreement on value.
No trade is made until there is
disagreement on value
and agreement on price.**

No market moves until there is new incoming information (Chaos). Most traders disagree with the purpose and function of the market and thus lose. Picking tops and bottoms is disagreeing with the market. And because we are all stubborn to one degree or another, we make following the trend of the market, which should be the easiest thing in the world, one of the most difficult tasks in speculating.

Most traders feel that what they need is some new "genius" who can create a trading system or indicator that will make sense of the "craziness" of the market. A muddle of conflicting indicators united by the force of greed is the worst possible instrument for trading the market. Irrevocable commitment to this kind of indicator is financial suicide.

We do not need a new indicator or strategy. We need a new experience—a new feeling of what it is to come from the right hemisphere and intuitively understand the market. One must take care not to confuse the image (chart) with fact, which would be like climbing up the signpost instead of following the road, or eating the menu rather than the meal.

WE ALL SWIM IN OUR OWN PARTICULAR LOGIC MAP

Our own personal ocean of logic started approximately 2,500 years ago, when a philosophical war was going on between two opposite camps represented on one side by Aristotle and on the other by Heraclitus. Aristotle basically seduced the world by saying that if you don't know something, you should go to people who know more than you do, and ask them.

That advice sounds quite reasonable, and it has been accepted by much of the earth's population for two and a half millennia. Acceptance does not necessarily make it true. Remember that the civilized world functioned adequately for hundreds of years while believing that the world was flat. Businesses and mapmakers flourished. But then Galileo and a handful of others looked through a telescope and saw round planets in orbits in the heavens. They knew that the flat-earth paradigm was wrong, but it took close to 200 years and much suffering on their part before the reality of a round earth was accepted.

The Aristotelian/Heraclitian dispute was much more insidious than the conflict involved in understanding the heavens. Because Aristotle won this intellectual war, your life is as it is today. Had Heraclitus won back then, we would have a completely different civilization. Aristotle influences almost every thought you have and each of your analyses of the markets. Why do you read the *Wall Street Journal* or listen to FNN or call your broker or the trading floor? Because you think THEY know more about the market than you do; after all, "They are in the business." Most likely, they don't! I do not know any broker who would be a broker if he or she could trade profitably. The designation of *broker* probably means that you are the *brokee.* Of the newsletter writers and market commentators you know, how many have made money in the markets? I have never met an economics professor who made a significant amount of money trading.

Aristotle believed in a *reductionist* approach: if you break anything down into its smallest primary parts, you can understand how that mechanism works. Thus began our search for the smallest part of the universe, which was thought to be the atom. However, with more sophisticated tools, we developed an entirely new science based on subatomic particles, and this subatomic research has totally changed our basic ideas about the universe. It is also interesting to note that all the subatomic particles that have been discovered were named long before they were discovered. The old questions return: Do we believe what we see? Or, do we see what we believe?

Aristotelian philosophy has influenced our legal system (precedence), our educational system (the teacher–student relationship: the student is dumb and the teacher is smart), medicine (double-blind studies), and science (reliability and validity). Following this path of reductionism has produced the concepts of cause and effect, "laws" of motion, "conservation" of energy, and entropy. The latest findings of modern science have proven all of these assumptions and concepts false.

Aristotle's philosophical counterpart, Heraclitus, felt that the universe was in constant flux, and stability and homeostasis were *not* the norm. Probably his most famous saying was: "You can't step in the same river twice," meaning that when you put your foot in and take it out and immediately place it back into the water, not only has the river changed, your foot has changed also. Heraclitus's most famous student, Clayitus, went even further. He said: "You can't step in the same river once": you and the river are changing during the *process* of putting your foot in.

Science in the twentieth century will be remembered for three very basic innovations that completely changed our way of viewing the world:

1. Relativity.
2. Quantum mechanics.

3. The Science of Chaos, which includes information theory, cybernetics, holography, nonlinear dynamics, and fractal geometry.

WHAT DOES EINSTEIN'S EFFECT ON CLASSICAL SCIENCE HAVE TO DO WITH WINNING?

If you follow the history of science, you will find nothing that predicted the introduction of the theory of relativity. Until the twentieth century, classical science dealt with four basic elements that were considered separate from each other: *mass, energy, space,* and *time.* Einstein, who seemingly came out of left field, introduced his theory of relativity, which basically states that space and time are really the same thing. He also pointed out that matter and energy can be converted from one state to the other and therefore are not different. He often stated that there are really only two components of the universe:

1. Nothingness.
2. Condensed nothingness, which we call form or things.

This led to undreamed-of innovations such as atomic energy and changed science's view of the world forever. About the only thing that Einstein left us as a constant was the speed of light. The next revolutionary development in modern science, quantum mechanics, took away even that constant.

QUANTUM MECHANICS

After the discovery of subatomic particles, our consentually logical world went haywire. Subatomic particles do not "behave" as they should, or at least the way we *think* they should. Our most basic assumptions came into doubt. A number of things apparently traveled much faster than the speed of light. In fact, there was evidence that some things travel so incredibly fast that they could be in two places at once. That was not supposed to happen, according to classical science.

In 1964, John Stuart Bell, a brilliant scientist, introduced a notion he called the nonlocality of causes. This cast doubt on the entire theory of cause and effect. Bell said individual causes could not be isolated.

This is quite a serious concept. Most of us tend to run our lives and our trading with cause-and-effect assumptions such as "Why did I catch that cold?" or, more particularly, "Why did I lose on that trade?" If, as Bell maintains, this is not the way the world really works, we might have our ladder of learning leaning against the wrong building. Thousands of experiments offer positive proof that Bell's theorem is indeed a more accurate description of how things really work. Bell maintains that everything in the universe is connected. You are a part of me and vice versa; whereas Aristotle maintained that everything had its own discrete boundaries and could be located and categorized.

The next science-changing innovator was another brilliant American scientist, David Bohm. Bohm was caught up in the terrible McCarthy hearings in the 1950s and chose not to live in a country that would allow such travesty of human justice. He moved to England and was a research professor at the University of London. Bohm went even further than Bell, maintaining that not only is everything in the Universe connected but *everything is actually the same thing.* Everything comes from the same shimmering quantum soup.

In the market, we are looking at a very non-Aristotelian world in which there are no discrete categories, no actual nouns, and no real long-lasting stability. In this new view of the world, everything is constantly changing and those very beautiful smooth shapes of Euclidean geometry are themselves aberrations and not the norm. The materials that scientists through the centuries had ignored as "random" variations are actually the cornerstones of reality.

As mentioned before, the two areas where classical science makes little headway are: turbulence and living systems. From the shoulders of relativity and quantum mechanics came a new approach whose goals were to study turbulence, living systems, and nonlinear behavior. The techniques were impossible to deal with mathematically before the advent of very powerful computers, but the questions had been asked centuries before.

FIFTEENTH-CENTURY CHAOLOGISTS

Before Columbus landed in America, the fifteenth-century mathematicians were asking questions about Chaos. Their theoretical questions concerned the various levels of Dimensionality. For example, a point has no dimensions, a line has one dimension, a plane has two, and a solid has three. They understood that even a crooked line has only one dimension as long as it does not cross itself and create a plane.

Suppose then that a *very* crooked line is placed on top of a rectangle (plane) and moves over the surface of that plane but never crosses itself. It is so crooked that it covers up 50 percent of the plane as it moves off to the other side. The mathematicians' question was, quite simply: What is the dimension of that line? It can't be one dimension because it covers half the plane (which is two dimensions), and it can't be two dimensions because it doesn't cover the entire plane. (Stay with me here because this concept has changed our world and will change it even more so in the future.)

In addition to this concept of higher dimensions, two other scientific developments have altered our worldview. One is the concept of *cybernetics,* which came from a Greek word meaning steersman—the man who holds a boat's rudder, and who can, with a small amount of force, move a much larger force (the boat). Cybernetics does not follow Newton's law of motion, which says that for every action there is an equal and opposite reaction. A small action on the rudder produces much more than an equal reaction.

Cybernetics came out of information theory, which was developed during World War II in an effort to get more communication through the existing cable that crossed the Atlantic Ocean between America and England. Basically, information theory points out that there are at least five parts to any communication: (1) a source, (2) an encoder, (3) a message, (4) a decoder, and (5) a receiver.

The important point here is that the decoder comes from and is attached to the receiver whereas the encoder comes from and is attached to the source. Any qualitative difference between the source and the receiver will always be distortion between the intended message and the received message. It is not an accident that we misunderstand each other; it is a miracle that we ever do.

Our personal decoder is the home of all our prejudices and preferences. That is where our categories (belief systems) and desires live and work. Our decoder is the filter that distorts incoming messages that do not fit into our existing beliefs (categories).

Another scientific breakthrough since the 1950s was the discovery of the hologram. The insight gained here is that information can be stored in ways yet to be discovered, and unbelievably large amounts of information can be stored in extremely tiny spaces. Before you were born, your entire body—including the size of your muscles, the number of hairs on your head, the shape and size of your teeth, the color of your eyes, the number of cells in your brain, how you will age, and, barring accidents, when you will die—were all stored in your RNA/DNA in a space so small it cannot be seen with the naked eye.

If you take a holographic 8 × 10-inch film and cut off one corner a slice smaller than 1/16 of an inch, it will still contain the same details as the 8 × 10-inch picture. Information theory, cybernetics, and holographic theory do not support the Aristotelian view of the world. When we say "Our world is changing," what we really mean is that *we* are getting a different view of it. And this is what the approach in this book is about: getting a different, more accurate view of what the market actually is and how it operates.

We do this by examining five dimensions of the market. These dimensions could be compared to looking through five different windows, each of which adds to the total picture. These dimensions are:

1. The fractal (phase space).
2. Momentum (phase energy).
3. Acceleration/Deceleration (phase force).
4. Zone (phase energy/force combination).
5. Balance line (strange attractors).

Each of these different dimensions gives unique insight into the underlying structure of the market and its behavior. The recent advent of extremely powerful computers has now permitted us to get more specific insights into this worldview that we now label as the Science of Chaos. If you knew everything there is to know about the Science of Chaos and you decided to give it a name that would confuse the most people, you probably would choose the name Chaos. Chaos is not craziness and it does not mean randomness; rather, it is an insight into a much higher form of order. (We will examine this new science, and how it can improve our trading, in the next chapter.)

WHY GORILLAS DON'T PROCREATE IN A CONTROLLED ARTIFICIAL SETTING AND WHAT THAT HAS TO DO WITH THE MARKET

A problem that has perplexed zookeepers for many years is why gorillas don't mate in captivity. It is not because they don't learn about sexual activity; it is because they don't have the proper environment. All animals must have risk to make life worthwhile. If there is no risk, we try to create some because risk and feeling alive are different sides of the same coin. Risk is what makes us alive. Life is not worth living in an environment where there is no risk.

In the past, depressions, wars, and conflict gave us a national purpose. We could risk everything for the common good. World War II brought Americans together and created a level of cooperation among us that has not been matched. Our risk was in seeing our enemies, looking them in the eye, and doing something about them. Then the atomic bomb made hand-to-hand combat obsolete. We no longer looked our enemies in the eye, and war became more scientific and less personal.

Even before World War II, most people had the risk of surviving during the Great Depression. Just getting by brought out the best in us. Because we spent most of our time surviving, we were relatively happy while dealing with this risk. Then modernization machinery and the postwar industrial revolution allowed us more leisure time than we were accustomed to having.

Today we have to spend that leisure time, and we have lost the opportunity to struggle. Most people fill the gap with TV, but you and I have the opportunity to fill this deep need by being in the market. First, we must understand our need and how the market interfaces with that need. Chaos provides us with unique tools. Chaos is the background from which we mine the material needed to make us feel good about ourselves, to learn about ourselves, and to progress toward realizing our own personal potential. We are forced to make choices, to abide by the results, and to learn from daily opportunities. Risk is a *turn-on* in life. We are not interested in haphazard risk. We are talking about the risk that produces research, allowing us to understand the markets better and to extract profits from our knowledge and understanding.

TRADING OUR BELIEF SYSTEMS

Your beliefs about the market create your reality of the market. Beliefs are *assumptions* about the nature of reality, and because you create what you believe in, you will have many "proofs" that the market operates the way you think it does. For instance, a trader who believes that the market is abundant and generous will act in such a way that he or she experiences abundance; a person who believes that no one can make money from the markets will not receive money from the market. Each trader will have many experiences to prove that his or her personal belief about the market is really a fact about the market. You can change what you believe and thus change your experiences in trading.

In this book, we are going to explore in detail how to trade each of the five dimensions. We will then put them all together for a profitable approach to decision making in the markets. We will also discuss our proprietary software, which eliminates most of the work and errors in analyzing the markets.

The biggest risk you can ever take
Is not betting on yourself.

SUMMARY AND PREVIEW

We have explored in this chapter the reason most traders lose, and we have introduced the idea that the new Science of Chaos can improve our market performance, allowing us to be consistent winners in the markets and in life. We also took a quick look at what I refer to as the real Holy Grail.

In the next chapter, we will examine the Science of Chaos from a practical everyday trading orientation. We will eliminate most of the complicated math and concentrate on profitable application of the theory. A number of books contain the mathematical underpinning of the Science of Chaos and Complexity, but few have successfully applied the theory to the investing and trading markets. I am proud to have you join me in this pioneering effort. The best is yet to come.

Let me again welcome you to the wonderful world of trading and investing, where anything is possible if you understand what is happening in both the *market* and *yourself.* Permit me to share with you other reasons I love trading the markets. It is the last bastion of free enterprise where you are rewarded generously for doing the easy, appropriate thing. You win or lose purely on your own decisions. If at the end of today, I have lost, THERE IS NO ONE TO BLAME. If, on the other hand, I win today, I DON'T HAVE TO SAY THANK YOU TO ANYONE. I am not obligated to anyone or anything. I do not have to be politically correct.

The reward is there for the taking; the only question is: Are you *conscious* enough to take it? My wife once wrote an article describing the market experience as "sliding down the razor blade of life." One young man whom we taught to trade successfully wrote, "It is the most fun I have ever had . . . with my clothes on." Yours can be a life of freedom and fun; the responsibility for that freedom lies solely within you. And now, let's take a closer look at Chaos, which you will find to be another word for FREEDOM.

2

FROM CHAOS TO COSMOS TO CASH

NEW DIMENSIONS IN TRADING

In the first decade of the twenty-first century, we have a choice to either be a part of the last generation of traders using linear (ineffective) techniques, or the first generation using effective nonlinear (chaotic) techniques.

My purposes in this chapter are: to introduce you to the basic concepts of Chaos in a relatively nonscientific manner, and to point out its applicability to profitable trading and investing. When I first started trading, over 40 years ago, the primary approach to understanding the markets was fundamental analysis. Poring over the company's financial statements, examining the crop reports, and gathering as much "expert" opinion as could be found were the standard procedures. They did not produce predictable or profitable results, but they were the only options if one did not have insider information. Through these past four decades, I have seen the personalities of both the stock market and the commodity markets change many times. Actually, they are in a constant state of flux. They form an example of "applied chaos."

In the 1970s, very few traders would admit that they used technical analysis. In those days, technical analysts were considered "weirdos." There has now been a complete turnaround. Today, most traders are proud to call themselves technical analysts—not because they have been successful, but because they are following the crowd.

TECHNICAL ANALYSIS BASICALLY DOESN'T WORK

The rise of the personal computer (PC) gave technical analysts a tool that allowed them to analyze immense amounts of data, then curve-fit and optimize the past data to show how they would have produced enormous profits in the past. The more they optimized and curve-fitted, the more the systems were predestined not to work in present time. During the early 1980s, hundreds of different "black box" systems were sold at prices averaging around $3,000 each. Today, not a single one of them is in use. Mechanical systems were touted because they "took the emotions out of trading." When technical analysis did not produce consistent, predictable profits, traders started looking in other directions.

One of these directions currently is *neural networks*. Basically, neural networks do not change any perspective paradigms in the markets. They, too, are still based on the false assumption that the future will be like the past. Neural networks do not give us any underlying change in our general paradigms. Neural networks are really only very elaborate calculators. They do not tap into the underlying structure of the markets.

The real reason these efforts have not paid off is that our approach is based on classical science, which has now been proven to contain vital errors in its approach to understanding the true nature of behavior. Let's examine what has happened in today's scientific knowledge and draw parallels to trading. Then we will demonstrate how this new approach can be used in your personal trading.

PRINCIPLES FROM THE SCIENCE OF CHAOS

The newest science on this planet is the Science of Chaos. In this chapter, we will explore the generalized principles derived from this science and apply them to life and particularly to trading on the stock and commodity markets. As pointed out earlier, the Science of Chaos deals primarily with natural phenomena. One of Mandelbrot's pregnant findings was that the fractal dimensions of rivers are similar to those of commodity and stock markets, which is an indication that the markets are more a function of nature than a process designed by the left hemisphere of the human brain. Our view is that economics fundamentals and technical/mechanical analysis do not draw an accurate map of the market's behavior.

The Science of Chaos provides three primary principles for the study of markets. Collectively, these principles govern the behavior of energy. As discussed fully in Robert Fritz's book, *The Path of Least Resistance,* these principles are:[1]

1. *Everything in the universe follows the path of least resistance.* The markets are like a river. As they move through each trading minute, they take the path of least resistance. That's what we all do—you, me, the markets, everything in nature. It is part of the inherent design of nature. While a river is running downstream, the path of least resistance determines its behavior. Gravity is energizing it as it flows around rocks and along curves in the riverbed. You are reading this sentence at this time because this was the path of least resistance when all your time management factors were examined. You are sitting wherever you are because that location was on your path of least resistance. In the market, you will exit from a losing trade when the pain of losing one more dollar becomes stronger than the pain of saying that you were wrong to be in the trade. The path of least resistance will win again.
2. *The path of least resistance is determined by an always underlying and usually unseen structure.* The behavior of a river, whether it is calmly flowing downhill or creating rapids, depends on the underlying structure of the riverbed. If the riverbed is deep and wide, the river will flow calmly downhill. If the riverbed is shallow and narrow, the riverbed will create rapids. The behavior of the river can be accurately predicted by examining the underlying riverbed. If you could see the bottom, you could accurately predict the behavior of the river at that point.

   Many traders who keep repeating their trading behavior produce losses. They often feel powerless and frustrated. They attend seminars, read books and underline appropriate passages, study NLP (Neuro Linguistic Programming), have

[1] Fritz, Robert. *The Path of Least Resistance.* New York: Ballantine Books, 1989.

private sessions with market psychologists, and then find themselves back in the same old losing rut. If that has happened to you, you simply haven't changed your underlying structure. Permanent changes happen only when you alter the riverbed, the underlying structure.

As a trader, you always know when you are trying to go against the path of least resistance. Tension immediately builds up in your body and mind. If you are tense about trading, you are not "floating down the river." Once you learn to determine the underlying structure of a market, you can make peace with the behavior of the market and simply "float like a butterfly, sting like a bee."

3. *The always underlying and usually unseen structure can be discovered, and it can be altered.* You can change the flow of your life and your trading. To do this easily and permanently, you must work with the underlying structure rather than the behavior produced by that underlying structure.

The basic concept derived from these three principles is this: you can learn to first recognize the underlying structure that is driving your trading, and then change it so that you can create what you really want from the markets.

Structure determines behavior. Structure determines the way anything behaves—a bullet, a hurricane, a cab driver, a spouse, a market. The way the pits are structured determines the behavior of the traders in the pits. The structures that have the most influence on your trading results are composed of desires, beliefs, assumptions, and, most of all, your understanding of the underlying structure of the market and yourself. As Robert Fritz notes, "You can't fool Mother Structure."

SCIENCE IS CHANGING FROM ARISTOTLE TO EINSTEIN TO CHAOS

As pointed out in the previous chapter, classical science began around 2,500 years ago and was based on Aristotle's assumption that the universe was similar to a smoothly running clock. The "natural" state of affairs featured smooth lines, round curves, and pleasing-to-the-eye structures. The unexplained divergences, considered "random" behavior, were neglected as essentially unimportant.

The scientific community ran into unexpected paradoxes in the study of subatomic particles. Nothing seemed to act as it should. The "laws" that had been accurate and permanent through the centuries were now on trial. The real world of atomic particles and the universe did not follow the laws that, through the centuries, scientists had so painstakingly prescribed. The question was: Do we keep the laws that make us comfortable, or do we allow the newly observed behavior to change our view of the world? What do we do with all this new information that does not follow our laws of physics?

When John Stuart Bell and David Bohm dropped their bombshells and proved that everything is really connected to everything else and there is no singular cause-and-effect relationship, our assumptions had to change. Their findings limited the scope of classical science to the laboratory. It could not explain turbulence nor living systems. The question "why?" has become irrelevant. Correlation and coincidences have replaced causality. They proved with thousands of experiments that appearances of individuality, including our individual brains, come from the same "quantum soup."

Coincidental with the changing of our scientific paradigms came information theory, which pointed out that we all live in parallel universes and all our perceptions must pass through a filter whose purpose is to keep our personal paradigms intact. This material is either rejected as being inappropriate or massaged to fit our previous opinions. The latest addition to this changing paradigm is the Science of Chaos.

THE SCIENCE OF CHAOS: THE HANDLING OF *NEW INFORMATION*

The Science of Chaos has proven that material traditionally neglected by classical science as being random behavior and/or unimportant measurement errors may be the most important causative factors in our search for understanding. It pointedly addresses areas that cannot be navigated by classical concepts. It specifically concentrates on what scientists formerly labeled as Chaos.

Chaos is one of those unfortunate misnomers that describes more of what IT IS NOT than what IT IS. Chaos is not random behavior. It is a much higher form of order. Instead of thinking of your usual connotation of the word Chaos, substitute instead the more accurate description: NEW INFORMATION. From now on, every time you hear the word Chaos, translate it in your mind to new information.

HOW WE HANDLE NEW INCOMING INFORMATION

The universally most common and most prejudiced way to handle new information is to fit it into old categories. We have done this so often that we consider it either the natural thing to do or, more commonly, the ONLY way to handle it. Upon receiving new information, our usual first approach is:

"What is it like? It reminds me of . . . ."

According to psychologists, any time you feel either overwhelmed or bored it is because you are attempting to fit new information into old categories. (Aha! What are you doing with this information at this moment?) Think about that when you are in the market and feeling either bored or overwhelmed.

Our first impulse when handling new incoming information is to organize it in some way. You are in the process of organizing this material that you are reading. Once anything, material or otherwise, is organized, it takes on a life of its own. When it takes on this life, its primary purpose and goal is survival. As this chapter is being written, there is a national outcry to do away with the IRS. What do you think the chances are? Before that happens, there will be blood in the street. For any organization, from the most complex to the very simplest, the first goal is to survive.

The four largest money gatherers and distributors in the world are:

1. War.
2. Medicine.
3. Insurance.
4. Religion.

These four institutions control more money than the most powerful country in the world. Why do they enjoy this position? Because they have to do with the survival of our most personal organization—ourselves. The purpose of war is to break things and kill people. The purpose of medicine is to repair those who aren't dead, so that they can fight again. The purpose of insurance is to take care of those left by the dead. The purpose of religion is to take care of those who do die. These institutions have the most money because they all have to do with our personal ultimate survival.

The real reason that most traders lose consistently is that they are fitting new information into old, inappropriate categories. If our usual way of handling new information is to fit it into old categories, what is the alternate choice? *Let the new information organize itself.* When that happens, we have a trance-ending experience of a higher form of order. The question then is: How is this done in trading the markets?

A NEW WAY TO HANDLE MARKET INFORMATION

The simplest organization I can think of is a hydrogen atom. It contains one proton made up of three quarks and one electron. It just doesn't get much simpler than that. Trillions of these gaseous atoms are floating around in the air in the room where you are sitting. Their first instinct, just like yours and mine, is to keep their current logic organization intact. They seek to remain hydrogen atoms. In this room, there are also trillions of oxygen atoms. They are much larger and more complex, and they, too, seek to keep their current organization intact.

As both of these gases circulate and bounce around the room, they occasionally will come into each other's gravitational field (Figure 2–1). This provides new information for both of them (the gravitational pull of the other). And even though they are infinitesimally small and are inorganic, they make what could only be called an intelligent choice—whether to keep their old organization as independent atoms or to permit the new incoming information to change their organizational structure. They keep their current structure 99.99999 percent of the time. About 0.00001 percent of the time, they let this new information (the gravitational pull of the other atom) reorganize their approach to the world. When that happens, these atoms TRANCE-END their old limitations and become something entirely new, with all new characteristics and a totally different organization. They have become H_20—water. Water has virtually no characteristics that are shared by the two former gases. They were compressible, light as air, invisible to humans and so on. Water is not compressible, is heavier than air, is visible, and exists in different states (solid, liquid, gas).

The point here is that there are only two ways of dealing with new information:

1. Massage (distort) it so that it will fit into an old organization.
2. Permit the new incoming information to organize itself into a new, different, and unpredictable organization.

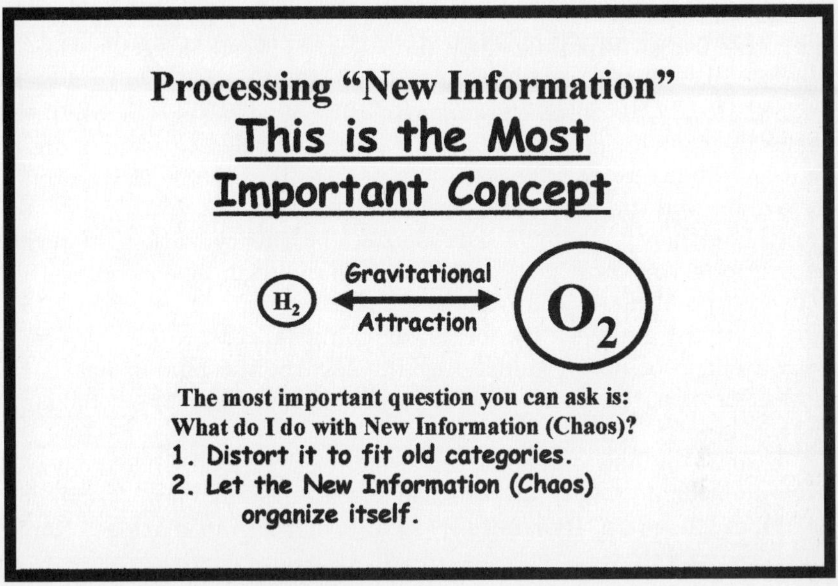

Figure 2–1 How do you handle new information (Chaos)?

Therein lies the difference between a successful approach to trading and the more common losing approach. Traders who let the new incoming information organize their trading will be in sync with the market and thereby will be winners. Attempting to fit new incoming information (Chaos) into old categories distorts both the information and the trading. The surprise that the Science of Chaos found was that there is an underlying structure to what seems, on the surface, to be random behavior or information.

MARKETS AND THE STRUCTURE OF REALITY

By understanding and appreciating the underlying structure in the cosmos, we can gain insight into the machinations of the markets. The first outstanding feature is that the "laws" of nature are flexible, not rigid as once thought by classical physics. This insight will expose the failure of traditional classical technical analysis, which falls into the same traps that classical physics has created over the centuries.

In fact, the modern "laws" of the universe are more closely allied with the Taoist–Buddhist view than that of western civilization. It seems that the nature and structure of the universe are in a never ending flux. Chaos theory supports this hypothesis. Chaos theory tends to focus on process; classical physics tended to focus more on content. Chaos tends to confirm the process philosophy of Kant (subjectivism) and the model put forth by Heraclitus.

Chaos theory, then, is a revolutionary theory with a historical backdrop of Kantian "possibility" and Heraclitian never-ending flux. This viewpoint more accurately explains the events of astronomy, biology, chemical and creative forces, dripping faucets, the earth's magnetic field, economics, galactic orbits, health, the human heart, the flow of traffic, the use of language, and, for traders, the behavior of the markets.

Examining how other researchers have described Chaos may give some additional insight into this new gestalt or worldview. Joseph Ford describes Chaos as "Dynamics freed at last from the shackles of order and predictability. . . systems liberated to randomly explore their every dynamic possibility. . . . Exciting variety, richness of choice, a cornucopia of opportunity."

Hao Bai-Lin, a physicist in China, describes Chaos as "a kind of order without periodicity . . . a newly recognized ubiquitous class of natural phenomena."

Roderick V. Jensen defines Chaos as "the irregular, unpredictable behavior of deterministic, nonlinear systems."[2] This brings up an interesting question: How can you have unpredictable behavior in a deterministic system? We are jolted back to the Aristotelian statement that something cannot be both A and not A. Chaos theory, like quantum science, takes issue with Aristotle, and many experiments show that some things both *are* and *are not* at the same time. It is almost a kind of mysticism if we follow the old Aristotelian logic. Douglas Hofstadter wrote: "It turns out that an eerie type of chaos can lurk just behind the façade of order and yet, deep inside the chaos lurks an even eerier type of order." All randomness has a pattern deeply imbedded in it. This is the underlying structure of both the world and the markets. My trading approach attempts to trade this

[2] This information is available via the internet at http://amath.colorado.edu/appm/faculty/jdm/faw.html.

underlying order rather than the seemingly random outcroppings we see on the computer screen.

Everyday examples of Chaos, other than in the markets, can be seen all around us in the weather, the flow of traffic, and the cycles of living. In the weather, for example, we can predict at a general level, but at another level the weather is random and unpredictable. We know that midsummer days are generally warmer than midwinter days. The ranges of temperatures for the summer season and the winter season are somewhat predictable. But the exact temperature is much less predictable. In the market, there are general long-term cycles that are somewhat predictable, but predicting the end of a current cycle is much less precise. One of the key findings of Edward Lorenz, a pioneer in Chaos theory at Massachusetts Institute of Technology, was that the "noise" that other meteorologists had discarded was really a primary part of the map being drawn by the data.

Most scientists and traders are trained in linear thinking and tend to explain all behavior in Newtonian terms, but Chaos has revealed that nonlinear thinking draws a more accurate map of puzzling situations. These scientists have found that "educated intuition" becomes an important factor in solving problems and can be of great benefit in extracting profits from the markets.

Lorenz coined the term "Butterfly Effect" in explaining how small changes in initial conditions change the outcomes of larger patterns. On the day that this is being written, the national unemployment was announced at a percentage that was slightly better than expected. This caused bonds to make an almost record-breaking downward move, and the Dow dropped over 114 points—the seventh largest drop in its recorded history.

This non-Newtonian behavior can also be seen in the flow of traffic. You usually can estimate how long it will take to go into town because the flow of traffic is about the same every day. But we know all too well how the Butterfly Effect takes over when there is an accident during rush hour.

According to Einstein, the universe is one extremely large piece of matter with the characteristic that it is unchanging in material mass but constantly changing in shape. Could that also be an accurate assessment of the markets? This conclusion comes from taking the $E = mc^2$ equation seriously. When you think about mass being energy, then everything is really the same thing, as so eloquently pointed out by David Bohm.

CHAOS VERSUS ANALYTICAL VIEWS OF THE WORLD AND THE MARKETS

Chaos theory stands in stark contrast with analytical theory. Analytical theory is exacting, but the area that it can accurately describe is quite limited. It is confined to that small domain of empirical, verifiable experience that can be broken down into smaller parts and then analyzed. It seeks "universal truths" within a very limited and specific domain. It can be useful in some contexts, but domains such as the behavior of the markets cannot be fully understood using these tools. Chaos theory also analyzes, but it demands few limits within the domain of human experience and behavior. Both classical and Chaos scientists study empirical data, but classical analysis tends to ignore data that Chaos acknowledges. In fact, the value of Chaos philosophy is that it finds real meaning in what classical analysts describe as random data.

We have a strong tendency to discard data simply because they do not fit into our preconceived categories when we describe behavior in turbulence and living systems. The classical approach to both science and the analysis of markets contains too many filters, stiff perspectives, and levels of intersubjectivity to teach us what is really going on "out there." Chaos points in the direction of finding patterns and structures within different levels of inquiry.

For example, are you just a collection of cells that operates like an ant colony? Where do you start your inquiry—with the whole or by analyzing each cell (ant)? In medicine, for example, we have foot specialists, knee specialists, internal organs specialists, and so on. If we put all of these observations together, do we get an accurate picture of a person? No. Neither can we get a picture of the market by adding up a number of technical indicators.

Chaos theory gives us the challenge of a new metaphysics. It focuses on what's happening right now, which deserves much more attention in market analysis. Chaos theory meets the challenge of looking at this larger picture, capturing the whole of the market-river as it flows ever onward, creating all sorts of little surprises along the way. Noting the ongoing changes in the flow is the challenge of real market analysis and is the antidote to dogmatism, the most fatal disease to traders. Chaos is the new and exciting way to view the changes in market movement.

CHAOS: THE ULTIMATE PARADIGM SHIFT

The discoveries of Chaos have proven that almost all of the pre-Chaos scientists were dead wrong in their basic view of the Universe. The old clockwork view does not accurately describe reality. The certainties that scientists formerly took for granted have turned out to be only probabilities. Laws that were supposed to act in very predictable ways, don't. Scientists previously thought that with knowledge of all of the initial conditions, accurate predictions could be made. The Universe was thought to be ruled by unchanging laws. Cosmos and causality reigned supreme. They also thought that this machinelike Universe would eventually wind down. They called this concept *entropy.* It basically states that, eventually, everything goes down the drain. Chaos has killed this paradigm. A whole new view of the Universe is emerging—a view that is more complicated and carries much more hope and spirit.

Our clockwork Universe started crumbling when Einstein and other physicists found that subatomic particles' behavior could not be predicted. However, old ideas die hard. Even Einstein clung to the clockwork view and could not believe that God would play dice with the Universe. His search for a Unified Field Theory was motivated by this need, as was his effort to explain away the chance and unpredictability of subatomic particles. Much of the physics world to this day wants to follow linear, orderly, and predictable clocklike processes. The conflict is passed off as an exception that proves the rule.

Chaos clearly shows that causality does not apply as previously thought (and still desired). James Gleick, in his book *Chaos,*[3] points out how science has, for centuries, fooled itself by ignoring tiny deviations in its data and experiments. The phrase "error in measurement" became the catchall for data that did not fit the causality paradigm. To keep their integrity, scientists began to limit their research and investigation to closed systems, even if they had to make them artificial, rather than tackle the turbulence of open systems such as the market and nature.

Causality was the prime assumption that they never questioned. Their imaginary game of perfect order and fudged experiments could not continue in the face of overwhelming evidence to the contrary. It began to crumble with the advent of superpowerful computers that

[3] Gleick, J. *Chaos: The Making of a New Science.* New York: Viking Press, 1987.

were capable of including aberrations that had been ignored in all previous scientific investigations. As the new information began to flow in, picturing a very different Universe, the blinders began to fall as more and more scientists in myriad fields found the new paradigm not just useful but revolutionary. Our understanding of our world and our personal lives will never be the same.

The evidence is now overwhelming. The world is not a gigantic clock, with everything happening as predicted. *Chaos has won!* Simple linear systems, causality, and predictability are the exceptions, not the rule. The Universe works in jumps and starts. Freedom and free will—Strange Attractors—more accurately picture the world. Does this new paradigm cause a chasm and will it destroy the cosmos? No; Chaos has always been here. Chaos brought us here and Chaos will take us further down the road of intelligent development. Out of Chaos comes a higher form of order, and it comes spontaneously and unpredictably. It is self-organized. Creation is an ongoing process. The world is not a clock, it is a game, and one of the best personifications of this game is the markets, which allow chance and serendipity, freedom and free will, and unpredictable creativity. Why not play the game to win, to have fun, and to get to know ourselves better?

The Universe is still governed by laws, but they are not the laws we previously thought we had identified. They are not written in stone; they are general and evolving, and they are much looser than we had previously assumed. Nature is flexible, and self-organization is the rule, not the exception. Physicist Paul Davies, in his book *The Cosmic Blueprint,* says:[4]

> There is no detailed blueprint, only a set of laws with an inbuilt facility for making interesting things happen. The universe is free to create itself as it goes along. The general pattern of development is "predestined," but the details are not. Thus, the existence of intelligent life at some stage is inevitable; it is, so to speak, written into the laws of nature. But man as such is far from preordained.

Apparently, Einstein never realized the organization that lurked just below the surface of what appeared to be nonstructured randomness. He never really saw how entities can self-organize to further

[4] Davies, Paul. *The Cosmic Blueprint: New Discoveries in the Nature's Creative Ability to Order the Universe.* New York: Cambridge University Press, 1987, p. 47.

evolution and to create entirely new symmetries and coherence. He did realize that time is not mechanical; time depends on space. If time is flexible, then it follows that it is not predictable but it is still useful over the long run. Chaos, while not totally predictable on a case-by-case basis, is still useful and workable over time spans.

Our current worldview is that we don't live in a clockwork space–time continuum. We have an intelligent Universe where everything not only thrives but evolves, creating a higher order from old decaying forms. It is now clear that the Universe is not the victim of entropy but creates neg-entropy; it is not winding down but being created anew each moment. God now has the appearance of a giant Strange Attractor. This new kind of order is based on a few basic principles from which many laws follow. The underlying structure is stable but does not stand still. The philosophic implications of Chaos are positive and encouraging.

FROM CHAOS TO COSMOS

The market can often seem as chaotic as our inner world, our stream of consciousness. To make sense of it all, we must first find the basic structure to reality and the market—an underlying structure that reveals the order underneath the chaos. The "Chaoticians," a label given to them in the movie *Jurassic Park,* are revolutionizing the world of science. Their discoveries are teaching us that Newton, and indeed almost all of the pre-Chaos scientists, were dead wrong in their basic view of the Universe (the way they organized incoming information). They believed that the world worked in fixed ways; that there was a predictable cause and effect for everything; and that everything happened according to fixed physical laws. They believed in certainties, not probabilities.

The Science of Chaos has found that all outer phenomena are governed by what are known as the four "attractors"—forces that bring order out of perceived disorder. They are:

1. The Point Attractor.
2. The Cycle Attractor.
3. The Torus Attractor.
4. The Strange Attractor.

The Universe goes from Chaos to cosmos through these attractors. An attractor can be thought of as a sort of a magnet that pulls energy in a certain direction. It is the force behind energy movements and behind changes in market prices. We will illustrate the four attractors here and will then apply them to trading in the market.

The market as a representative of the real world is fundamentally disordered and free. Chaos reigns over predictability. Simple linear approaches to trading the market do not work. The market is infinitely complex. Freedom and free will—Strange Attractors—prevail over rules and determinacy. Chaos is not the enemy. From out of Chaos a higher order always appears, but this order comes spontaneously and unpredictably. It is self-organized just as hydrogen and oxygen self-organize from gas to water.

THE GEOMETRY OF CHAOS

Benoit Mandelbrot (Chaos's most visible pioneer) made a great breakthrough that can be summarized by a simple mathematical formula:

$$z -> z^2 + c$$

The arrow (−>) means iteration—the feedback process where the end result of the last calculation becomes the beginning constant of the next: $z^2 + c$ becomes z in the next repetition. Like life, this is a dynamic equation, existing in time. It is not a static equation.

When iteration becomes a squaring process, the results are predictable and will reach infinity quickly: $1.1 \cdot 1.1 = 1.21 \cdot 1.21 = 1.461 \cdot 1.461 = 2.14358$, and so on. The same is true for any noncomplex number that is less than one. It quickly becomes infinitely small: $.9 \cdot .9 = .81 \cdot .81 = .6561 \cdot .6561 = .43046$, and so on.

However, by adding a constant c (a complex number) to the squaring process and starting z from zero, stable iterations that go to neither infinitely large nor infinitely small become possible. These numbers are contained within the black area of the Mandelbrot set (see Figure 2–2).

THE MANDELBROT SET ON A COMPLEX PLANE

Like the weather, the stock and commodity markets, and other chaotic systems, negligible changes in quantities (such as may appear in the

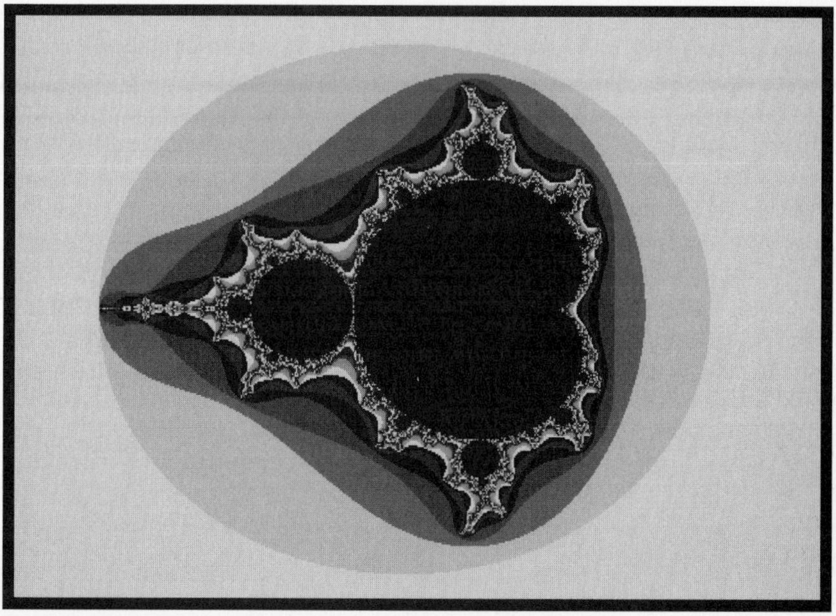

Figure 2–2 The Mandelbrot set on a complex plane ($z -> z^2 + c$).

unemployment report), coupled with feedback, can produce unexpected effects. This mirrors the behavior in the fourth dimension, the real world where Chaos is obvious and is the underlying structure of the most ordered systems.

The Mandelbrot set, the formula named after its inventor, could not have been invented without the use of computers and computer graphics. Many scientists believe this formula is the most important mathematical breakthrough during the twentieth century. Again, it is a dynamic calculation based on the iteration (a calculation based on constant feedback) of complex numbers with zero as the starting point. The result of this formula can only be seen by a computer calculation and graphic portrayal of these numbers. The formula summarizes many of the insights Mandelbrot gained into the fractal geometry of nature—the world, or the fourth dimension. This is in absolute contrast to the idealized world of Euclidean forms: the first, second, and third dimensions.

The fractal as a geometric figure not only has irregular shapes (as does a stock or commodity chart), but lurking in the disorder of these irregular shapes is a hidden order. This was the hidden order that

Gann, Elliott, and other pattern-recognition pioneers were looking for but did not have the computer power to actually find or define.

An understanding of how the fourth dimension includes the infinity of intervals between the other dimensions can be gained by visualizing a couple of the better known fractal dimensions (called the Hausdorff dimensions by mathematicians). One of the more famous ones lies between the zero dimension and the first dimension, the point and the line. It is created by erasing the middle third of the line. This leaves two lines. We then erase the middle third of each of those lines and continue this process to infinity. What remains after all the middle-third removals is called by Mandelbrot: "Cantor's Dust." It consists of an infinite number of points, but no length. Figure 2–3 is an example of the beginning of this process.

What remains at infinity is not quite a line but is more than a point. This dimension is calculated to have a numerical value of .63, interestingly close (12/1000ths) to the famous Fibonacci number of .618. This was considered an anomaly and was avoided by most mathematicians in the early part of the twentieth century as a "useless monstrosity." In fact, this is a vital part of the real world in inorganic matter, plants, animals, and markets. Understanding this phenomenon allowed Mandelbrot to solve a perplexing problem for IBM: how to overcome apparently random errors in data transmission by simple redundancies in the transmission. Without this insight, the Internet would not be workable.

The next well-known fractal dimension lies between a line and a plane, the first and second dimensions. Named the Sierpiniski Gasket after another mathematician, Waclaw Sierpiniski, it has a fractal dimension of 1.58 (32/1000ths away from another Fibonacci number of 1.618). You start with an equilateral triangle and use half of the side lengths to form the beginning triangle. The area

Figure 2–3 "Cantor's Dust."

that is left accommodates three half-size triangles. Repeat this process to infinity and you end up with a form that has infinite lines but is less than a plane.

Fractal forms and these same relationships are found in your body. The best known examples are the arteries and veins in mammalian vascular systems. The bronchi of the human lung are self-similar over 15 successive bifurcations. The Mandelbrot set has far-reaching implications ranging from the markets to the delicate functioning of our brains.

Fractal theory offers a new geometry of the Universe, one that represents the realities of the markets and permits more profitable operations in both investing and trading. This is the same science that Air Force reconnaissance pilots use to tell the difference between tanks and trees when their altitude does not allow visual identification. Psychiatrists are studying the relationship between mental health and fractal patterns in the brain. Kinesthesiologists are using self-reflective geometry of the human body to help their patients heal. High-tech video animation producers use fractals to create spectacular 3D explosions and other-worldly scenes. Textile designers weave fractal symmetry into their products. Electronic engineers use fractal graphics to lay out complex circuit-board routing. And now speculators are using nonlinear techniques for investing and trading.

Fractals are the markets' new toys. Fractals are the way the markets organize themselves. A specific fractal organization is produced by what are known in the Science of Chaos as attractors. Think of all preexistence as a universe-wide quantum soup. Everything that exists is drawn out of this quantum soup by attractors. These attractors act like magnets. They pull the cosmos out of Chaos.

We usually experience a convoluted flow of happenings and events. The fragmented, fractal nature of everyday reality is one of the basic problems. To use thinking to sort things out, to start making sense of it all, we must first find the basic structure of reality. That structure would reveal the order underneath Chaos. There are four nonlinear functions that help us find that order in our own consciousness. Chaos scientists have found that seemingly chaotic, lawless actions in the outer world actually follow a hidden order. The order they have discovered is fourfold: all outer phenomena are governed by what they call the four attractors—forces that bring order out of disorder. As noted earlier, they are called the Point Attractor, the Cycle Attractor, the Torus Attractor, and the Strange Attractor.

These four attractors form the basic structure of the outer world, the nature of behavior, and the machinations of the market.

With this brief background, we can examine these four attractors that bring order out of Chaos in the markets. As traders and human beings living in the fourth dimension, we are at our best when we follow the spontaneity and freedom of the Strange Attractors. Only in this way can we live and trade autonomously in the moment, in tune with what the Chinese call the Tao—the Way, the flow of forces in the fourth dimension.

THE POINT ATTRACTOR

The Point Attractor (Figure 2–4) is the simplest way to bring order out of Chaos. It lives in the first dimension of the line, which is made up of an infinite number of points. Whenever this point attractor is controlling, a person is drawn to one particular activity, or repelled from another. A newborn baby is an illustration of the Point Attractor. The baby is attracted to food when hungry and repelled by wet and dirty diapers. Its responses are similar to the positive and negative poles of electromagnetic energy. The middle of the attraction/repulsion continuum is known as the saddle point. There, all the energies are in balance, just before one or the other forces becomes stronger and directs the energy toward one side or the other. In human behavior, the Point Attractor produces a psychological fixation on one desire (or revulsion), and all else is put aside until it is satisfied (or destroyed). A young male dog around a bitch is another good example of the type of behavior this fractal produces. The Point Attractor is a black–white,

Figure 2–4 The Point Attractor.

good–bad, single-minded attractor, except at the saddle point. This is the first-dimension attractor, and it can be used to trade the markets. The exact techniques for trading the stock and commodity markets are examined and explained in later chapters.

THE CYCLE (CIRCLE) ATTRACTOR

The characteristic of the Cycle Attractor (Figure 2–5) is a back-and-forth movement, like a pendulum or a circling magnet. It attracts, then repels, then attracts again, and so on. It lives in the second dimension of a plane, which is made up of an infinite number of lines. It is characteristic of a range-bound or bracketed market where the price moves up and down in a range over a period of time. This attractor is more complex than the Point Attractor and becomes the underlying structure for more complicated behavior. One activity automatically leads into another activity in a repetitive manner; it mirrors how the light of day is followed by the dark of night. In nature, it can be seen in a number of ways—for example, in predator/prey systems where the respective predator or prey populations

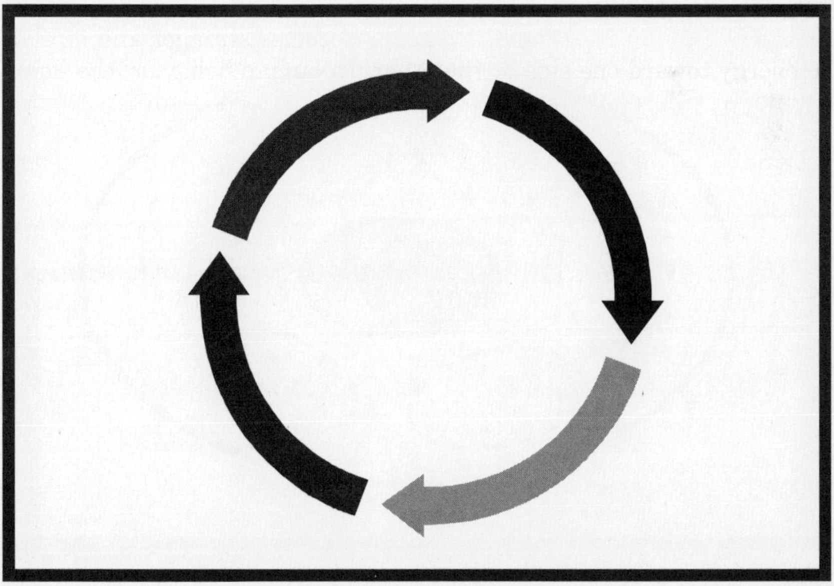

Figure 2–5 The Cycle (Circle) Attractor.

cycle up and down in relation to each other. In the grains market, it can be seen on a yearly basis. One year of high prices produces more plantings the next spring, which produces low prices. The farmers then cut their planting acreage to yield higher prices. In computers, the electric current provides these iterations.

The Cycle Attractor produces a structural tension between the two poles and opens the way for integration between the two opposites. Synthesis comes from combining the thesis and antithesis; the neutron is produced by the proton and electron. In the human brain structure, the two parts of the brain make possible the third integrating, inspirational part.

THE TORUS ATTRACTOR

The third and more complicated attractor is known as the Torus Attractor (Figure 2–6). It begins a complex cycling that repeats itself as it moves forward. It lives in the third dimension, which is

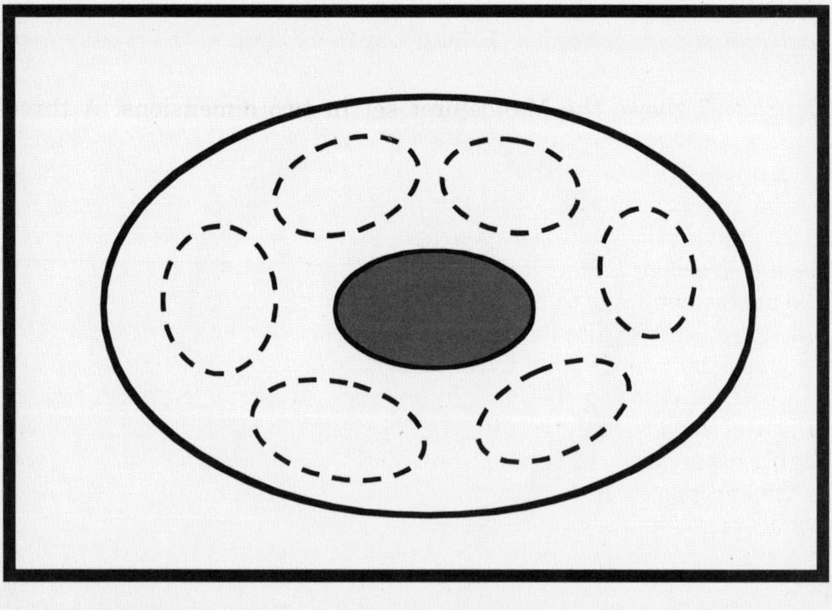

Figure 2–6 The second-dimensional Cycle Attractor (Torus).

made up of an infinite number of planes. Compared to the Cycle and Point Attractors, the Torus Attractor introduces a higher degree of irregularity and the patterns are more complex. At this level, predictions are more precise and the patterns tend to be more finite. Graphically it looks like a donut or a bagel. It contains spiraling circles on a number of different planes and sometimes will turn back on itself to complete full revolutions.

Its main characteristic is the repeating function. One is attracted to cycling and hiking in the summer and skiing in the winter. It tends to produce a sort of irregular homeostasis—for example, how the insect population affects the frog population. The presence of more insects will produce larger frogs, and the larger frogs will eat more insects, which reduces the insect population. Having less food then creates smaller frogs. Its effects can also be seen in how the world's assets seek a safe haven. If the bond interest goes up, it attracts more investors. Bond prices then go up, which lowers the interest rate and makes bonds less attractive, and so on.

We now come to the attractor that most affects human behavior. It is very aptly labeled the Strange Attractor.

THE STRANGE ATTRACTOR

Figure 2–7 shows the Mandelbrot set in two dimensions. A three-dimensional representation would show a beautiful world of spontaneity and freedom coming from the Strange Attractor. It allows an escape from the confines of old paradigms. The Strange Attractor from the fourth dimension becomes self-organizing. It is the birthplace of freedom and of understanding how the market really works. The surface appears to be pure Chaos, with no apparent order at all. But there is a definite underlying order based on the Strange Attractor when the view is from the perspective of the fourth dimension.

Another characteristic of the Strange Attractor is its sensitivity to initial conditions, sometimes known as the Butterfly Effect. The slightest variation in the beginning can make enormous differences in the end result. In our own trading, we have found that instituting trades based on varying initial conditions can raise the profitability of a trading system by a factor of five. In other words, taking trades based on sensitive initial conditions can increase profits by 500 percent. Edward Lorenz discovered the importance of initial conditions

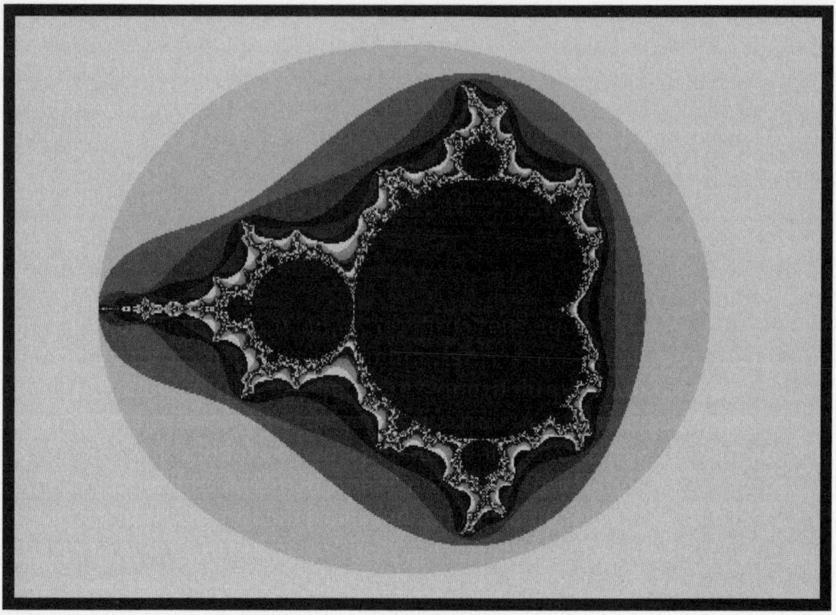

Figure 2–7 The Strange Attractor.

while researching the predictability of weather. He used this now famous example of the Butterfly Effect:

> **The wing movement of a butterfly in Peru may later, through an extremely complex series of unpredictably linked events, magnify air movements and ultimately cause a hurricane in Texas.[5]**

This sequence has only recently been scientifically proven and verified, but it is really a rediscovery of long-held folk wisdom. As James Gleick points out, sensitive dependence on initial conditions is an old idea that can even be found in nursery rhymes:

For want of a nail, the shoe was lost;
For want of a shoe, the horse was lost;

[5] As quoted in Gleick, J. *Chaos: The Making of a New Science.* New York: Viking Press, 1987, p. 8.

For want of a horse, the rider was lost;
For want of a rider, the battle was lost;
For want of a battle, the kingdom was lost!

Following the same principle, a trader must be closely attuned to any changes in the initial conditions of the market. Current technical analysis pays virtually no attention to the importance of initial conditions. My trading approach involves five different perspectives:

1. Momentum.
2. Change in the speed of current momentum.
3. Appearance of an initiating fractal.
4. Zonal influences.
5. Balance Line differentials.

By surveying all five dimensions of the market, the trader becomes very sensitive to important initial conditions before the market moves.

When we are subject to the first three attractors, we are manipulated and we become predictable. Only in the range of the Strange Attractor can we really be free. The Strange Attractor allows us to participate in the ebb and flow of the market and of life. We can add our own butterfly wing to the weather of the market. We can base our trading, as well as our life, on Strange Attactors. As Don Juan explained to Castenada, we then live in "the crack between the worlds." When we enter the flow (in athletics, the "zone") we are in tune with the Strange Attractor. We then see the hidden order. Time stops, and we have a flowing peak experience where all seems to go right by itself. Effort becomes effortless, and we *know* without knowing how we know. We reach Levels 4 and 5 of expert trading. Mandelbrot gave us an accurate map for navigating this "crack between the worlds," which, in the markets, is a space–time continuum of turbulence and chance.

When you have a loss in the market, then stop that activity (you are out of tune with the current activity, so cut your losses short) and choose to let go of thinking of it as a failure. Choose again to take a chance, which, in Chaos terms, means returning to zero, where the inspiration for new action comes from the market and not from your desires or your former organization. Remember how the hydrogen atom *let go* and became a more complex organization known as water.

Will you end up a winner? Absolutely. What will winning mean to you? That depends on your categories and your belief systems. You get in touch with the Strange Attractor only through *experience* backed up by *awareness*. You learn by trial and error with feedback, by learning from your mistakes, and always by beginning anew from Awareness. Letting Chaos organize your life and trading will allow you to TRANCE-END to the next higher level. In the land of Chaos, you get better by letting go, not by strenuously climbing hills.

If this new action is rewarding—if it leads to greater order and coherence (cosmos)—then continue to follow it. Enjoy the fractal beauty of living on the edge. Like failure, an established success should lead to freedom, to a new activity in an unknown future. Trading is the most efficient psychotherapy and growth technique available, when done with the right attitude and the right tools. It allows us to personally pioneer the frontiers of cosmos in the midst of Chaos.

Remember that the hidden order may not appear immediately. It may become obvious much later, through a series of synchronous other events. Mandelbrot's own life, which had many career changes, seems to have been necessary to lead him to the unfolding of this new order. It is important here to point out the difference between chance and choice, and chance and chance. Chaos "for the hell of it" is a dead end.

THE DIFFERENCE BETWEEN A FRACTAL AND A HOLOGRAM

A hologram has the characteristic that each small part contains the entire hologram (with just a bit less detail). It is uniform; each point contains the same pattern as every other point. In a fractal, slight variations are found. A fractal is similar to a hologram in that the hologram contains identical repetitions of the exact same pattern while in fractals there is only self-similarity, not identity. A fractal does not repeat the exact same pattern but it still contains and reflects the whole, like a hologram. Because the Universe is a fractal rather than a hologram, it permits creativity and invention. Spontaneity and freedom are displayed every day in the markets. When we view various markets and time frames, we can see similarities, yet each part, on further examination, tends to be very individualistic and different from any other part. That is the great joy—the freedom and beauty—in our fractal Universe as well as our fractal markets.

With the markets' ever-changing personality, our best hope is to learn how to learn. Only a few basic principles must be combined, bent, and moved to create more profitable ways of following the markets' movements. That's why we will never be bored with the markets and there will always be more to know. Within the basic parameters and the given structure, the content is still unpredictable in the absolute sense. Only the overall pattern and statistics can be predicted. Again, that is the great joy of the markets. The rules of the game may be given and limited, but the trades we choose to make within the confines of those rules are limitless, and the outcome of each individual trade is unknown.

SUMMARY

In this chapter, we have looked at the Science of Chaos from a trading standpoint. We eliminated the nonlinear feedback calculus, which is a rather awesome mathematical exercise, and instead condensed our 15+ years of intensive study and application of Chaos principles and techniques in investing and trading in the markets. In the following chapters, we will go through each of the five dimensions we use to analyze the markets, looking for entry and exit strategies based on nonlinear dynamics and fractal geometry.

In the next chapter, we will explore how we use the phase space between the Strange Attractors to filter out the more potentially profitable trades from those that have not broken the stalemate of being balanced between the attractors.

WHAT YOU SHOULD UNDERSTAND BEFORE GOING FURTHER

At this point in our journey, you should understand that this approach you are studying is not the consensus opinion of the majority of traders. You should understand that no individual or company is large enough, strong enough, or smart enough to control the markets. They are beyond even the muscle of the central and international reserve banks.

You should also understand that to win consistently in the markets you must get to know them and how they process incoming information. Your best strategy is to relax you own personal goals and spend that energy in understanding and getting in tune with the markets. You should understand that we all trade our own personal belief systems. If you want to change your results in the markets, the most efficient approach is to change your beliefs about the markets and the world. You should understand that Chaos is really FREEDOM if you are in step with it rather than fighting against it. Finally, you should begin to realize that any sort of organization is itself, by definition, a resistance to Chaos.

So let's open up, relax, and begin to have fun with the markets and with the Universe. They are twins.

3

THE ALLIGATOR

OUR COMPASS AND ODDS MAKER

One of the keys to profitable trading is to take only those trades with the most potential and stay out of situations where there is marginal potential. My trading group has completed fifteen years of intensive research into applying the new Science of Chaos, along with quantum physics, holography, cybernetics, nonlinear dynamics, information theory, and fractal geometry, to the world of stock and commodity trading.

When this research started, we were using super computers. Through a process of literally millions of iterations, we devised a process that will work on ordinary personal computers. The Alligator is basically a compass to keep you trading in the appropriate direction no matter which way the immediate *price* is moving.

The Alligator is a personification of this process and influences every signal in my trading group's arsenal. We will demonstrate both the setup and how to use this valuable tool while trading. In this chapter, we will describe the Alligator, what it does, how to construct it, and how to trade it.

TRADERS' BIGGEST PROBLEM

Trading is likely the most exciting way to make a living and/or accumulate a fortune. You are your own boss and your own worst enemy. You alone must deal with the frustration of your own choices. If you lose, there is no one else to blame. You made the losing decision, even if that decision was to let someone else make your decisions or to follow someone else's approach. On the other hand, if you win, you don't have to say "Thank you" to anyone. You are not obliged to anyone but yourself. There is no politics nor anyone to whom you must cater. You are truly "sliding down the razor blade of life."

But here is the problem. Most of the time, the market goes nowhere. Only 15 to 30 percent of the time does the market trend, and traders who are not on the floor make nearly all of their profits in a trending market. My grandfather used to say, "Even a blind chicken will find an ear of corn every now and then." We call trending trades "blind-chicken trades" because all you have to do is "be there." Through the years, we have developed an indicator that helps keep our powder dry until we can get into one of those "blind chicken trades."

Figure 3–1 shows typical "generic" market action in both stocks and commodities. The typical market spends from 70 to 85 percent of its life going nowhere. In that portion of market action, most traders lose. About the only ones making profit in those times are traders on the floor and specialists in the stock markets. The most crucial point in Figure 3–1 is at the last low point, just before the large move upward.

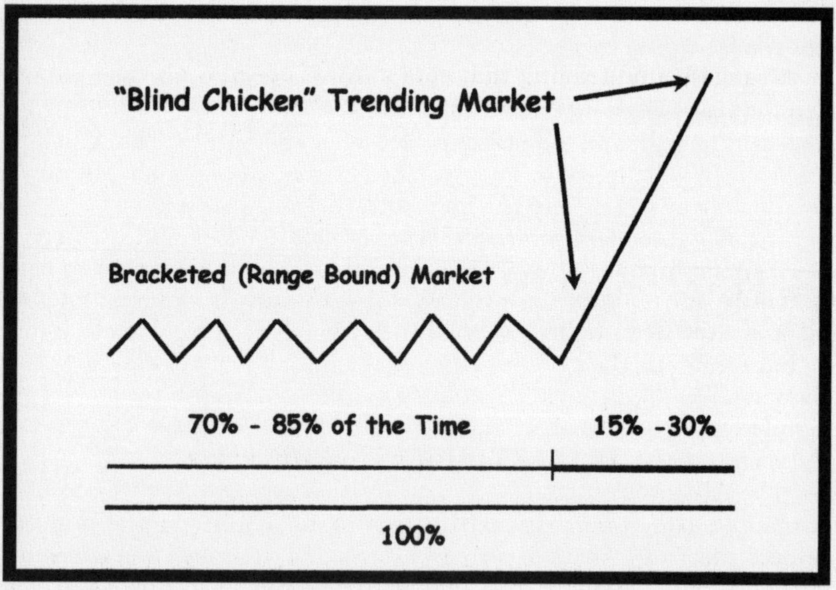

Figure 3–1 A typical stock and/or commodity trading market.

- **An integrated approach to monitoring the market's momentum**
- **A simple indicator to trade only with the current trend**
- **A protection device to not lose money during bracketed markets**

Figure 3–2 What is the Alligator?

The Profitunity techniques, including the five magic bullets, are the best yet in finding this ideal starting point for trading.

Here is our problem: we don't want to spend our time entering and exiting a market that is going nowhere. If the market is going nowhere, then opportunity is NO-WHERE. We want to change that to opportunity is NOW-HERE. Our technique for moving that hyphen over one letter is the Alligator.

The Alligator will help us to get in on a real trend and stay out of most range-bound trading that eats away at our profits. Let's look at exactly what the Alligator is (Figure 3–2). Later, we will examine the Alligator's behavior patterns.

WHAT IS THE ALLIGATOR?

Basically, the Alligator is a combination of Balance Lines using fractal geometry and nonlinear dynamics. The *Blue* line (Alligator's Jaw) on Figure 3–3 is the Balance Line for the time frame that the chart is showing. The *Red* line (Alligator's Teeth) is the Balance Line for one significant time frame lower. The *Green* line (Alligator's Lips) is a Balance Line for one more significant time frame lower.

The Alligator's Lips, Teeth, and Jaws show the interaction of the various time frames. Because markets trend only about 15 to 30 percent of the time, we want to go with the trends and stay out of the bracketed or range-bound markets. We have found the Alligator an excellent guide. When all three lines are intertwined (see Figure 3–3),

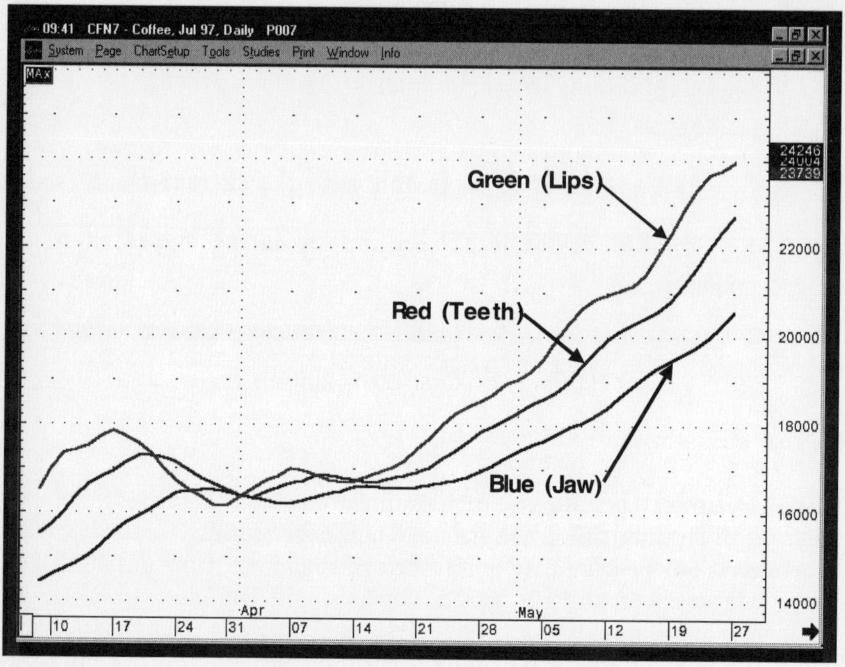

Figure 3–3 Alligator Anatomy 101.

the Alligator is sleeping and the market is range-bound. The market is taking back what we gained during the last trend move.

The purposes of the Alligator are to:

1. Provide an integrated approach to monitoring the market's momentum.
2. Provide a simple indicator for when to trade only with the current trend.
3. Create a protection device so as to not lose money during a bracketed, range-bound market.

Here is our basic strategy: we want to wait for the trend to prove itself by giving us a fractal that is above/below the Alligator's mouth (the fractal signal will be explained in the next chapter). Ideally, but not always, all five highs (or lows, in a down move) should be on the same side (higher for buys and lower for sells) of the Blue Balance

Line (the Alligator's Jaw). We take that fractal as our first entry and then add on aggressively in that direction for any of the five dimensional signals, including the zone trades.

We place our first Stop to Exit (not a SAR—Stop and Reverse) just inside the Alligator's Teeth (Red line) on a Stop Close Only order for the dailies and Stop Close Only for the close of the bar on any other time frame. If the market goes our way, we trail a stop after we have had five consecutive bars of the same color. This technique is covered in Chapter Seven.

ALLIGATOR ANATOMY 101

A full explanation of the Balance Line—what it means and how to use it—will be presented in Chapter 8. Basically, the Blue Balance Line is where the price would be if there were no new incoming information. The original calculations for this Balance Line were done mathematically using a super mainframe computer. It is constructed by plotting a 13-bar smoothed moving average that is offset 8 bars into the future. Again, we refer to this as the Jaw of the Alligator.

The Teeth of the Alligator is the Balance Line of one significant time frame lower. The computer figures the exact time frame (roughly, about a five-to-one ratio). If the Blue line is on the dailies, the Red line (Teeth) is roughly on an hourly basis. The Red line is constructed using an 8-bar smoothed moving average that is offset 5 bars into the future. The Green line (Alligator's Lips) is another significantly lower time frame. It is constructed using a 5-bar smoothed moving average that is offset 3 bars into the future.

Therefore our construction is as follows (Figure 3–4):

Blue line—a 13-bar smoothed moving average offset 8 bars into the future.

Red line—an 8-bar smoothed moving average offset 5 bars into the future.

Green line—a 5-bar smoothed moving average offset 3 bars into the future.

These averages are available on most retrieval machines and are also available on Investor's Dream, our proprietary software. The averages create three different Balance Line time frames on the same chart.

- **Jaw [Blue]: This is the Balance Line for the current time from displayed on the chart. It is a 13-bar Smoothed moving average offset 8 bars into the future.**
- **Teeth Line [Red]: This is the Balance Line for one significantly shorter time frame. It is an 8-bar Smoothed moving average offset 5 bars into the future.**
- **Lip Line [Green]: This is the Balance Line for still one more significantly shorter time frame. It is a 5-bar Smoothed moving average offset 3 bars into the future.**

Figure 3–4 The Alligator setup.

THE ALLIGATOR ON THE PRICE CHART

Figure 3–5 is the same chart as Figure 3–3, but prices have been added. Notice that when the offset moving averages are intertwined, the Alligator is asleep, and the longer he sleeps the hungrier he gets. When he wakes up from a long sleep, he is very hungry and chases the price (Alligator food) much farther because it takes more prices to fill his stomach.

Whenever the Alligator has had enough, he starts to close his mouth and loses interest in eating. (Eating here is signified by an open mouth; sleeping, by a closed or intertwining mouth.) This is the time you want to start taking profits from the trend move. Then you simply sit back, let the Alligator take a nap, and get back into this market when the Alligator starts to awaken.

Figure 3–6 is a Coca-Cola stock chart. During August and early September, the only logical position was to be short this market. Notice that the mouth started to close in early September, telling us to take profit and wait to see whether the Alligator would take a nap.

We have found that the Alligator technique gives us fewer losing trades and improves our win–lose ratio. It keeps us out of choppy markets and gets us into every significant trend.

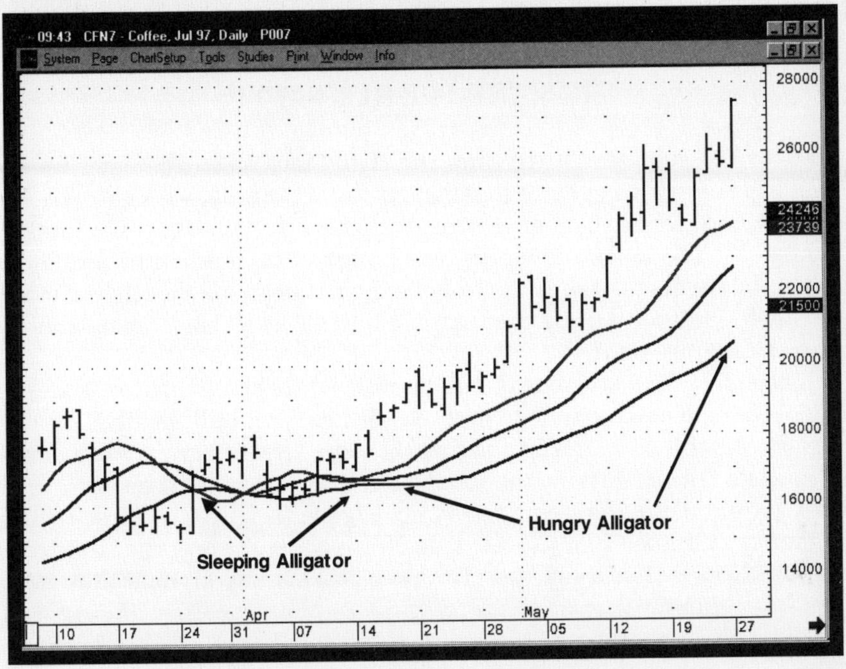

Figure 3–5 The Alligator on a coffee price chart.

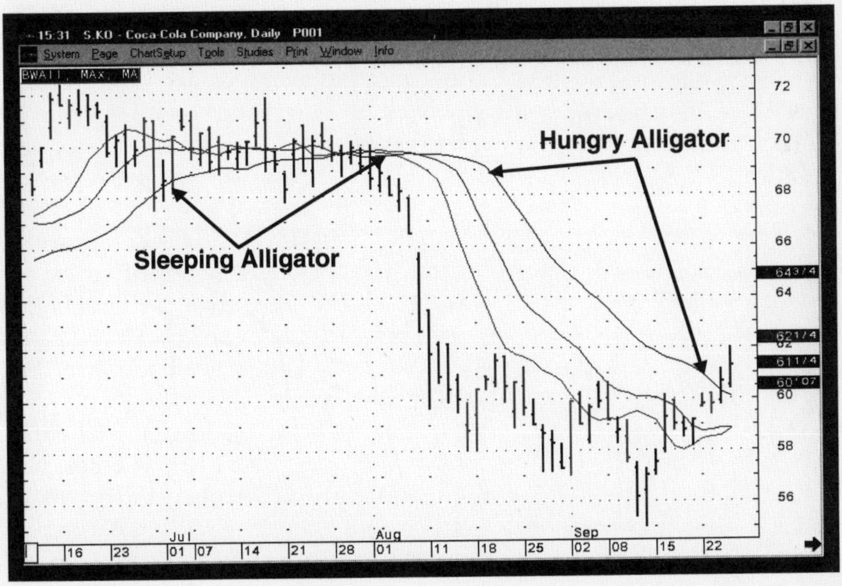

Figure 3–6 The Alligator on a bearish Coca-Cola stock chart.

TRADING THE ALLIGATOR

Here is the strategy for trading the Alligator. When the Jaw, Teeth, and Lips are closing, close together, or intertwining, we know the Alligator is going to sleep or is already asleep. As he sleeps, his hunger increases. The longer he sleeps, the hungrier he is when he awakens. When he wakes up, the first thing he does is open his mouth and start to yawn. He then smells food, either bull meat or bear meat, and he starts chasing it.

Normally, we stay out of the market while the Alligator is sleeping. We basically want to bet on either the bull or the bear—whichever the Alligator is chasing. For our first entry, we wait until there is a fractal outside the jaw. The fractal signal will be explained in Chapter Four. You can see it on Figure 3–7, at the first ^ just under the number 1 on the left side of the chart. This is the first fractal up. Notice that there are five more fractal buy signals that were hit later during this up trend. Figure 3–7 is for coffee. Figure 3–8 shows the same type of situation in a Dell Computer stock chart.

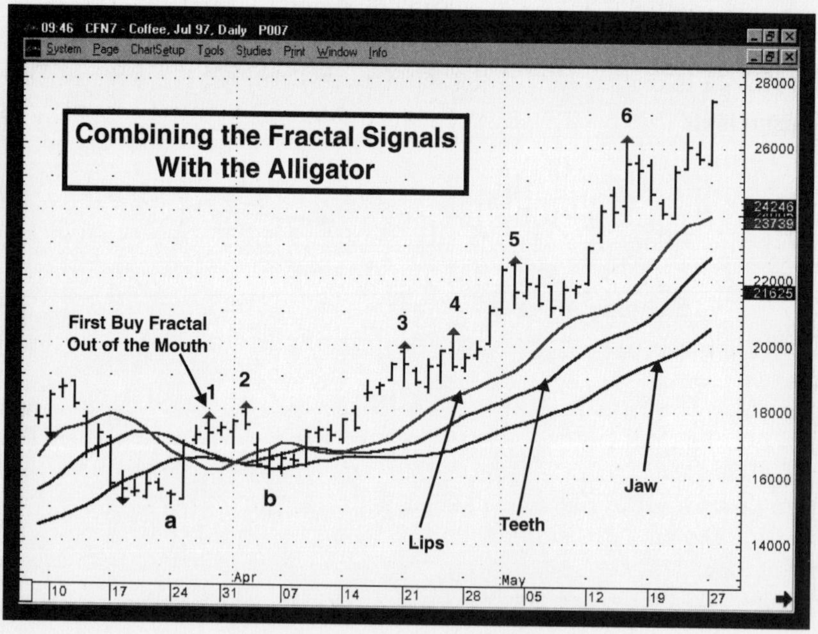

Figure 3–7 Trading the Alligator.

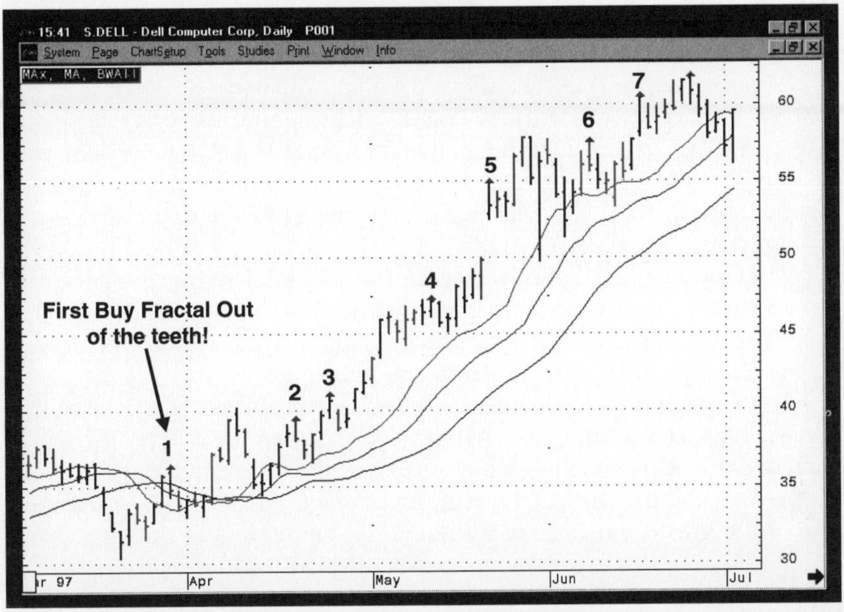

Figure 3–8 Trading outside the mouth in Dell Computer stock.

Throughout this book, you will see both commodity and stock charts. There is no difference in trading strategy when you use the concepts from the Science of Chaos.

ALLIGATOR BEHAVIOR

Our trading strategy is to not trade until the first fractal breakout outside the mouth. This entry will be fully explained in the next chapter. After the first fractal breakout has been triggered, we take any and every signal from all five dimensions in that direction. For example, if the price is above the Alligator's mouth, we would only take buy signals and would not go short. We would have profit-protecting stops trailing the up move. On the down side, we would only take sell signals below the Alligator's mouth and would only buy to exit a position, not to go long. Exit procedures are fully explained in Chapter Nine.

It is just that simple. Above the mouth we only go long, and below the mouth we only go short. This guarantees that we will not be left out of any significant trend and our whiplashes will be kept at a minimum.

Another simplification allowed by using these Balance Lines is that we can trade the Elliott Waves without the necessity for accurate counting. If the current price is outside the Alligator's mouth, we are in an impulsive wave of one degree or another. If the price is meandering around the Balance Lines, we are in a reactive wave of one degree or another.

Figures 3–9 and 3–10 illustrate the power of using the Alligator for a compass and odds maker in trading both stocks and commodities. These unusually good examples demonstrate the power of this approach to gleaning profits from the markets.

The two Figures illustrate the power of combining all five trading dimensions and using the Alligator as a compass. The Alligator clearly delineates which signals to take and which ones to leave alone. Figure 3–10 marks all the fractal, Awesome Oscillator (AO), Acceleration (AC), and Balance Line signals. You can see how the aggressive

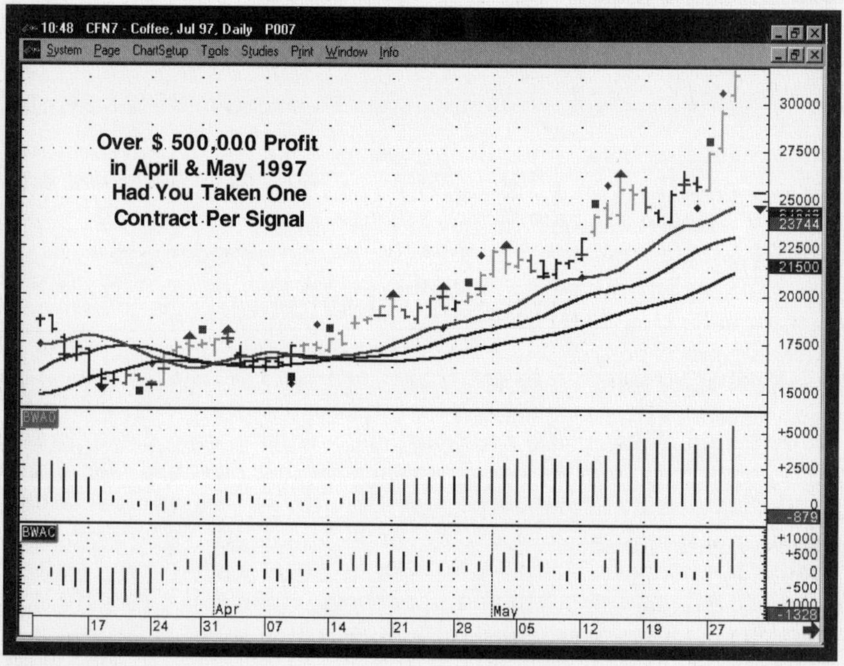

Figure 3–9 Trading all five dimensions during April and May in coffee.

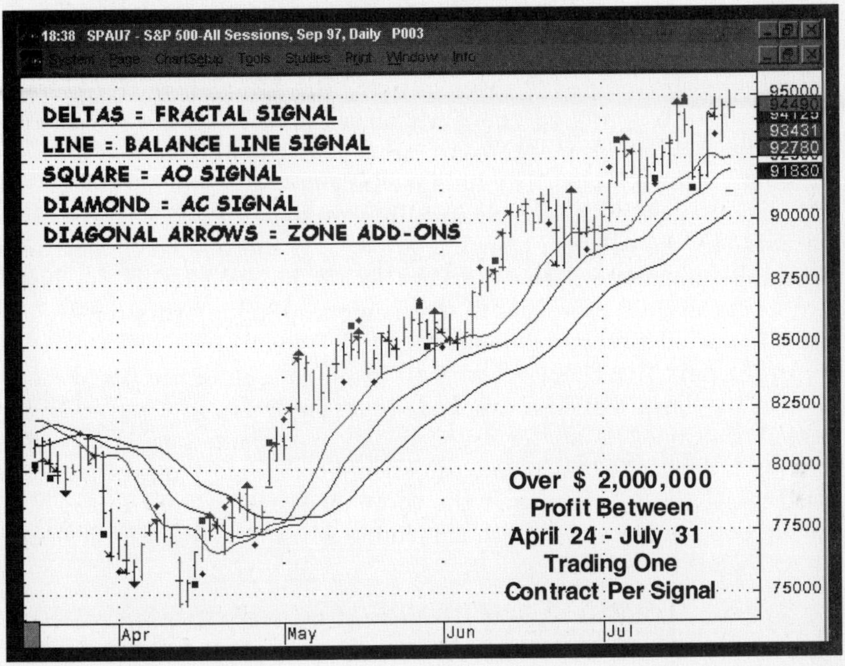

Figure 3–10 Trading all five dimensions in 3½ months in the S&P dailies.

add-ons during a trend move give you an exponential profit curve. (AO and AC are explained in later chapters.)

The coffee move (Figure 3–9), which covered less than two months, generated a profit of over $500,000 based on trading one contract for each signal. This five-dimensional strategy allows us to have the reachable profit goal of 3 to 5 times the trend move. In other words, if a trend is 200 points, our goal is to take 600 to 1,000 points from that move, based on trading one contract per signal.

The S&P chart (Figure 3–10) shows the signals that would have been taken using the Alligator as the compass while trading just over three months of the S&P 500 on a daily chart with no intraday trades. Again, it should be pointed out that these are especially good results and using these techniques has proven to be consistently profitable.

All these signals are easy to recognize and can be generated automatically using our software, which is available for use on most price formats.

SUMMARY

This chapter introduced the idea of using the Alligator to sharpen up entries and exits and to cut down on whiplashes. What moves the commodity and stock markets are traders responding to new incoming information (Chaos). The Balance Line is where the market would be if there were no new incoming information. In other words, the markets only move when Chaos is present. If there is no Chaos (new incoming information) the markets would be static. Our job is to ferret out the characteristics of this new incoming information and to use it to our advantage while trading.

In the next five chapters, we will examine each of the five dimensions of the market and how to trade them for profit. In Chapter Nine, we will use Chaos theory for squeezing the maximum amount of profit from each trade. At this point, you should thoroughly understand the workings of the Alligator and the three different Balance Lines. You should also understand how to determine when the Alligator is sleeping and when he is hunting.

4

THE FRACTAL—THE BREAKAWAY TRADE

Many experienced traders say that making money in trading the markets is easy; what is difficult is keeping it. The pattern of all markets is that they spend most of their time going nowhere and only a small amount of time (15 to 30 percent) in identifiable trends. Traders who are not on the floor and/or not specialists have a tough time while the market is not moving. Most traders have a tendency to place their stops too close to the market and consequently get whiplashed. Still, the greatest potential for profits occurs when the markets are trending. Therefore, our first consideration is to *not be left out* of any significant trend move. Remember, this is the first of our five entry systems, and it is the first signal we take after the Alligator starts to awaken.

FRACTAL BREAKOUT

As we saw in Chapter Three, we want to stay out of the market and "keep our powder dry" until the Alligator is hungry and starts his search for food (either higher or lower prices). We do not take any trades until this first fractal is triggered. Let's take another look at a typical stock and/or commodity market (Figure 4–1).

A Typical Trading Market

Figure 4–1 shows typical "generic" market action. The market spends from 70 to 85 percent of its life going nowhere. In that portion of

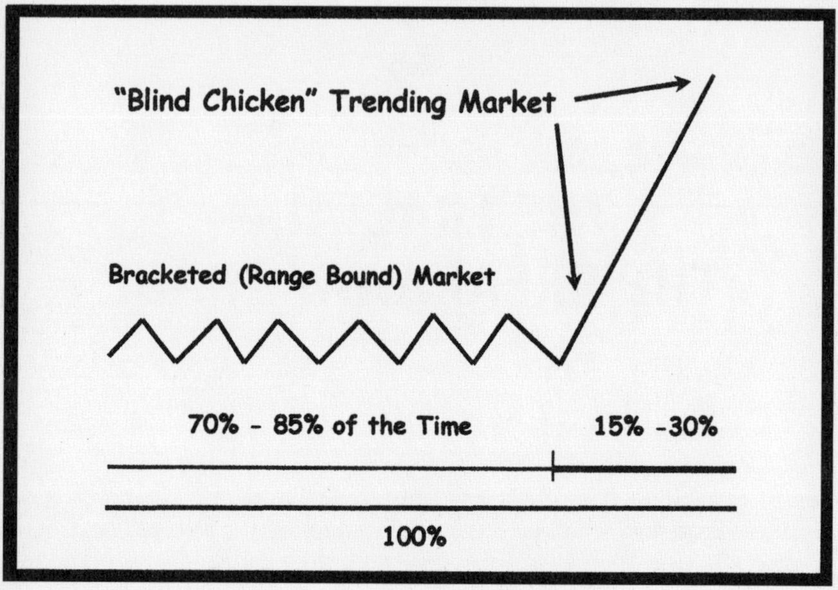

Figure 4–1 A typical trading market.

market action, most traders lose; about the only ones making profit are traders on the floor who are fading the market in a very short time period. The most crucial point is where the last bottom (low point) occurs. My trading techniques, including the five magic bullets, are the best we have ever seen for finding any bottom or top.

The Alligator will help us to get in on a real trend and stay out of most range-bound trading that eats away at our profits.

THE FRACTAL PATTERN

The fractal pattern is a simple one. The market makes a move in one direction or the other. After a period of time, all the willing buyers have bought (on an up move) and the market falls back because of a lack of buyers. Then some new incoming information (Chaos) begins to affect the traders. There is an influx of new buying, and the market, finding that place of equal disagreement on value and agreement on price, moves up. If the momentum and the buyers' strength are strong enough to exceed the immediately preceding up fractal, we

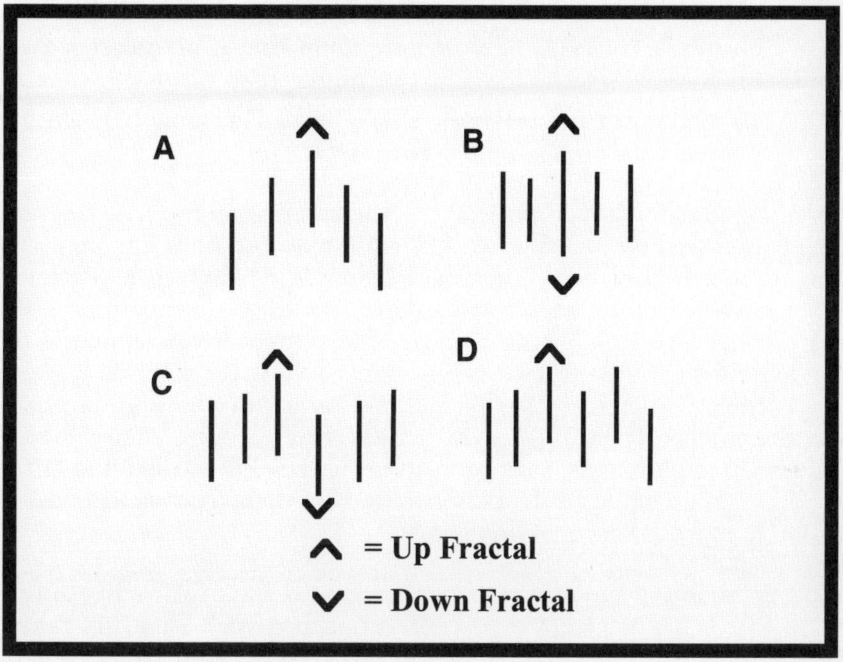

Figure 4–2 The fractal pattern.

would place an order to buy one tick over the high of the fractal. Let's examine some typical fractal patterns.

In Figure 4–2, you see an idealized fractal setup in Pattern A. The technical definition of a fractal is: a series of a minimum of five consecutive bars where the highest high is preceded by two lower highs and is followed by two lower highs. (The opposite configuration would be applicable to a sell fractal.) One way to visualize this is to hold your hand outstretched in front of you with your fingers spread and your middle finger pointing up. Your fingers are your five consecutive bars, and your middle finger is the highest, creating a fractal formation. In an up fractal, we are interested only in the bars' high, and in a down fractal, we are interested only in the bars' low. It is important to note the following restrictions:

1. If the current bars' high is the same height as the middle or high bar, it does not count as one of the five bars necessary to form a fractal. For a buy fractal, you must have a high that is

preceded by two lower highs *and* followed by two lower highs. For a sell fractal, you must have a low that is preceded by two higher lows *and* followed by two higher lows.

2. Up and down fractals may share bars. The same bar can be part of both an up and a down fractal.

Note that Pattern B fulfills all the requirements for a fractal. The two preceding and the two following bars can have any high, so long as that high is not higher than the middle bar (finger). Pattern B then is both an up fractal and a down fractal because both preceding bars and both following bars are inside bars when compared to the middle bar of the fractal.

Pattern C shows another formation that creates both an up fractal and a down fractal. As shown, these fractals may "share" bars. Pattern D requires six bars to form an up fractal because the fifth bar has a high equal to the previous highest high. The working definition is repeated here for emphasis:

A fractal must have two preceding and two following bars with lower highs (higher lows in a down move). In a buy fractal, we are interested only in the bars' high. In a sell fractal, we are interested only in the bars' low.

Fractals tell us a great deal about the "phase space" of the market's behavior, but we can improve our trading by knowing how a fractal's behavioral functions change as the market moves from high to low and back again. Once a fractal is formed, it will always be a fractal, but the role it plays depends on its location in relation to the Alligator's mouth. Figure 4–3 shows both a buy and a sell fractal. If the buy signal is above the Red Balance Line (the Alligator's Teeth), we would place a buy stop one tick above the high of the up fractal. If the sell signal is below the Red Balance Line, we would place a sell stop one tick below the low of the fractal sell signal.

It is essential to understand that we would not take a fractal buy signal if, *at the time it is hit,* the price is below the Red Balance Line. Likewise, we would not take a fractal sell signal if, *at the time it is hit,* the price is above the Red Balance Line. This is the best method we have found to filter out nonprofitable fractal trades.

Once a fractal signal is formed and is valid in relation to its position outside the Alligator's mouth, it remains a signal until it is hit or until a more recent fractal signal is formed.

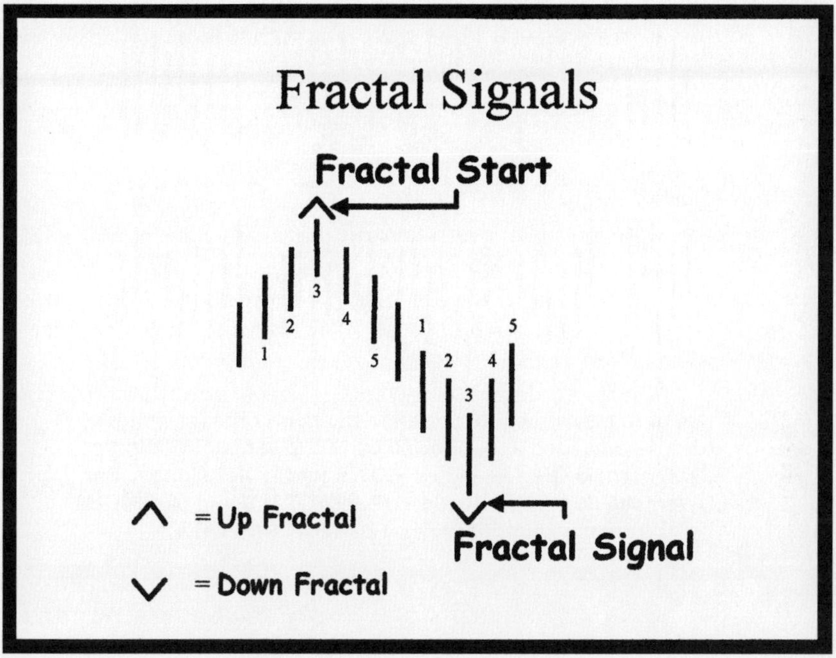

Figure 4–3 The initiating fractal.

Figure 4–4 shows a variety of fractal patterns. Fractal buys are in the upper section and fractal sells are in the lower section. Remember that although a fractal formation may be triggered, it has to be filtered through the Alligator. In other words, you would not take a buy if the fractal is below the Alligator's teeth, and you would not take a sell if the fractal is above the alligator's teeth.

Figure 4–5 provides a quick review of fractal characteristics. The underlying structure of the market is the Elliott Wave, and the underlying structure of the Elliott Wave is the fractal. Being able to locate fractals properly allows a trader to be profitable trading the Elliott Wave without having to know which wave the market is currently in. A fractal is always a change in behavior that is caused by new incoming information (Chaos). A fractal is always a breakout signal, so you would expect some satisfaction soon because you are buying the high or selling the low. (In other words, you have the world's worst trade location with the greatest potential loss.) In later

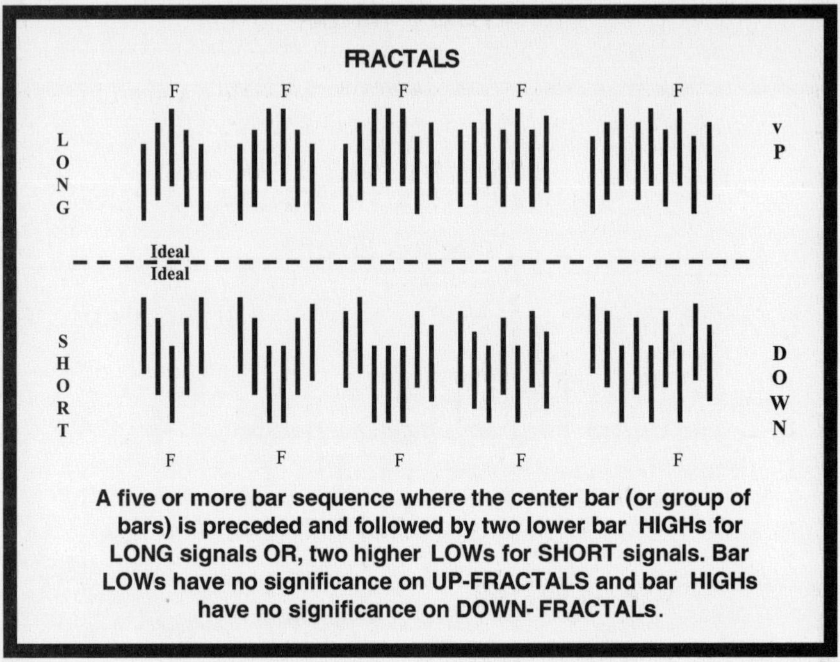

Figure 4–4 Various possible fractal formations.

- What happens between an up and a down Fractal is always an Elliott Wave of one degree or another.
- A Fractal is always a change in behavior, it is displayed as a five-bar sequence where the center bar (or group) has higher HIGHS for UP FRACTALS or, lower LOWS for DOWN FRACTALS.
- One way to trade the FRACTAL is: whenever the market exceeds the outside extreme HIGH on UP FRACTALS and LOW on DOWN FRACTALS, go with the outside direction/Fractal point.

Figure 4–5 A review of fractals.

chapters, you will see how to overcome this possible disadvantage and turn it into what we refer to as the "low rent district."

Practice in Locating Fractals

Mark the following fractals on Figure 4–6:

A. Locate the one buy fractal and the two sell fractals that are inside the box.
B. Locate the buy fractal and sell fractal inside the box.
C. Locate the two buy fractals and sell fractals.
D. Locate all the buy and sell fractals.

Check your answers against the answers in Figure 4–7.

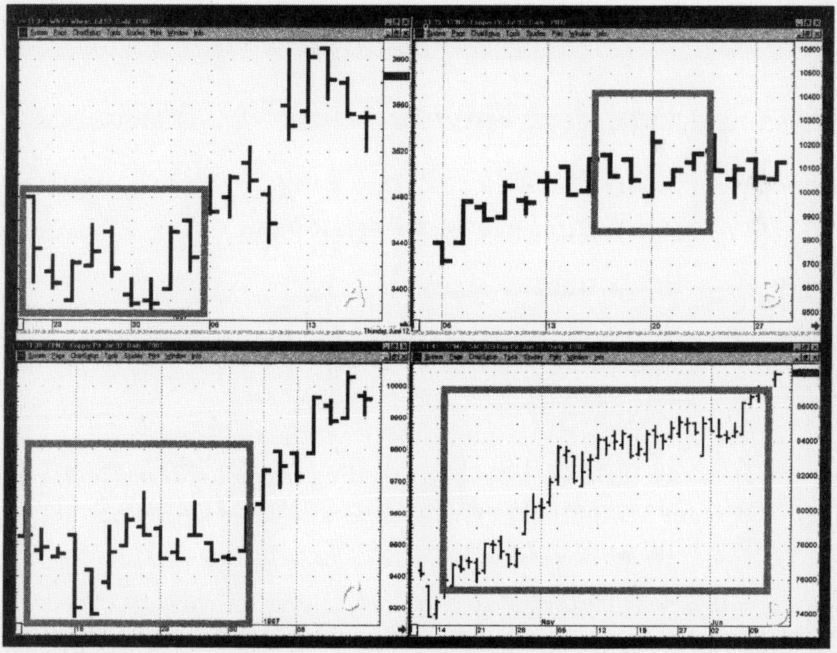

Figure 4–6 Fractal practice page.

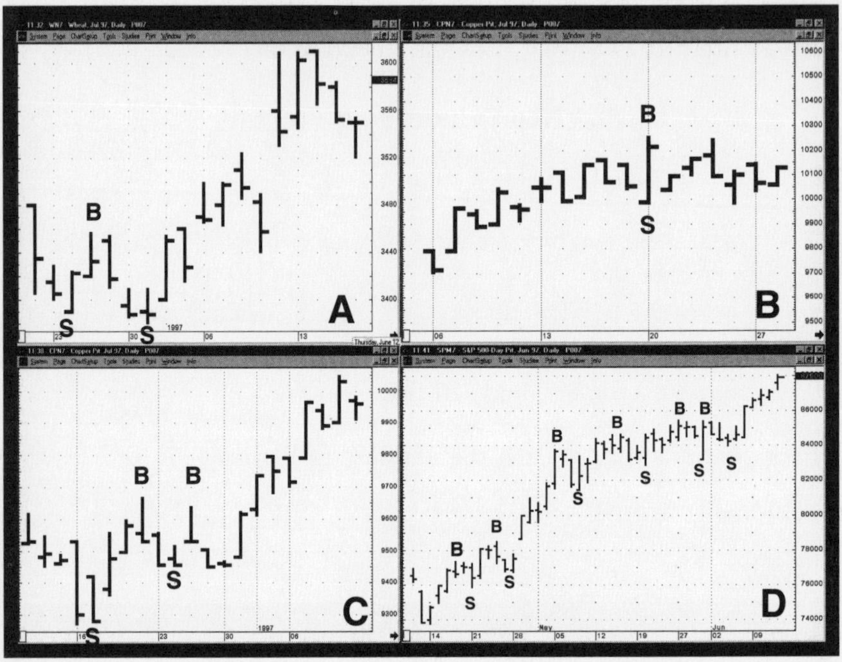

Figure 4–7 Answers to fractal practice page.

Answers to Practice Page

As shown in Figure 4–7:

A. There is one buy (B) and two sells (S).
B. There is a buy and a sell on the same bar.
C. There are two buys and two sells inside the box.
D. Here is a good example of a trending market. Note that all the fractal buy signals were hit but none of the fractal sell signals was hit.

In this practice exercise, we are not taking into account the location of the Alligator. Our purpose at this point is to gain the ability to recognize the fractal buy and sell signals. Now let's examine another practice chart and locate the fractal buy and sell signals.

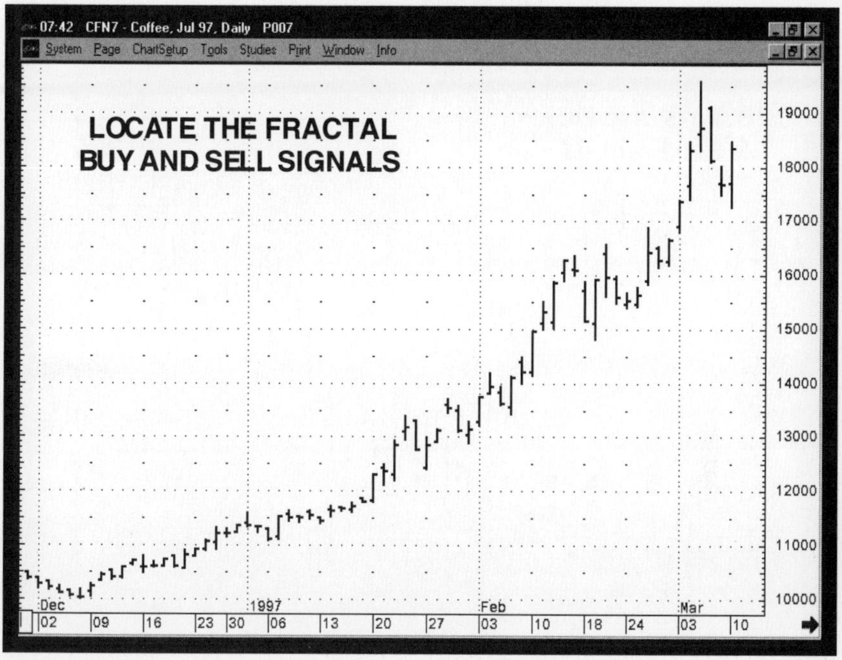

Figure 4–8 Practice page to locate fractal buy and sell signals for coffee.

Figure 4–8 is another chart to practice on. Remember, we are not considering the Alligator at this point. Try to learn how to recognize the fractals quickly and easily. Pay particular attention to all the fractals that are hit.

Figure 4–8 is a good bullish example. Had you traded this coffee market on a daily basis, using all five dimensions outlined in this material, you would have realized profits of over $500,000 in two months. In Figure 4–9, you will see how the fractal signals contributed to this very profitable trade.

Study Figure 4–9 carefully. The market constantly gives opportunities like this coffee move. Using my trading techniques and/or software, you will know exactly what order to place, where to place it, where to protect your equity, how to allocate your assets, and when to take profits.

Both the buy and sell fractals are marked in Figure 4–9. Notice that during the entire 3½ months none of the fractal sell signals was hit and all of the fractal buy signals were hit except the very highest

Figure 4–9 Answers to the practice page.

bar. Table 4–1 indicates the entry dates and profit from the fractal signals on the coffee chart shown in Figure 4–9.

In Figure 4–10 (coffee) and Figure 4–11 (Dell Computer), we have combined fractal signals with the Alligator to aid us in trade discrimination. Remember from Chapter Three that we only want to take signals outside the Alligator's mouth, and we always wait until the first buy or sell fractal is hit before taking any of the other four possible signals. In Figure 4–10, notice that the fractal buy at number 1 was the first fractal outside the Alligator's mouth that was hit. Notice also that points a and b are both sell fractals outside the Alligator's mouth but neither of these was hit. After the first fractal buy, we would take any and all buy signals that are hit. As long as the prices stay on the top of the Alligator's mouth, we would not even bother to determine where the sell signals are because we will not take any sell signals when the price is above the Alligator's mouth. This makes taking signals very easy, simple, and efficient.

TABLE 4–1 Results of Trading Only the Fractal Signals on Figure 4–9 (December 16–March 10).

Date	Pos.	Fractal	Points
16-Dec	L	10825	6240
2-Jan	L	11605	5640
8-Jan	L	11655	5590
23-Jan	L	13405	3840
29-Jan	L	13725	3520
4-Feb	L	14205	3040
14-Feb	L	16390	855
20-Feb	L	16605	640
26-Feb	L	16905	340
10-Mar	SAR-S	17245	
		Total Pts.	29705
			$111,393.75

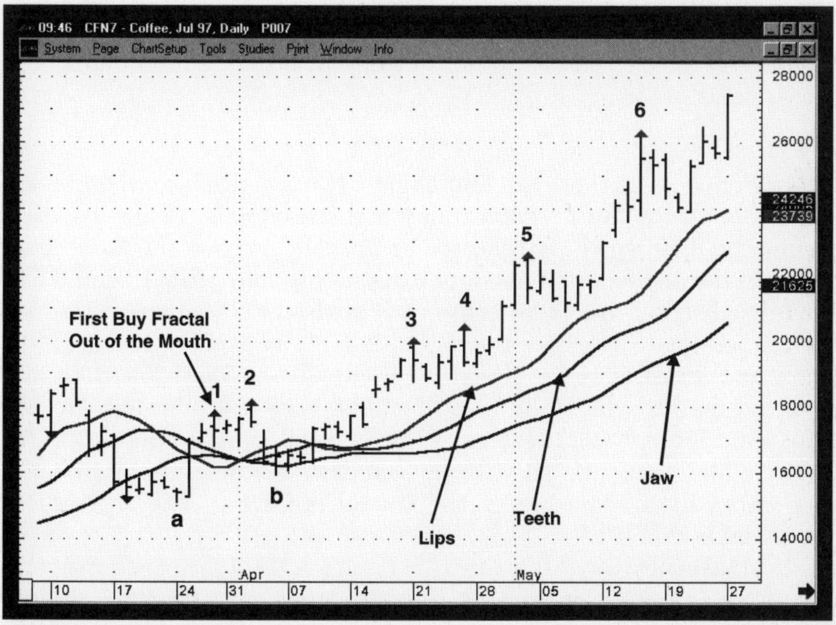

Figure 4–10 Combining the fractal signals with the Alligator in coffee.

Figure 4–11 Combining the fractal signals with the Alligator in a Dell Computer stock chart.

In Figure 4–12 there are four charts. For practice, see whether you can locate all the "valid" fractal buy and sell signals. Remember that the middle line (which we color red on actual charts) is the Teeth line, and we take any fractal buy signal that is hit above this line and any fractal sell signal that is hit below it. It is also vital to understand that the critical factor is where the signal is HIT, as opposed to where the signal is FORMED. If the signal is hit outside the Teeth, we take that trade no matter where the fractal might have been formed. On the charts in Figure 4–13, these valid buy and sell signals outside the Alligator's teeth are marked with up and down arrows. The arrows signify where the middle bar of the fractal is located. The entries are when that signal is hit.

In the Harley Davidson chart in Figure 4–14, there are nine valid fractal signals. Remember that a valid signal must be moving away from the Alligator's mouth. All the price bars are above the Alligator's mouth, so we would not take any sell fractals. We do not want to feed

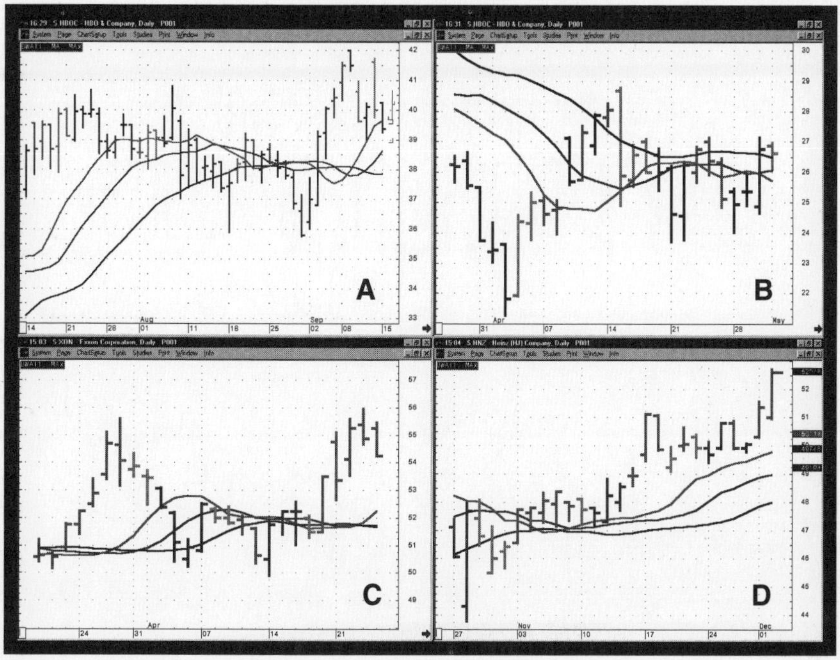

Figure 4–12 Finding the fractal buy and sell signals that are validated by the Alligator.

the Alligator. It should be obvious at first glance that we would not want to be short at any point during the time period of this chart. (The answers are shown on Figure 4–15.)

The numbers on Figure 4–15 locate the nine valid fractal buy signals for the Harley Davidson stock during this period. To test yourself, identify nine fractal sell signals that would not have been taken because they are above the middle line (Teeth) of the Alligator's mouth. Using the Alligator as your "odds maker" should greatly enhance your trading profits and keep you in tune with the current movement of any markets in either stocks or commodities.

FRACTALS "INSIDE" THE ALLIGATOR'S MOUTH

To make sure that you understand trading inside the Alligator's mouth, here are a couple of charts demonstrating how to trade in this situation.

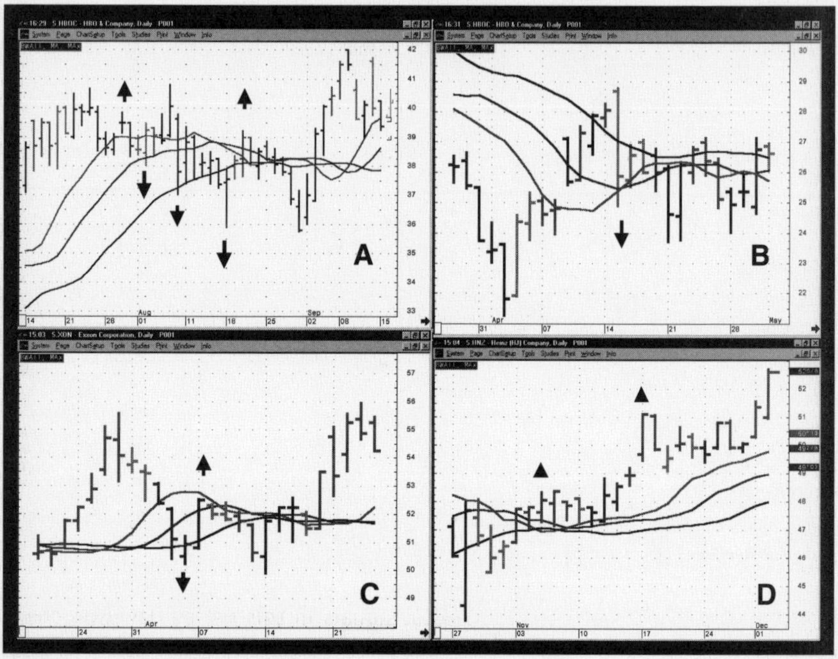

Figure 4–13 Answers to the valid fractals in Figure 4–12. Only the fractals that are hit are marked with arrows.

In Figure 4–16, a Coca-Cola stock chart, point A is not a valid buy fractal because, on the last bar, the fractal price is still below the middle (Teeth) line of the Alligator's mouth. Point B, however is a valid fractal sell signal because it is below the Alligator's Teeth (middle line). Figure 4–17, a chart of Liz Claiborne Inc., illustrates how an invalid fractal signal becomes a valid fractal signal.

In Figure 4–18, the buy fractal is below the middle line (Teeth) of the Alligator and, when formed, is not a valid buy signal. However, after the fractal is completed on the bar previous to the one labeled 1, it becomes a valid buy fractal signal because the middle line (Teeth) is below the fractal buy signal. Had any one of the bars numbered 1 through 5 gone above the fractal buy, it would have been taken.

Figure 4–18 is another example of how an invalid fractal signal becomes valid. A fractal buy signal at point 2 is well below the Alligator's middle line (Teeth) when it is triggered at point 3. Point 3 forms another buy fractal signal at the vertical line labeled A. The intersection between horizontal line 3 and vertical line A is just below the

Figure 4–14 Find the nine valid fractal signals in this Harley Davidson chart.

Figure 4–15 The nine valid fractal buy signals on the Harley Davidson chart.

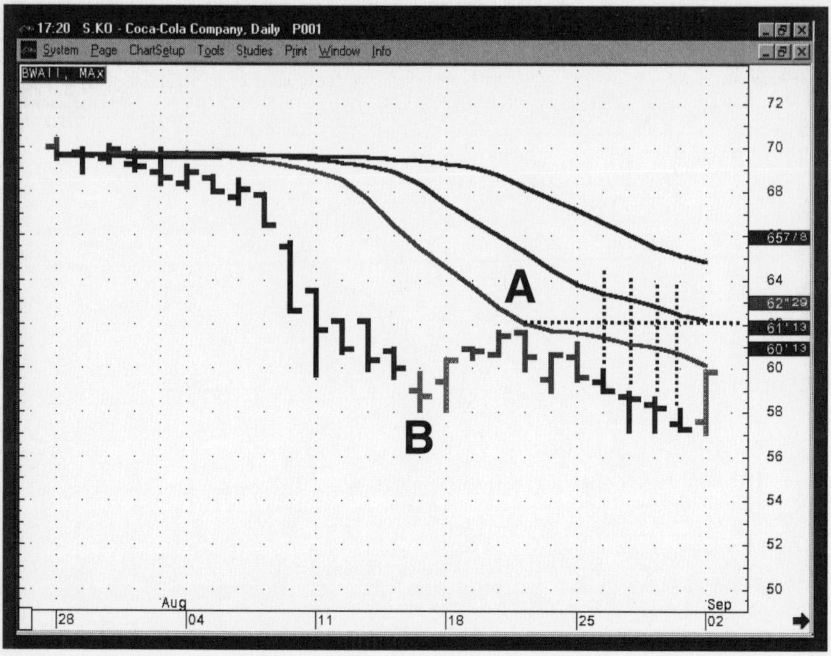

Figure 4–16 Fractal in (A) and out of (B) the Alligator's mouth.

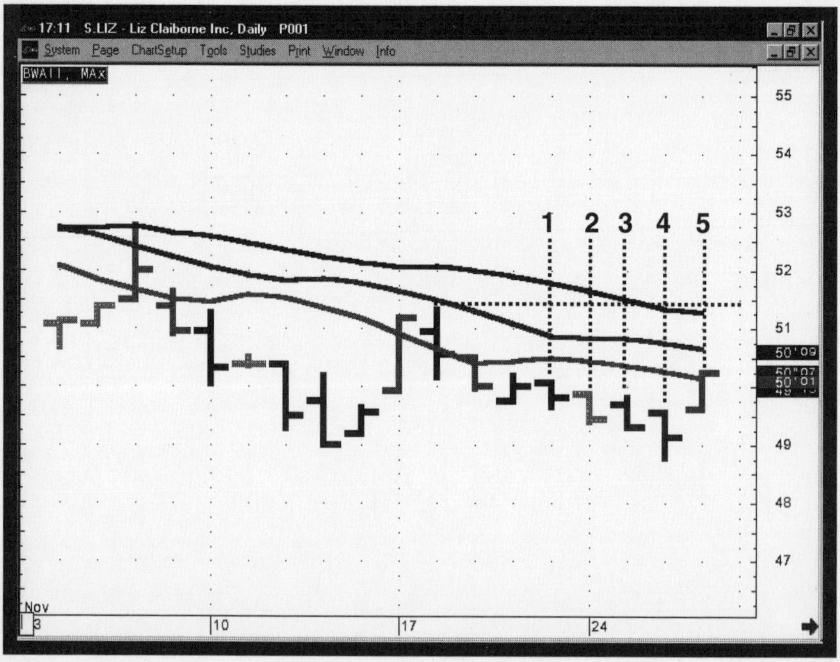

Figure 4–17 How an invalid fractal buy signal becomes valid.

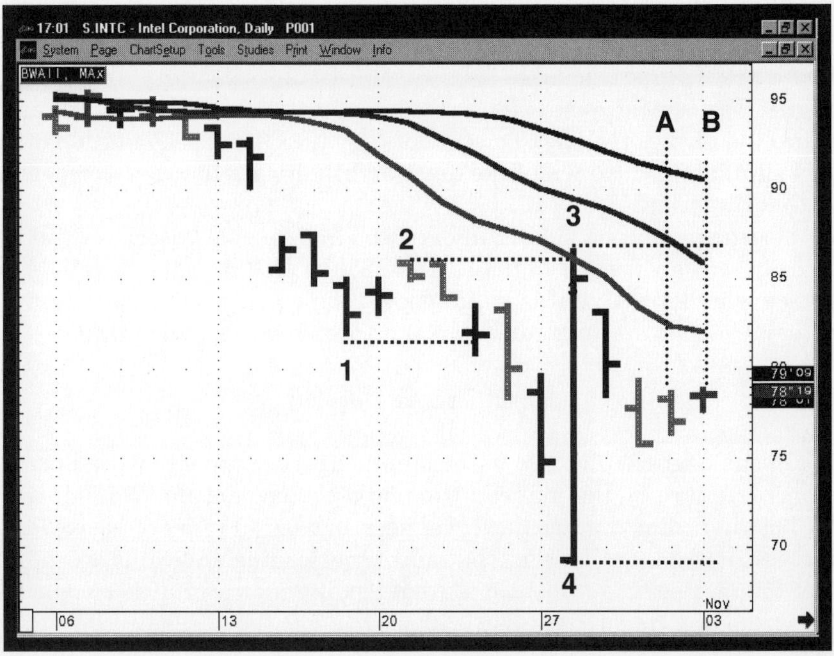

Figure 4–18 How an invalid fractal signal becomes valid.

Alligator's middle line (Teeth) and therefore is not a valid buy signal at line A. However, at line B, it becomes a valid signal because, if it were triggered, it would be above the Alligator's middle line (Teeth).

This example, combined with the previous examples, should illustrate how the Alligator becomes your decision and odds maker when trading either the stock or commodity markets.

You may wish to download our free fully functioning demo from the Internet and practice with other charts. It is very important to be able to recognize all fractal buy and sell signals and to determine whether they are valid.

SUMMARY

In this chapter, we have examined the "phase space" signal we label as a fractal. A fractal is a behavioral change and must be evaluated according to what is happening in the overall view of a market. The technical definition of a fractal is: **A minimum of five consecutive bars where the highest high is higher than the previous two bars' highs and also higher than the following two bars' highs.** The opposite is a sell fractal. Our first signal entry into any market is always the first fractal outside the Alligator's mouth. Once this signal is hit, we will take any and all signals that are triggered in that direction.

At this point, you should understand and be able to locate quickly any buy or sell fractal signals. You should also be able to tell at a glance whether a signal is valid, depending on its relationship to the Alligator's mouth. Remember to keep this slogan in your mind:

Do not feed the alligator!

In the next chapter, we will examine another aspect of the underlying structure of the market: the market's momentum. We will use the best indicator that we have ever seen in over 40 years of active and successful trading. This is the only true leading indicator we have ever found. Because it is such a great leading indicator, it is comparable to reading tomorrow's *Wall Street Journal* today. The reason this works so well is: price is actually the last thing that changes in the market. Momentum changes before price, and we will learn to use momentum in the next chapter. I strongly urge you not to read further until you have made fractal recognition second nature to you.

5

THE AWESOME OSCILLATOR

We now come to the second of our five trading dimensions: the Awesome Oscillator (AO). It is, without doubt, the best momentum indicator available in the stock and commodity markets (Figure 5–1). It is as simple as it is elegant. Basically, it is a 34-bar simple moving average that is subtracted from a 5-bar simple moving average. It is possible to be a profitable commodity and stock trader using only this oscillator, as we will explain in the next section.

The **Awesome Oscillator**

(The **Second Dimension)**

Measuring the
Momentum of the Market
is like reading tomorrow's
Wall Street Journal

Figure 5–1 The Awesome Oscillator (AO).

The Awesome Oscillator provides us with the

"KEYS TO THE KINGDOM"

The AO measures the immediate momentum of the past 5 price bars, compared to the momentum of the last 34 bars.

It is a 34-bar simple moving average of the bar's midpoints (H-L)/2 subtracted from a 5-bar simple moving average of the midpoints (H-L)/2, plotted in a histogram form.

The AO tells us exactly what is happening with the current momentum.

Figure 5–2 What is the AO?

UNDERSTANDING THE AWESOME OSCILLATOR

The Awesome Oscillator (AO) provides the "keys to the kingdom" when AO is properly understood. The AO can be used in trading both stock and commodity markets. It measures the immediate momentum of the last 5 bars and compares it to the momentum of the last 34 bars (Figure 5–2). It is a very close approximation to the continuing Market Facilitation Index (MFI). (See *Trading Chaos,* pp. 121–132.)[1]

We know that price is the very last thing to change in the markets. What changes before price is momentum, and what changes before momentum is the speed of the current momentum, and what changes before the speed is the volume, and what changes before the volume is all of us traders and investors making chaotic decisions about our activities in the markets.

[1] Williams, Bill M. *Trading Chaos: Applying Expert Techniques to Maximize Your Profits.* New York: John Wiley & Sons, pp. 121–132.

The AO is a 34-bar simple moving average of the bar's midpoints (H – L)/2 that is subtracted from a 5-bar simple moving average of the midpoints (H – L)/2. This tells us exactly what is happening with the current momentum. When understood and used properly, this is the best and most accurate indicator we have found in over 40 years of trading. If you really know how to use this indicator, it should be worth at least seven figures to you in the next few years.

Figure 5–3 shows how we display the Awesome Oscillator. As stated earlier, it is possible to trade profitably using only this oscillator and without even knowing what the current price is. For example, when the oscillator turns down, you simply call your broker and say, "Sell at the market." You stay short until it turns up, and then call and say, "Buy at the market." Unbelievable? Try it on a couple of charts and you'll see. Please understand, I do not recommend this because you can get much more precise with your trades. But think about other trader's reactions when you say that you can trade profitably without even looking at a price chart or asking about the current price.

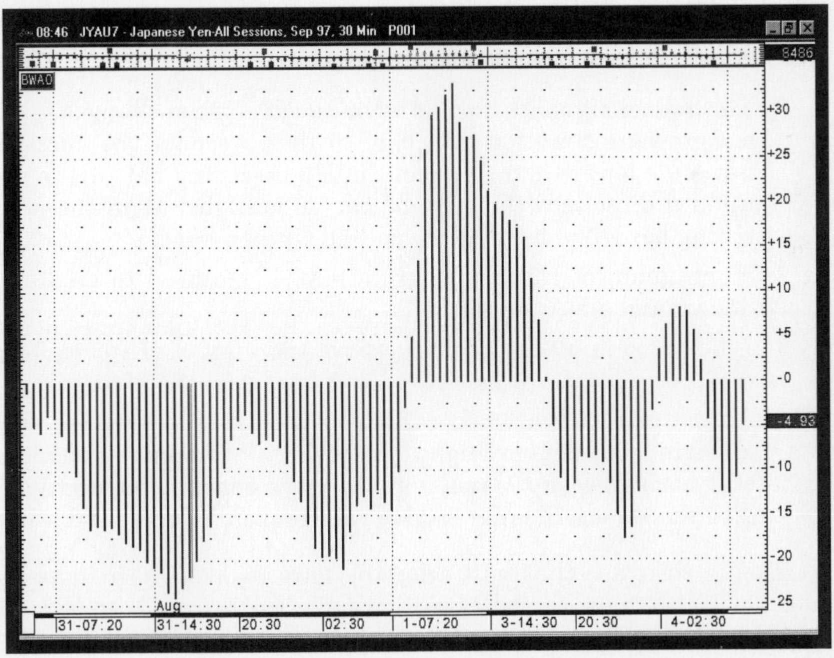

Figure 5–3 The Awesome Oscillator on a chart.

In the Profitunity software, we color green any histogram bar that is higher than the previous histogram bar, and we color red any histogram bar that is lower than the previous bar. This makes it very easy to see a change in momentum; all you do is look for a change in color.

The Awesome Oscillator creates three possible buy signals and three possible sell signals. We will first examine the three different buy formations and then the three different sell formations. It is important to remember that we do not take any AO signals until the first fractal buy or sell signal is triggered outside the Alligator's mouth. This was thoroughly explained in Chapter Four. If you have any gaps in your understanding of how the Alligator and the fractal combine to create buy and sell signals, do not go further until you review and thoroughly understand the previous chapter.

THE AO SAUCER BUY SIGNAL

This is the only buy signal when the histogram is above the zero line. We label it the *Saucer* buy signal (Figure 5–4). The main points to remember are:

1. The Saucer signal is created when the *histogram* changes from a downward direction [the bar (b) that precedes the current bar (c) is lower than the immediately preceding bar (a)] to an upward direction [the current bar (c) is higher than the preceding bar (b) and therefore will be a green bar].
2. A minimum of three histogram bars is required to create a Saucer and a buy signal.
3. A buy stop is placed one tick above the high of the price bar that corresponds to the first higher bar (c) on the histogram.
4. Almost any software can color bars with lower highs red and all bars with higher highs green. The Profitunity software will mark the buy signals on the price chart itself and will give you the exact order to give your broker.

Having software that will color the bars makes the histogram super simple. Review the rules in Figure 5–5. You only have to look for a change in color to alert you to a buy or sell Saucer signal. Remember that with the Saucer buy signal, all AO bars must be above the zero line. Note that in Figure 5–6 there are two Saucer buys.

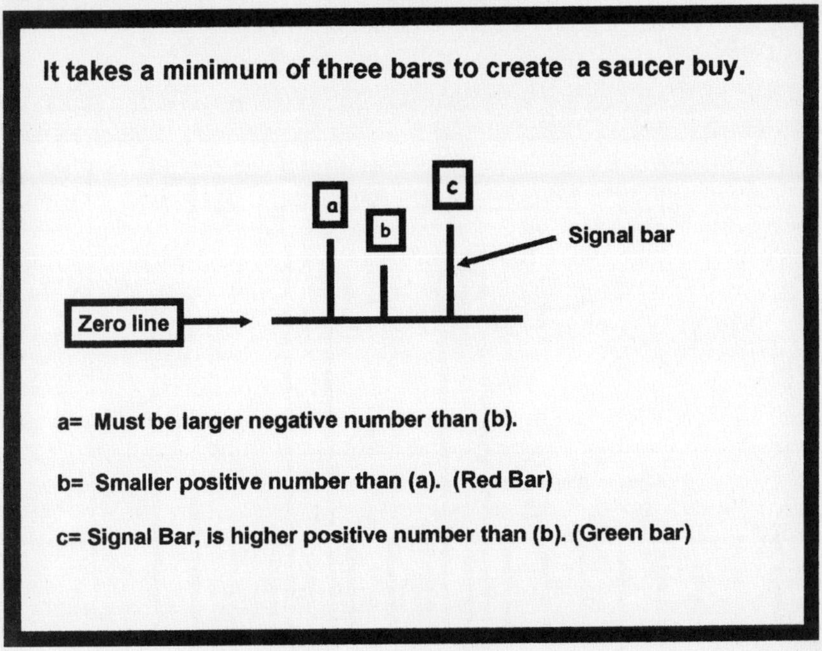

Figure 5–4 The Saucer buy signal.

Always read from left to right.

It takes a minimum of three bars to create a signal.

There is no limit to how many bars can be inside a saucer.

All bars in a Saucer must be above the zero line

The signal bar will be a Green Bar

You can not have a buy and sell at the same time.

After creating a signal, you MUST have a change of direction (color) before creating another signal.

Once you have created a signal, go to the corresponding price bar and add/subtract 1 tick to the high/low.

Figure 5–5 Rules for the Saucer buy signal.

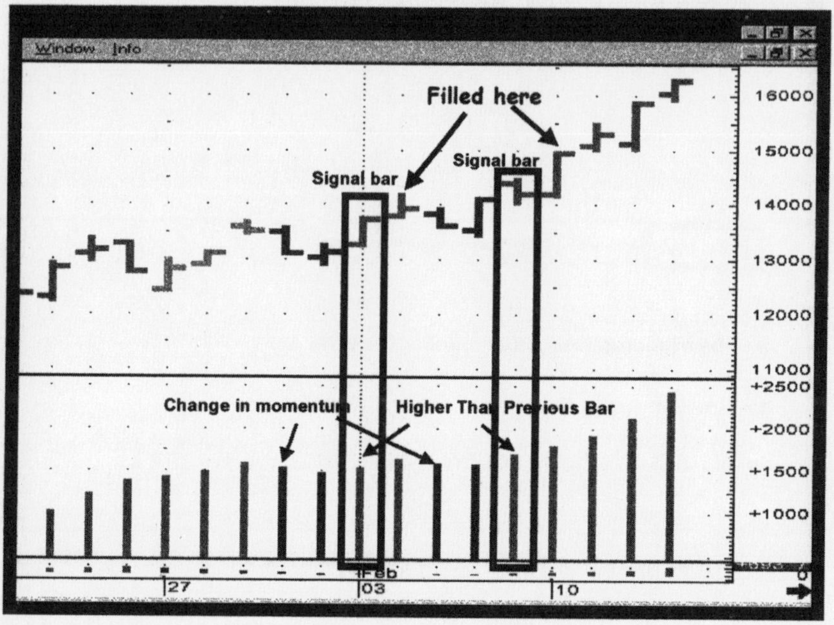

Figure 5–6 The AO Saucer buy signal on a coffee chart.

Figure 5–7 shows a variety of Saucer buy signals. In the illustration on the right, a, b, c, and d are all buy signals. Remember that the buy stop will be placed one tick above the price bar that corresponds to the buy signal on the AO histogram. Also note that we only take the most recently generated signals of that particular dimension.

The next AO signal we will examine occurs when the momentum is crossing the zero line on the AO histogram. This is the second of three possible AO buy signals.

THE AO CROSS BUY

If you buy when the histogram is "crossing" the zero line, you are using the histogram cross buy signal (Figure 5–8). The main points to remember are:

1. A buy signal is created when the histogram changes from a negative number to a positive number. This happens when the histogram bar *crosses* the zero line.

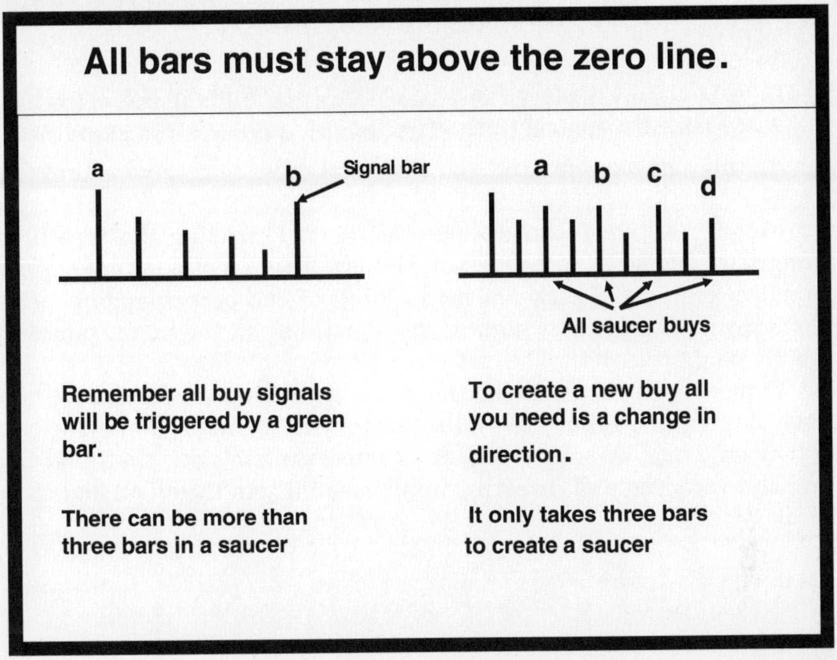

Figure 5–7 A variety of Saucer buys.

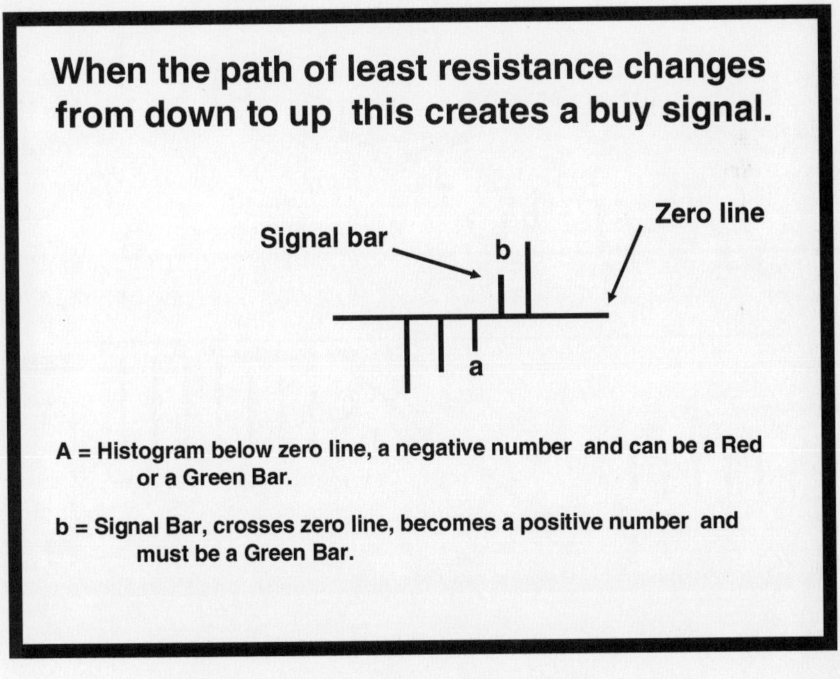

Figure 5–8 The AO histogram cross buy signal.

2. A buy stop is placed one tick above the high of the price bar, which corresponds to the first bar that crosses the zero line.
3. Our software can tell you the exact order to give your broker.

Figure 5–9 shows an example of the AO crossing the zero line, going from negative to positive territory. This creates a buy signal, which is placed one tick above the high of the corresponding price bar. On an AO cross buy signal, the signal bar on the histogram will always be a green bar.

Figure 5–10 summarizes the rules governing an AO histogram cross buy signal. Figure 5–11 illustrates an AO histogram cross buy signal on Time Warner stock. It is important to note that this approach to trading and investing applies equally to the stock and commodity markets.

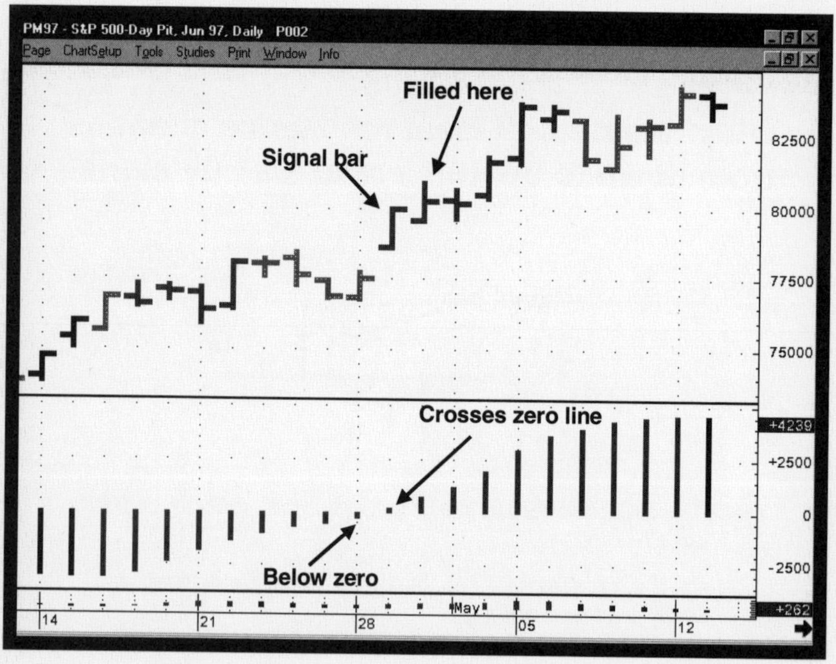

Figure 5–9 AO histogram crossing zero buy signal.

- **Always read from left to right**
- **It only takes two bars to create this signal.**
- **First bar must be below the zero line, second bar must cross above the zero line. (From a negative number to a positive number.)**
- **You can not have a buy and sell signal at the same time.**
- **Once a signal is created, go to the corresponding price bar and add 1 tick to the high for your buy stop.**

Figure 5–10 Rules for the AO histogram cross buy signal.

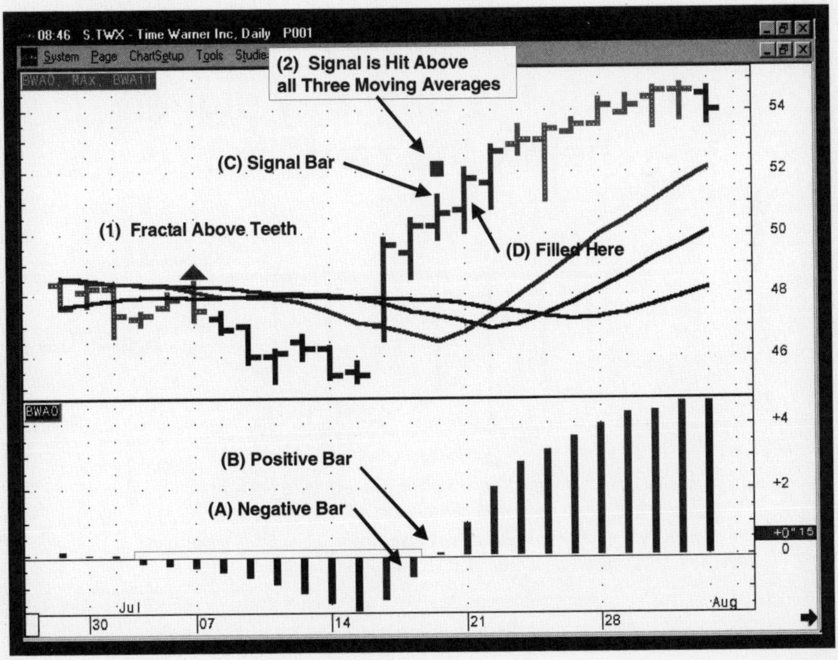

Figure 5–11 The AO histogram cross buy signal on Time Warner stock.

THE TWIN PEAKS BUY SIGNAL

The third buy signal that is created by the Awesome Oscillator is the Twin Peaks buy signal. This is the *only* buy signal that can be created while the AO histogram is below the zero line (Figure 5–12). Here are the main points to remember:

1. This signal is created when you have a downward peak (lowest low) below the zero line followed by another downward peak that is higher (smaller negative number, therefore closer to the zero line) than the previous downward peak.
2. The histogram must stay below the zero line between the two peaks. If the histogram crosses the zero line between the peaks, the buy signal is invalidated. However, crossing the zero line creates a buy signal.
3. Each new histogram peak must be higher (smaller negative number, closer to the zero line) than the previous peak. Our software will give you the exact order to place with your broker.

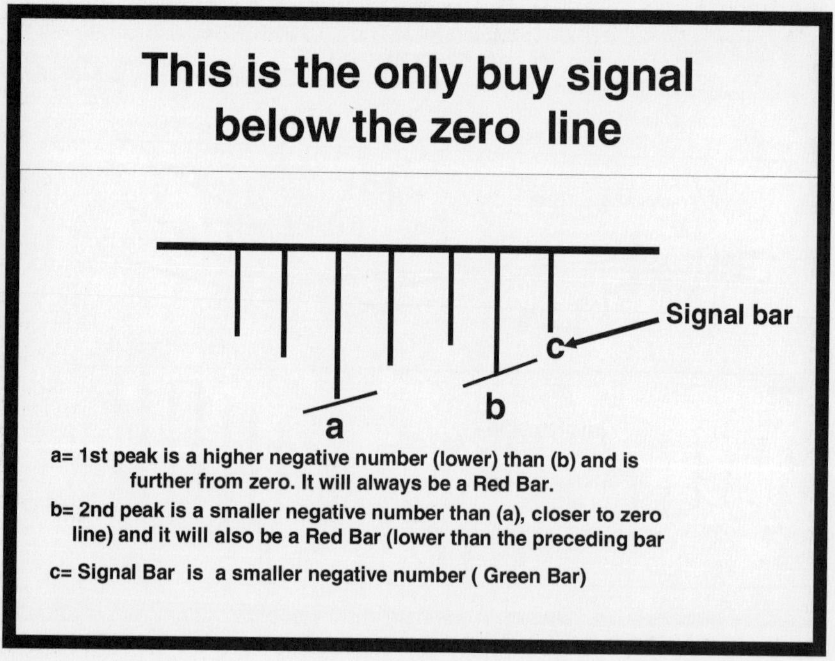

Figure 5–12 Buying when the AO is below the zero line.

4. If an additional higher peak (closer to the zero line) is formed and the histogram has not crossed the zero line, an additional buy signal is created.

Figure 5–13 illustrates the placement of a Twin Peaks buy signal. Remember that the signal histogram bar must be green. If the AO histogram bar is green, you cannot generate an AO sell signal. If it is red, you cannot generate an AO buy signal. Another important point is that if a buy or sell signal is generated but not hit on the current bar and the next histogram bar changes color, that signal is canceled. Figure 5–14 provides a full list of the rules for the AO Twin Peaks buy.

Review of the AO Buy Signals

There are three possible AO buy signals: (1) the Saucer, where the histogram must be above the zero line; (2) the histogram cross where the histogram bars are crossing the zero line; and (3) the

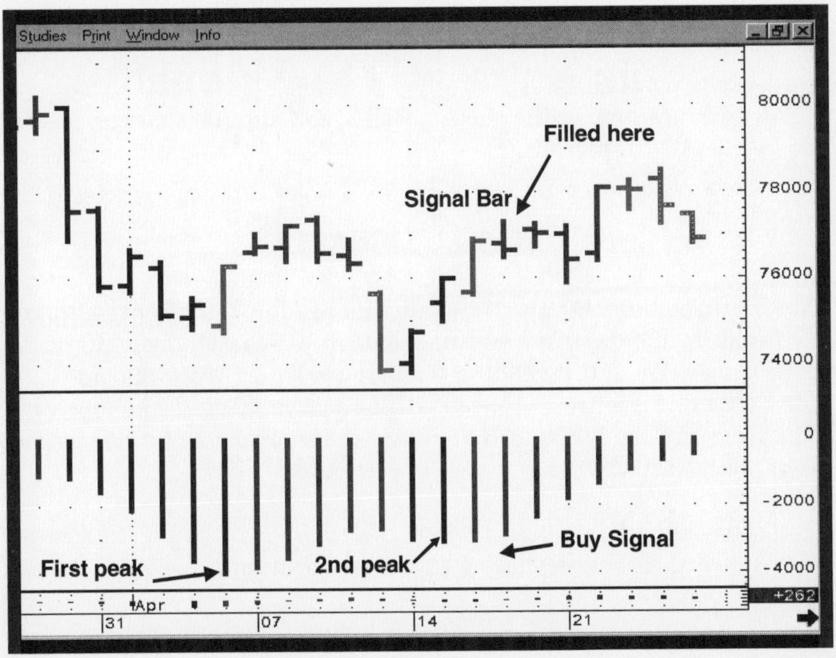

Figure 5–13 The AO Twin Peaks buy signal on a chart.

- This is the only buy signal below the zero line.
- The first peak must be a larger negative number than the second peak.
- Your trigger bar will be a Green Bar and a smaller negative number than either peak.
- If any bars cross the zero line in the Twin Peaks, the signal is invalid.
- A Saucer sell will be created before a Twin Peaks buy.

Figure 5–14 Rules for the AO Twin Peaks buy signal.

Twin Peaks buy, which can only be generated when the histogram bars are below the zero line and these bars cannot cross the zero line between the peaks.

We will now look at the three possible sell signals that can be created by the AO histogram.

AO SELL SIGNALS

Like the three buy signals, these signals are important because they are based on momentum, and momentum always changes direction before prices. We call it reading tomorrow's *Wall Street Journal.*

As shown in Figure 5–15, you will be *selling when the histogram is below the zero line.* A *Saucer sell signal is the opposite of a Saucer buy signal.* These are the main points to remember:

1. This signal is created when the histogram changes from an upward direction (bars a to b) to a downward direction (bars b to c).
2. A minimum of three histogram bars is required to create a Saucer and a sell signal.

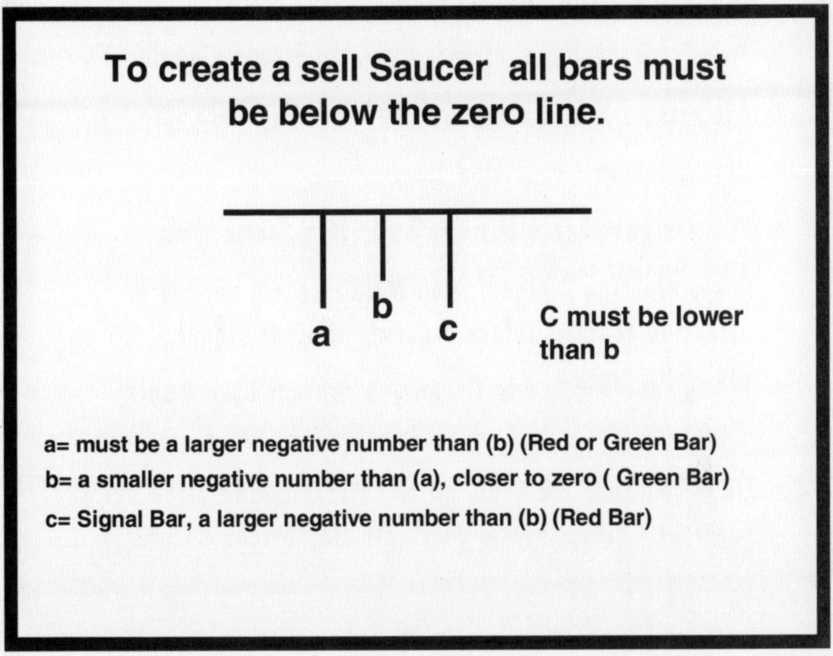

Figure 5–15 A schematic of an AO Saucer sell signal.

3. A sell stop is placed one tick below the low of the price bar, which corresponds to the first bar down (bar c on the histogram).

The rules for the Saucer sell are provided in Figure 5–16.

In Figure 5–17, you can see two sell signals created by two Saucers. Both signals were created by the AO's going higher (turning the AO bar green), which was followed by a lower bar (creating a red AO histogram bar). Note that the AO must stay below the zero line between peaks—a necessity for a Saucer sell.

In Figure 5–18, note that a Saucer sell signal is created by a Saucer on the AO below the zero line. Figures 5–17 and 5–18 illustrate that the same exact trading and investing tactics work on both stocks and commodities, in all time frames. We will now move on to the second AO sell signal: the AO histogram crossing the zero line sell signal.

- Always read from left to right.
- It takes a minimum of three bars to create signal.
- All bars in the saucer must be below the Zero line.
- Signal bar will be a Red Bar.
- You can not have a buy and sell at the same time.
- After creating a signal, you MUST have a change of direction (color) before creating another signal.
- If your current bar is Green you can not have a sell signal.
- Once you have a signal, go to corresponding price bar and subtract 1 tick, this is your sell stop price.

Figure 5–16 Rules for selling when the AO histogram is below the zero line.

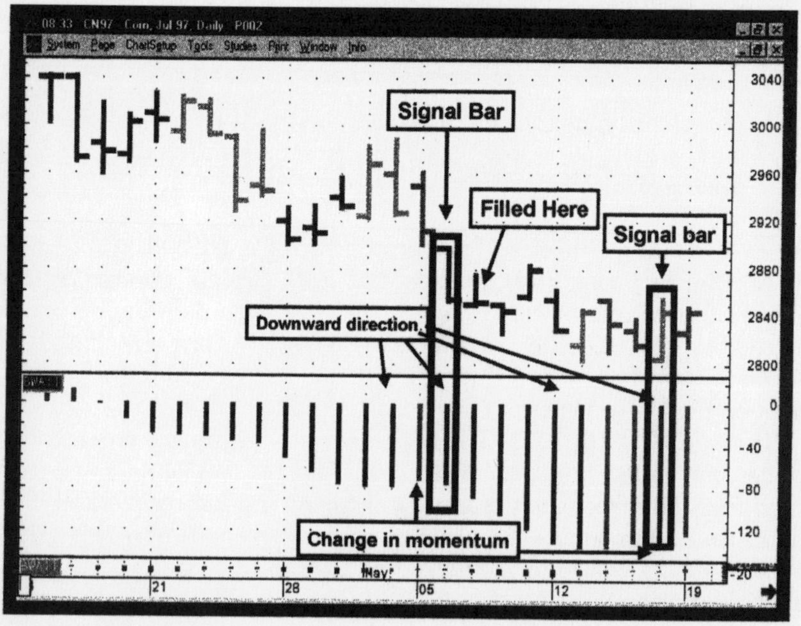

Figure 5–17 Two AO Saucer sell signals on a corn chart.

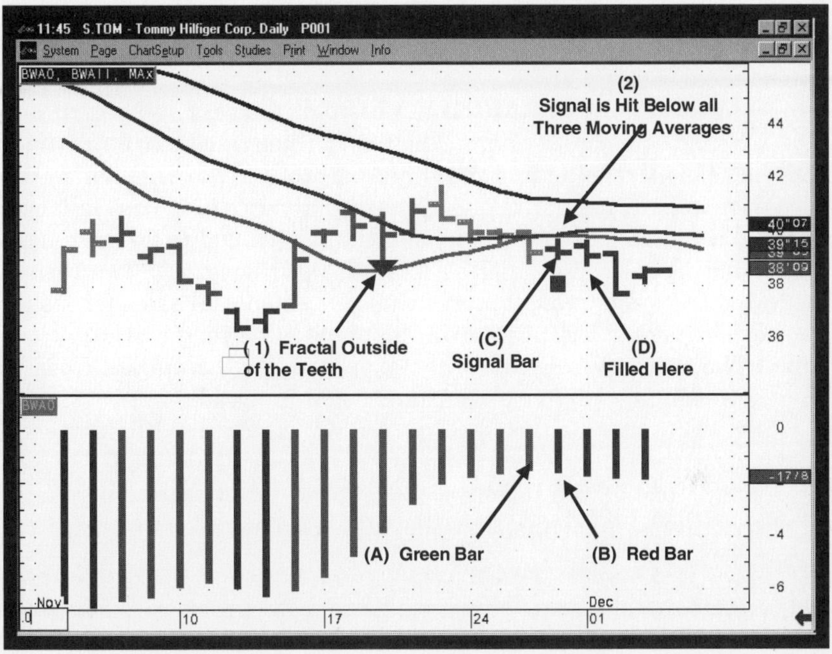

Figure 5–18 Saucer sell signal on Tommy Hilfiger Corp. stock.

THE AO HISTOGRAM CROSSING THE ZERO LINE SELL SIGNAL

When you employ the histogram cross sell, you will be selling when the histogram is "crossing" the zero line. Remember these main points:

1. A sell signal is created when the histogram changes from a positive number to a negative number. This happens when the histogram bar *crosses* the zero line.
2. A sell stop is placed one tick below the low of the price bar, which corresponds to the first histogram bar that crosses the zero line.
3. Our software also gives you the exact order to give your broker for this signal.

Figure 5–19 is a schematic of the requirements to create an AO histogram crossing the zero line sell signal. Figure 5–20 lists the rules for taking this trade.

Figure 5–21 illustrates the AO histogram cross sell signal on a Swiss Franc commodity chart. The chart illustrates two Profitunity concepts for increasing and maximizing profits. You will notice that the following bar did not take out the signal bar's low. That following bar had a higher low and the momentum continued to go more negative, creating what we label as a "blue light special." (The term is borrowed from department stores that put on special sales for a short period of time for the people who happen to be in the store at that time.) The market gives those who are watching the market closely a chance to sell at a higher price than the first signal.

The wheat stock chart in Figure 5–22 is another illustration of how these techniques work on all markets. This fulfills "self-similarity," one of the primary characteristics of fractal geometry. In the markets, it means that the various dimensions in nonlinear

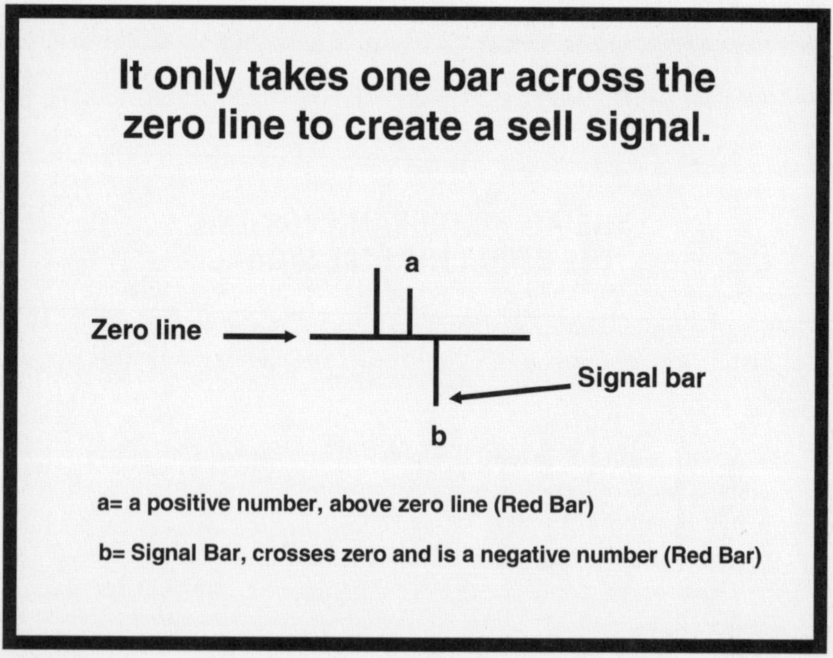

Figure 5–19 A schematic of the AO histogram crossing the zero line sell signal.

- **Always read from left to right.**
- **It only takes two bars to create this signal.**
- **First bar must be above the zero line, second bar must cross below the zero line. (From a positive number to a negative number.)**
- **You can not have a buy and sell at the same time.**
- **Once a signal has been created, go to the corresponding price bar and subtract 1 tick; this is your sell stop price.**

Figure 5–20 Rules for the AO histogram crossing zero line sell signal.

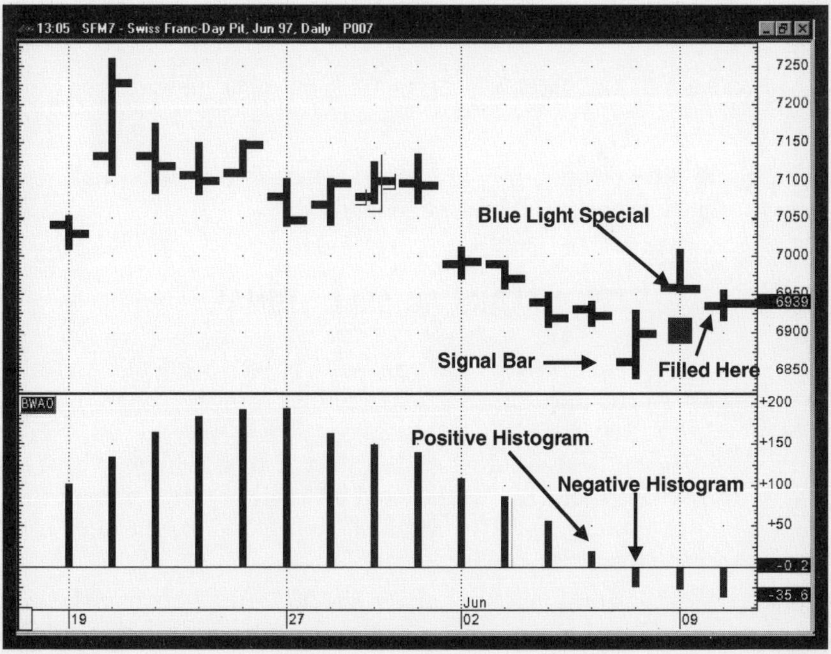

Figure 5–21 The AO histogram crossing zero sell signal on a Swiss Franc chart.

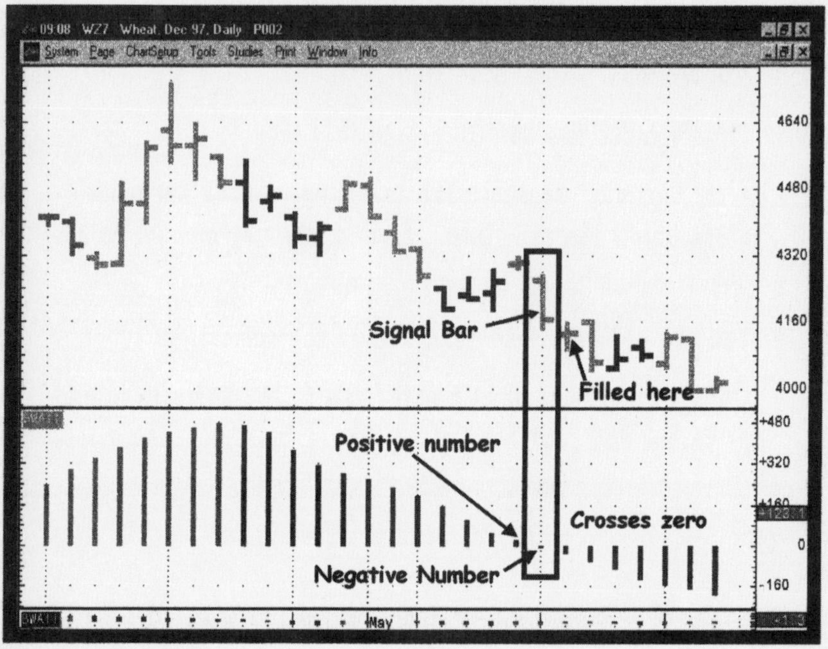

Figure 5–22 The AO histogram cross sell signal in wheat.

dynamics must work not only across all markets but also in all time frames—a requirement of fractal geometry.

TWIN PEAKS AO SELL SIGNAL

With the Twin Peaks sell signal, you will be selling when the histogram is above the Zero Line. The key points are:

1. This signal is created when you have a upward peak (highest high) above the zero line followed by another upward peak that is lower (smaller positive number and closer to the zero line) than the previous upward peak.
2. The histogram must stay above the zero line between the two peaks. If the histogram crosses the zero line between the peaks, the sell signal is invalidated. However, crossing the zero line would create an AO cross the line sell signal.

3. Each new histogram peak must be lower (smaller positive number and closer to the zero line) than the previous peak.
4. Most software can be configured to color the histogram bars for simple and easy observation.

Figure 5–23 is a schematic of the elements that are necessary to create an AO histogram Twin Peaks sell signal. This is the only sell signal possible when the AO histogram is above the zero line.

Figure 5–24 summarizes the rules for a Twin Peaks AO sell. It is a mirror of the AO Twin Peaks AO buy signal when the AO is below the zero line.

Figure 5–25 shows the Twin Peaks sell signal as it appears on a histogram chart. Notice that point (A) was a peak and the AO histogram turned down from that point. It continued lower until three bars to the left of point (B). It then went higher, forming another peak at point (B) but lower than the peak at point (A). At point (C),

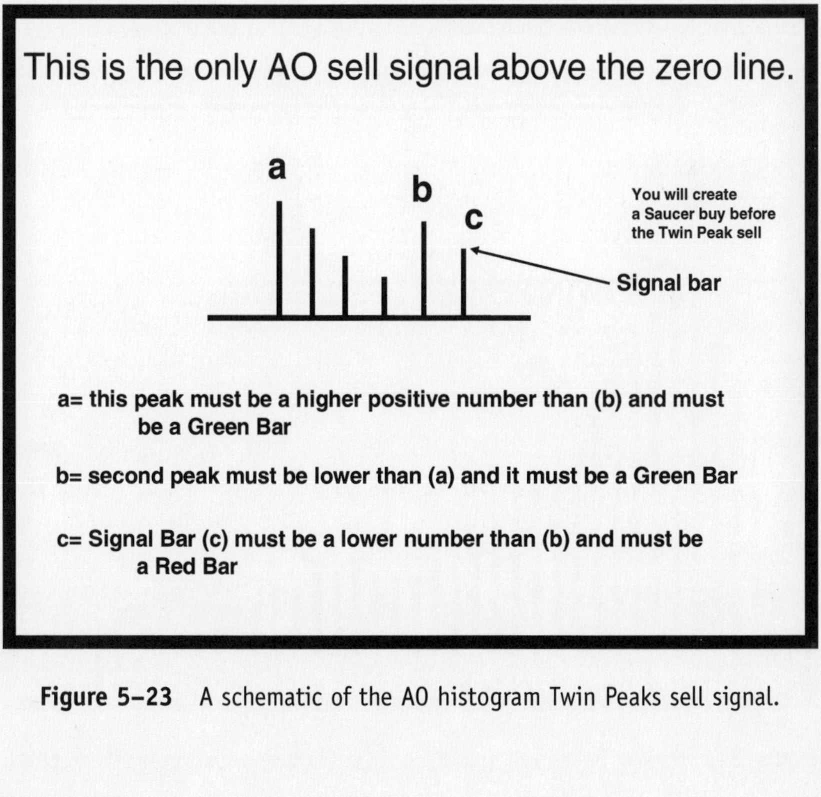

Figure 5–23 A schematic of the AO histogram Twin Peaks sell signal.

- Always read from left to right.
- This is the only sell signal above the zero line.
- The first peak must be a larger positive number than the second peak.
- Your trigger bar will be a Red Bar and a smaller positive number than either peak.
- If any bars in the Twin Peaks cross the zero line, the signal is invalid.
- A Saucer buy will be created before a Twin Peaks sell.
- Once a signal has been created, go to the corresponding price bar and subtract 1 tick; this is your sell stop.

Figure 5–24 Rules of the Twin Peaks sell signal.

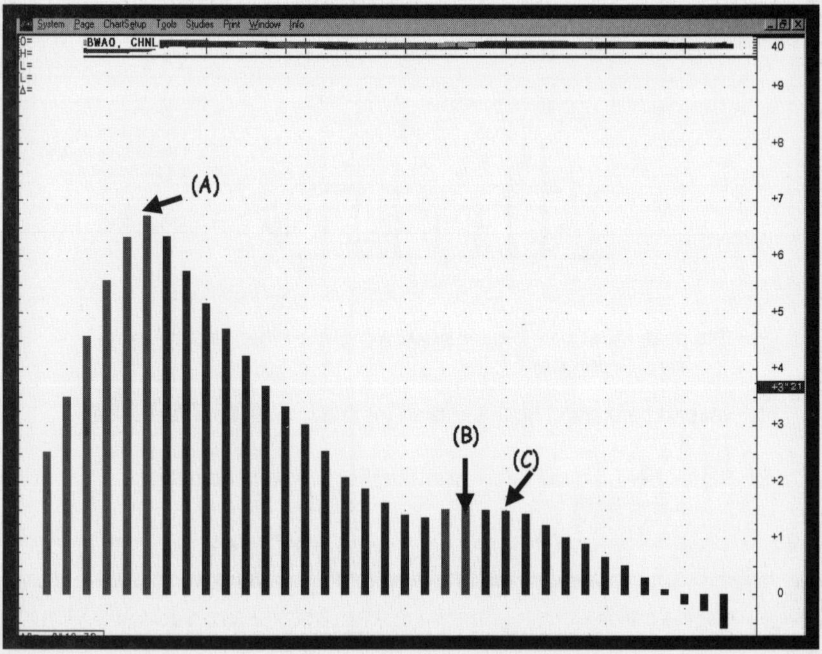

Figure 5–25 Twin Peaks sell signal on a Liz Claiborne histogram stock chart.

the histogram turned lower, creating a Twin Peaks sell signal at one tick lower than the low of the price bar that corresponds to the bar at point (C). Now let's put the price chart up to see how this plays out in this stock.

Figure 5–26 duplicates Figure 5–25 but adds the price bars. Note that at point (C) we place a sell stop just below the low of that price bar. That signal was not triggered on the following bar because its low was higher than the signal bar's low. Also note that all three bars at Point (D) had progressively higher lows. This formed a "blue light special," allowing us to sell at a higher price than was first signaled. It is very important to note that, during these time periods, the histogram continued to fall, creating red bars. This stock was finally sold at the first bar that made a lower low (circled on the price chart). Had the histogram turned upward (the bar would be painted green), this sell signal would have been canceled. Repeating for emphasis: You cannot sell on an AO signal if the current histogram bar is green, and you cannot buy any AO signals if the current histogram bar is red.

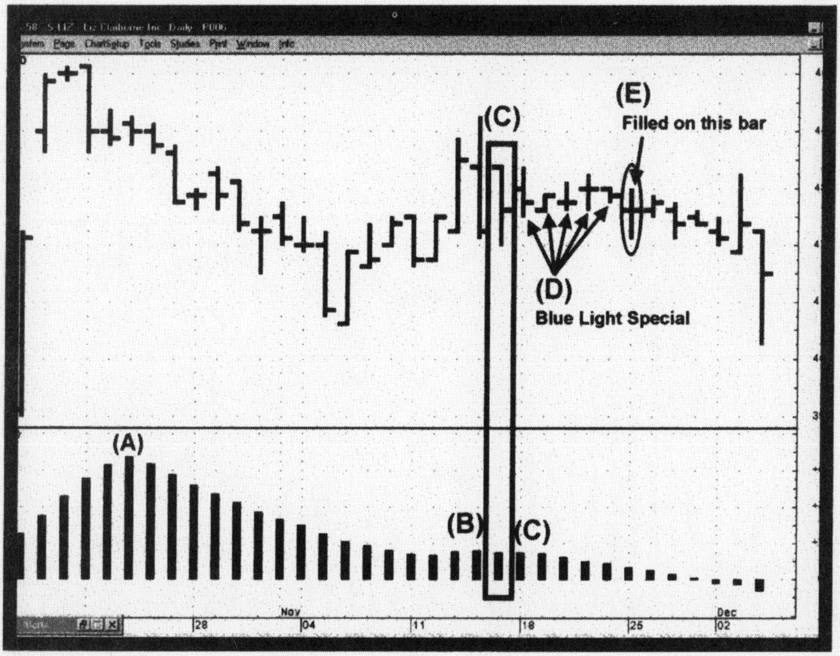

Figure 5–26 Price record and histogram for Liz Claiborne stock chart.

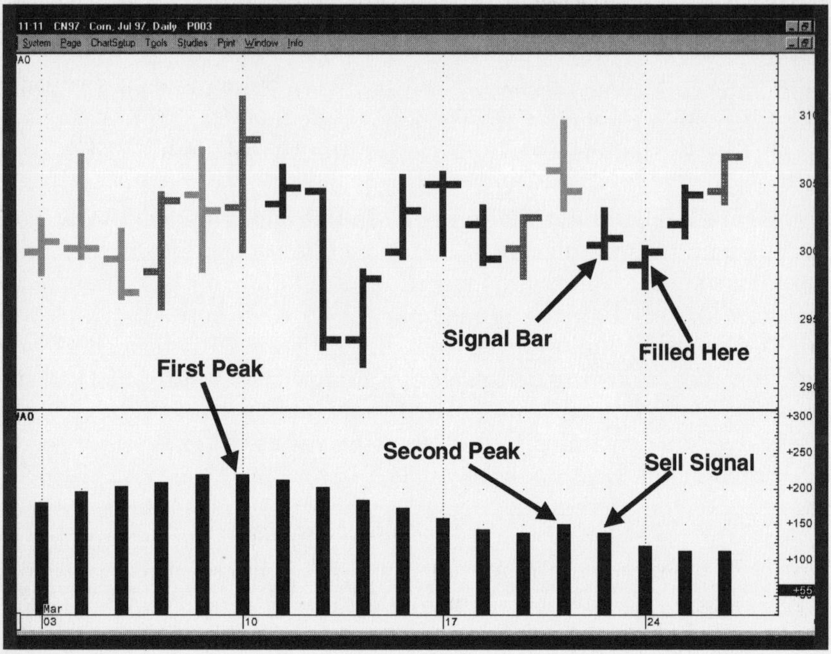

Figure 5–27 The AO histogram Twin Peaks sell signal on a corn chart.

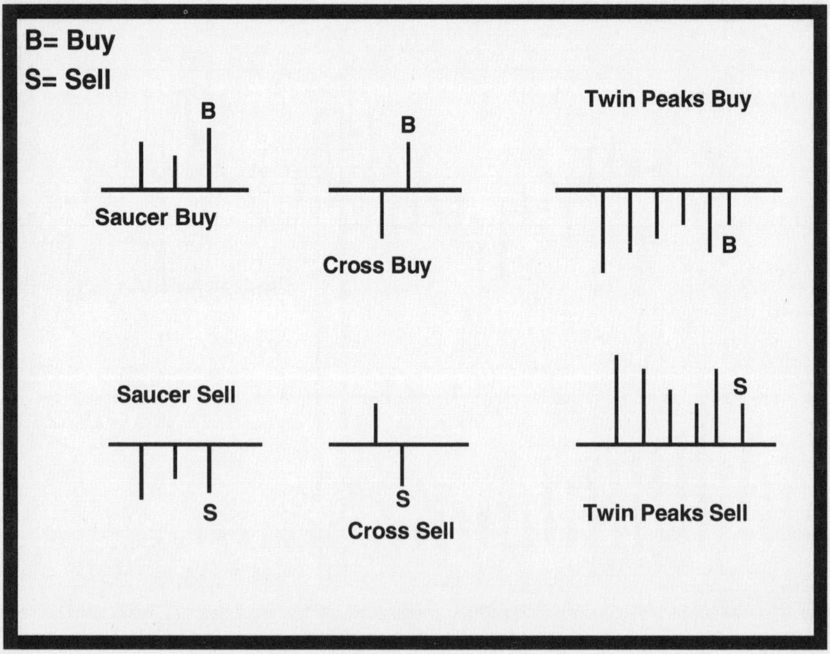

Figure 5–28 All the AO buy and sell signals.

In the corn chart shown in Figure 5–27, you can see a situation that is similar to the Liz Claiborne chart. Remember: This is the only AO sell signal that can be generated while the AO is above the zero line. At this point, it is a good idea to review all the buy and sell signals that are created by the Awesome Oscillator (Figure 5–28).

AWESOME OSCILLATOR PRACTICE PAGES

The following pages provide several charts for you to practice finding the AO buy and sell signals. Mark all the buy and sell signals you can find in Figure 5–29 before you look at the answers in Figure 5–30.

How many of these signals in Figure 5–29 were you able to find and identify properly?

A. Cross the zero line sell.

B. Saucer sell.

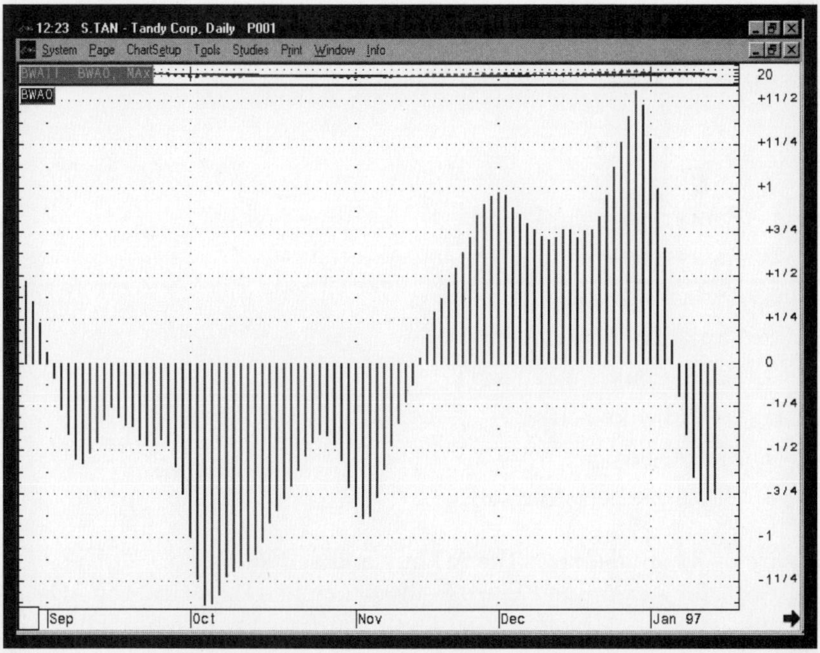

Figure 5–29 Find all the AO buy and sell signals.

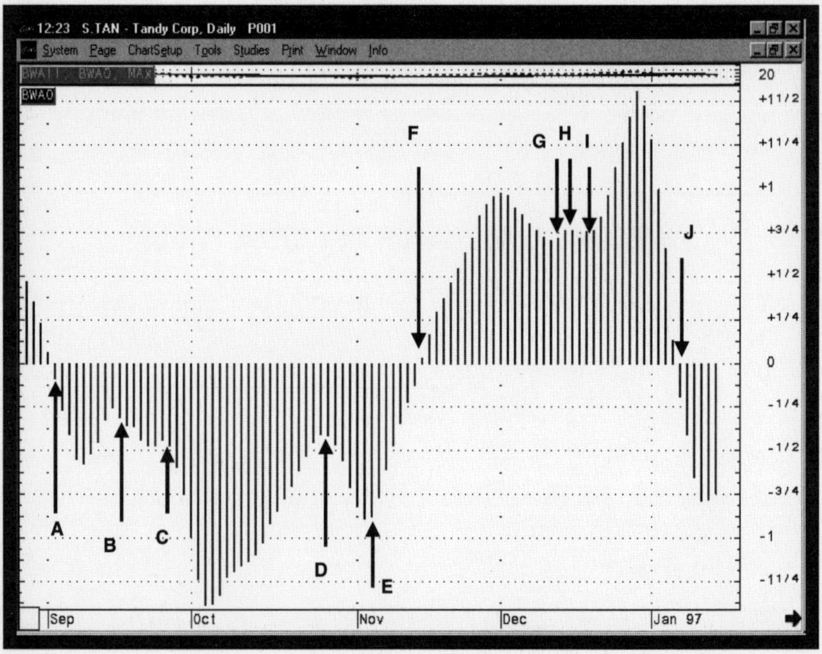

Figure 5–30 Answers to the practice chart in Figure 5–29.

C. Saucer sell.
D. Saucer sell.
E. Twin Peaks buy.
F. Cross the zero line buy.
G. Saucer buy.
H. Twin Peaks sell.
I. Saucer buy.
J. Cross the zero line sell.

Figure 5–31 summarizes the AO buy and sell signals.

Next, let's examine Figure 5–32, which has the price, the AO histogram, and the Alligator. See if you can find the seven AO buy signals. Be sure to locate the Alligator and to look only for AO signals that are leading away from the Alligator's mouth.

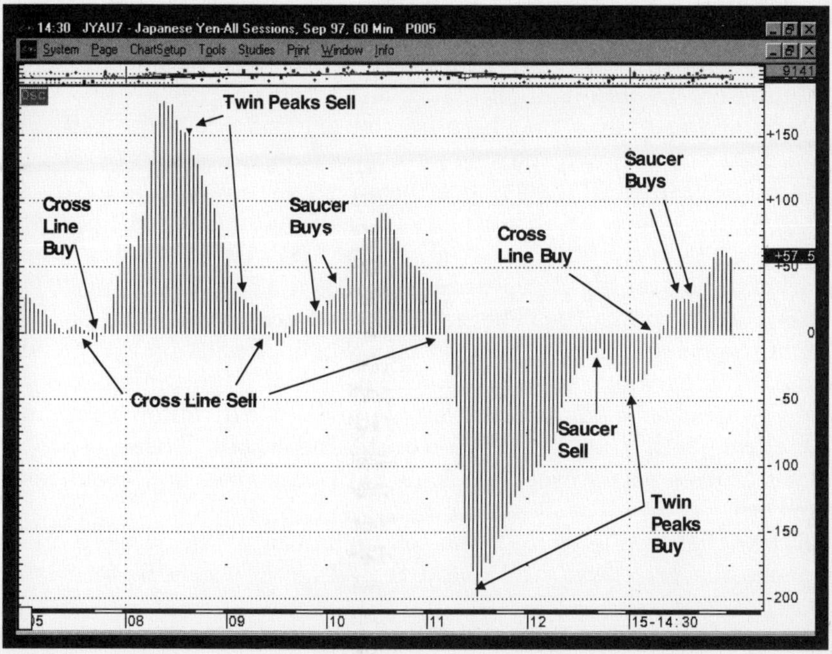

Figure 5–31 Summary of AO buy and sell signals.

Figure 5–32 Find the seven AO histogram buy signals.

Check your work against Figure 5–33. Did you find all seven signals? Did you realize that because the AO was above the zero line across the entire chart, the only possible AO signal was an AO Saucer buy and therefore all were Saucer buys?

Now, let's look at an example of real trading in real markets. Figure 5–34 is a history of trading the S&P dailies during a bull market. The trading dates were from April 17 through July 31, a little over three months. There were no intraday trades and no looking at the market during the day. Had you done nothing except take the AO histogram trades, you would have had outstanding results. This is a rather exceptional example and we will follow this market throughout the other Profitunity indicators. These types of opportunities occur every week in both the stock and commodity markets.

Note that on Figure 5–34 no sell signals of any kind were taken because the price was well above the Alligator's mouth. In a later

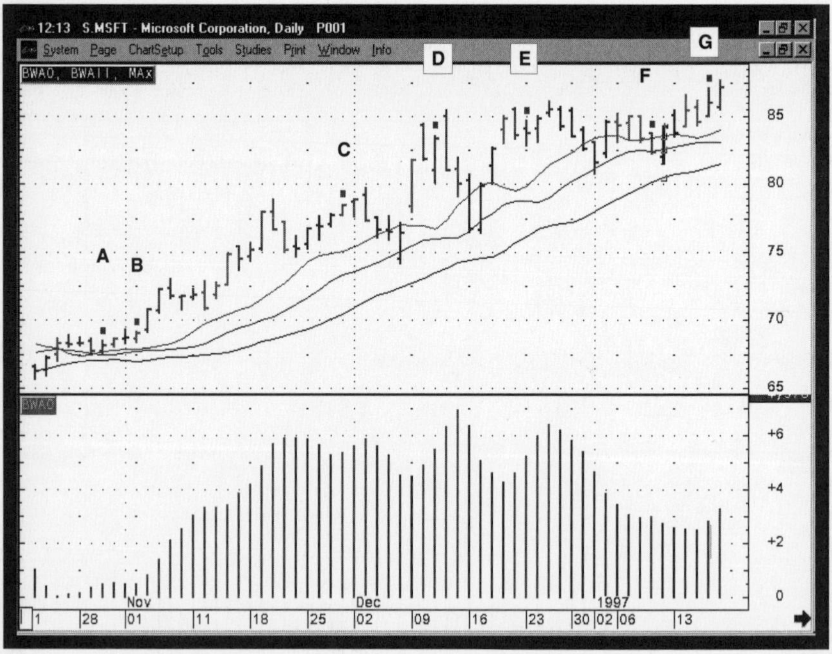

Figure 5–33 Answers to the seven AO buy signals.

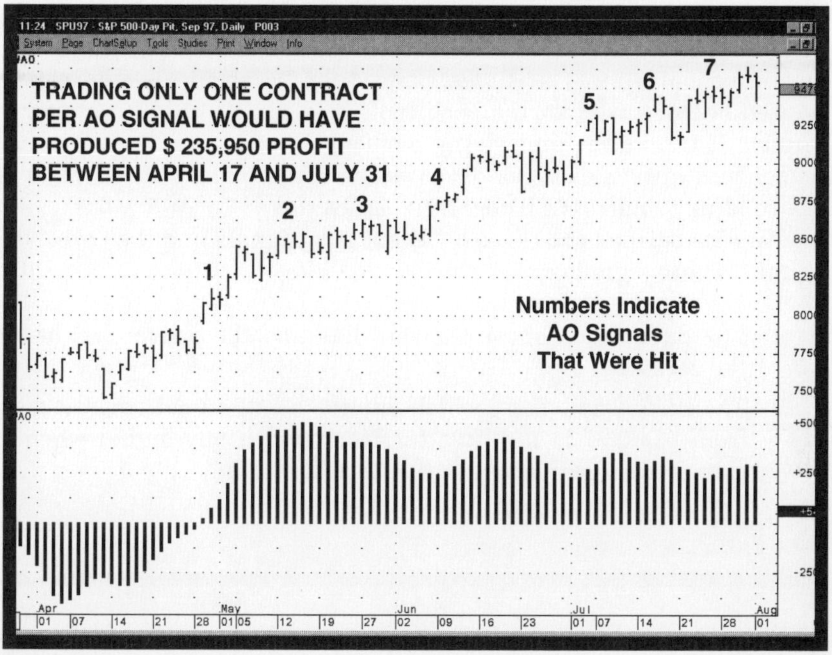

Figure 5–34 Results from trading only the AO signals for just over three months.

chapter, we will examine this same chart and identify all five dimensional signals.

Table 5–1 is a list of these signals, when they were formed, when they were taken, and the profits from trading the S&P for just over three months in a daily time frame. There was no intraday trading.

TABLE 5–1 Trading the S&P "AO" Signals.

#	Date	Signal	Date	Filled	P/L Points	P/L $	Cum. $
1	29-Apr	808.15	30-Apr	808.45	149.50	74,750.00	74,750.00
2	14-May	854.75	15-May	854.90	103.05	51,525.00	126,275.00
3	28-May	862.65	30-May	882.65	95.30	47,650.00	173,925.00
4	11-Jun	880.75	12-Jun	884.50	73.45	36,725.00	210,650.00
5	3-Jul	929.05	7-Jul	929.35	28.60	14,300.00	224,950.00
6	17-Jul	944.25	23-Jul	944.55	13.40	6,700.00	231,650.00
7	29-Jul	949.05	30-Jul	949.35	8.60	4,300.00	235,950.00
	Close	31-Jul		957.95	471.90	235,950.00	

SUMMARY

In this chapter, we have described the Awesome Oscillator and pointed out why it is such a good tool. It is truly a leading indicator because it tracks the underlying momentum of the market. Because momentum always changes direction before price, we say the AO is like reading tomorrow's *Wall Street Journal.*

We also defined the three different buy signals and the three sell signals. Those signals are:

1. The Saucer buy above the zero line and the Saucer sell below the zero line.
2. The histogram cross, which creates a sell signal when it goes from positive to negative territory and a buy signal when it goes from negative to positive territory.

Recap

The Awesome Oscillator measures the immediate momentum of the last 5 price bars as compared to the last 34 price bars.

Three types of signals are generated by the AO:

The Saucer, the Cross, and Twin Peaks

Above the Zero Line, the only signals generated are a Twin Peaks sell, a Saucer buy and a buy Cross.

Below the Zero Line, the only signals generated are a Twin Peaks buy, Saucer sell, and a sell Cross.

Figure 5–35 Recap of the AO signals.

3. The Twin Peaks buy signal, which is the only buy that is created below the zero line, and the Twin Peaks sell signal, which is the only sell created above the zero line.

For quick reference on the chapter's key points, Figure 5–35 is a recap.

In the next chapter, we will examine the AC, which is a more precise measure of the *change in speed* of momentum. One of the most valuable clues in trading is knowing when to anticipate a change in trend. Before a change in trend can happen, there must be a change in the direction of the momentum. Before there can be a change in the direction of the momentum, there must be a slowing down of the momentum—and that is what this next dimension is about. If understanding momentum is like reading tomorrow's *Wall Street Journal,* knowing how to use this next dimension is like reading the day after tomorrow's *Wall Street Journal.*

6

THE MARKET ACCELERATOR

So far, we have examined the Science of Chaos and how it relates to trading the stock and commodity markets. We explained how we use our primary decision and strategy maker—The Alligator—to filter out the bad trades and to add on to winning trades. The Alligator is the best asset allocator we have ever found. We then looked at how to get started in any embryo trend on a fractal breakout signal. This keeps us out of the whiplashes in a range-bound market and, at the same time, guarantees that we will not be left out of any significant trend move. In the previous chapter, we saw that we can get great timing advantages by using the *momentum* for signals rather than the *price.* This advantage comes from knowing that momentum will always change before price.

In this chapter, we are going to use a *derivative/integration* of the momentum so that we create an even further advantage over other traders. Imagine rolling a bowling ball down a street. The weight and momentum of the bowling ball will cause it to continue on its path. If that path encounters an uphill portion of the street, the momentum will start slowing down. From a physics standpoint, the instant it starts to slow down it is really accelerating in the opposite direction. In other words, before the price can change direction (we traders label this as a *trend change*), the momentum must come to a complete stop and turn in the opposite direction, either up or down. However, by monitoring the acceleration/deceleration of the momentum, we can get an even earlier warning of what the market has in mind. As I pointed out earlier, trading the momentum is like reading tomorrow's *Wall Street Journal* and trading the acceleration/deceleration (we label this indicator the AC) is like reading the day after tomorrow's *Wall Street Journal.* What an advantage to any trader!

THE AC SIGNALS

Acceleration/Deceleration (AC) is the third dimension of our market analysis. Remember that the price is the last item to change. Before the price changes, the momentum changes: and before the momentum changes direction, there must be a deceleration of momentum until momentum comes to zero. Then it starts accelerating in the opposite direction, before the price can change direction.

That is what the AC measures, the Acceleration and Deceleration of the *current* Momentum. The AC will change direction before the Momentum and Momentum will change direction before price. Understanding the AC as an early warning signal gives you an obvious advantage over other traders.

Figure 6–1 is a condensation of the rules for trading the AC. Basically, the zero line is the place where the momentum is balanced with the acceleration. If the AC is above zero, it will usually be easier for the acceleration to continue to move upward (and vice versa

In order to create a signal you must have a change in acceleration, (color change).

It's easier to buy above the line, therefore only a couple of bars are needed to create the signal.

Crossing zero is NOT a signal alone, it only affects the number of bars needed to create a signal.

You can not have a buy if the current bar is Red.

You can not have a sell if the current bar is Green.

This is the most sensitive signal we have. Acceleration will change before momentum, and momentum will change before price. Knowing that, we can use this signal as our first indication of where the market is heading .

This may help you remember the rules:

2 Bars with momentum
3 Bars against momentum

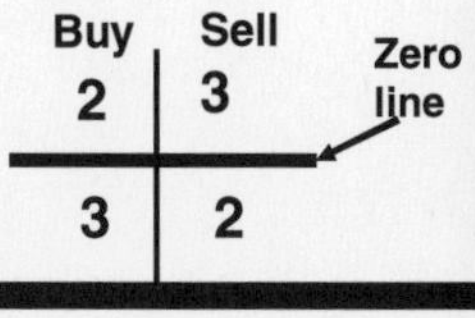

Figure 6–1 Rules for the AC signals.

below zero). Unlike the AO, *crossing* the zero line *is not* a signal. If your equipment allows you to color the histogram bars, then you only need to look for a change in color to know that you need to monitor the market and possibly take action. To eliminate spurious thinking, just remember: With the AC, you cannot have a buy if the bar is red, and you cannot have a sell if the bar is green.

Whenever the momentum and acceleration are both in the same direction, the momentum is not only moving in that direction but is also gaining speed and accelerating in that direction. This, of course, is the best of all worlds: the market is going your way and picking up speed at the same time.

Because this is a very sensitive signal, we want to give it a bit more room than we gave the AO. Check out Figure 6–1 and you will see, at the bottom right corner, how we do that. If the momentum is with us (it is above zero and we are buying, or below zero and we are selling), we want to enter aggressively and we need only two green bars for a buy (two red bars for a sell). If the momentum is against us (it is below zero and we are buying, or above zero and we are selling), we want confirmation so we require one extra bar. In this case, we would require three red bars to sell above the zero line and three green bars to buy below the zero line. Let's examine these signals more closely.

AC Buy above the Zero Line

All AC signals come from a change in the direction of the AC histogram. The AC histogram is a 5-bar simple moving average of the difference between the 5/34 momentum histogram and a 5-bar simple moving average of that difference. If the current difference between the 5/34 AO oscillator and the 5-bar moving average is greater than the average difference for the last 5 bars, the momentum is accelerating. If it is less, the momentum in that direction is slowing. Here are the key points you should remember:

1. A buy signal is created when there are two consecutive histogram bars with higher highs than the most recent lowest low (a down peak). (See Figure 6–2.)
2. A buy stop is placed one tick above the high of the price bar, which corresponds (in the same time frame) to the second higher high.

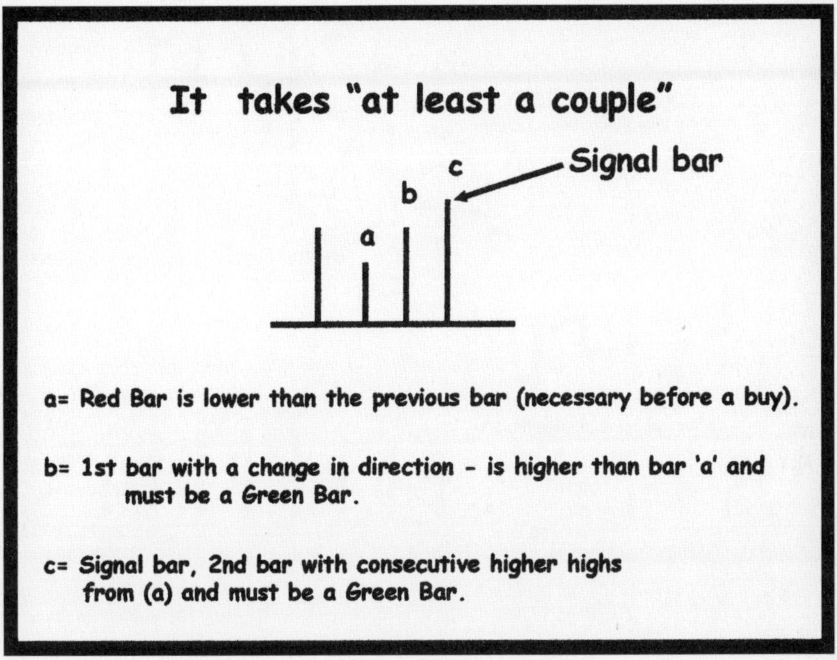

Figure 6–2 AC buy signal above the zero line.

3. A second buy signal cannot be created until the histogram moves at least one bar lower, creating a red bar. A new buy signal can then be created after two higher (green) bars.
4. In the software, this is easy to spot because it requires at least one red bar followed by two green bars on the AC histogram.

Figure 6–3 is an example of buying when the AC is above the zero line. The bar labeled "Down Peak" is the lowest bar on the current AC histogram. That is followed by a change in acceleration (noted at point 1), and the next bar (point 2) continues the upward acceleration. Because the Accelerator is above the zero line, we need only two higher highs (two green bars) to establish a buy signal. The buy is placed one tick above the high of the price bar that is in the same time frame as point 2. Notice that it was filed on the opening gap of the next bar (day). Figure 6–4 shows the same signal on Philip Morris stock.

In the next section, we will look at the requirements to place a buy stop when the Accelerator is below the zero line.

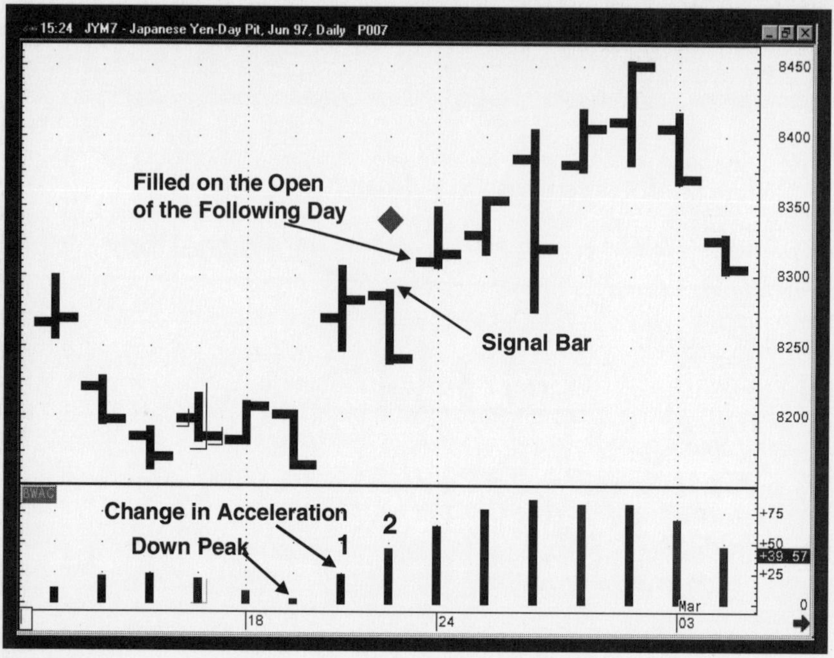

Figure 6–3 AC buy signal above the zero line in the Japanese Yen.

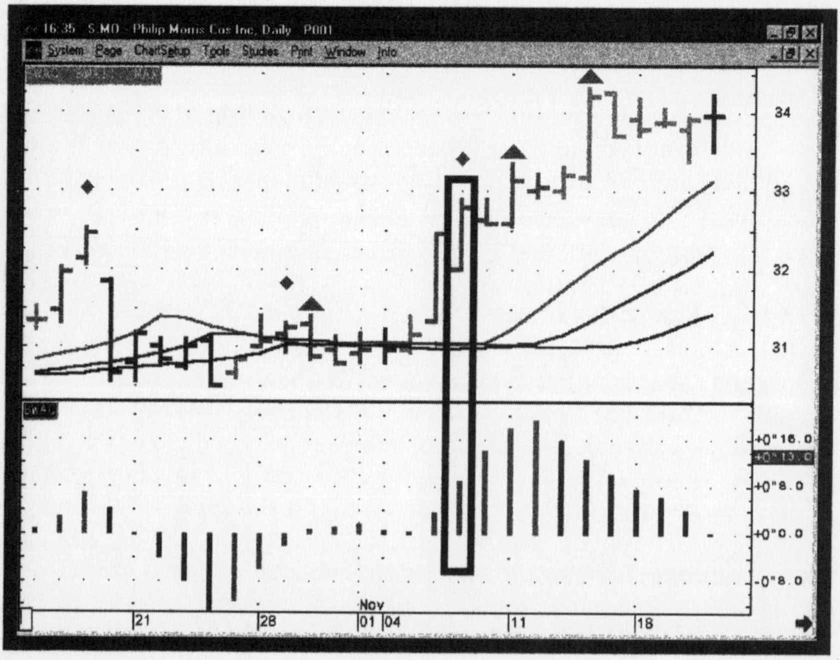

Figure 6–4 AC buy signal above the zero line in Philip Morris stock.

AC Buy below the Zero Line

How does the buy change if the Accelerator is below the zero line?

Figure 6–5 illustrates an Accelerator buy when the Accelerator is below the zero line. This means that the momentum is accelerating up (which is the same as the downward momentum slowing down as it falls) against the current momentum. This is similar to when you are approaching a traffic light and put on the brakes. Your momentum is still forward but it is slowing down. From a physics standpoint, you are really accelerating in the opposite direction.

Here are the AC rules for buying when the histogram is "below" the zero line:

1. A buy signal is created when the histogram forms *three* bars that have higher highs than the most recent lowest low (a down peak). All three must be green bars.

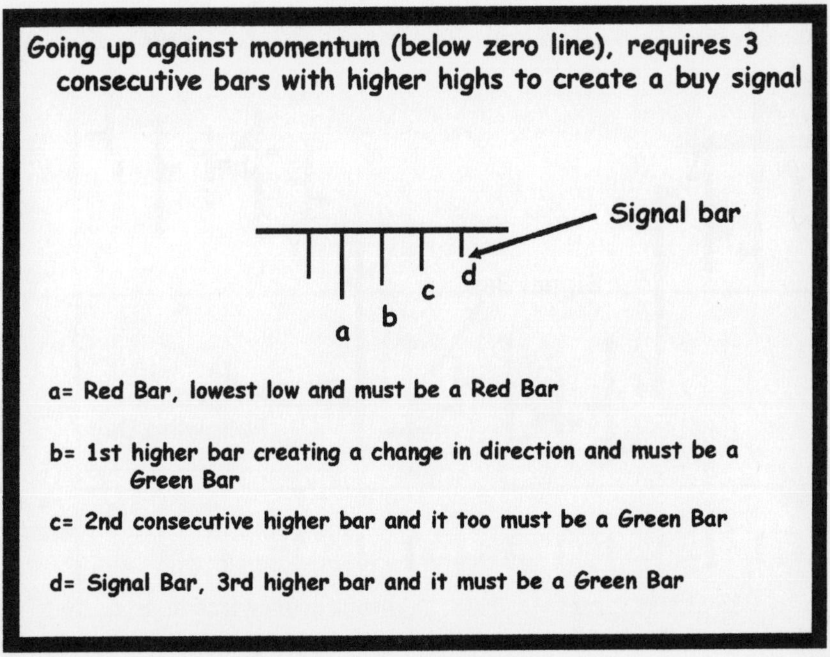

Figure 6–5 AC buy signal below the zero line.

2. A buy stop is placed one tick above the high of the price bar, which corresponds (in the same time segment) to the *third* higher high.
3. In our software, this is easy to spot because it requires at least one red bar followed by three green bars on the AC histogram.

Figure 6–6 shows the buy signal when the AC is below the zero line. Here, it takes three green bars because the momentum is against us, as determined by the AC's being below the zero line. Our buy stop would be one tick above the high of the price bar that corresponds to the same time period as the third higher high on the AC.

Both the coffee and the Intel Corporation charts (Figures 6–6 and 6–7) show a buy when the AC is below the zero line. Remember that it takes a base (B in Figure 6–7), which must be the most recent histogram low plus three higher lows. The easiest way to see this is to program your charting software so that an up move in the histogram is colored green and a down move is colored red. Then you

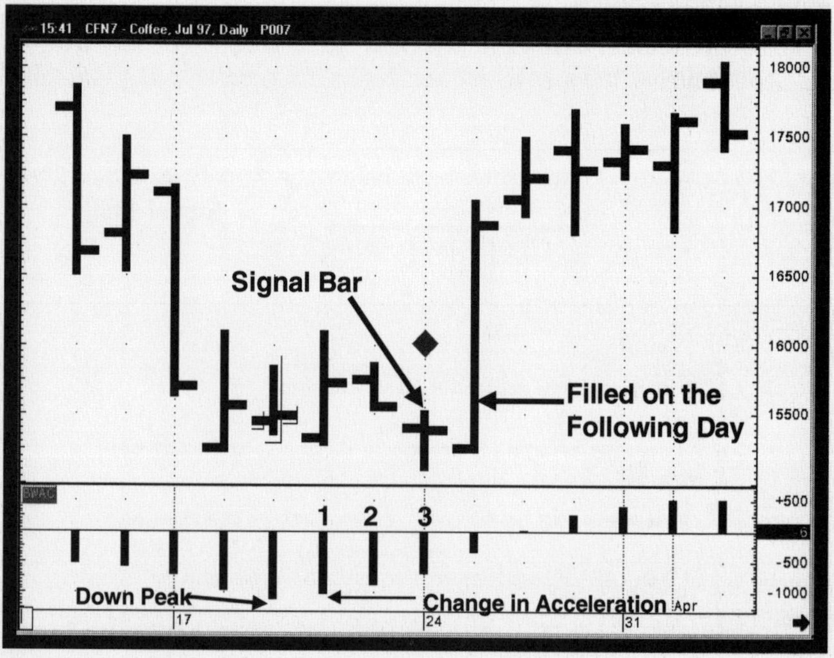

Figure 6–6 AC buy signal below zero line—coffee.

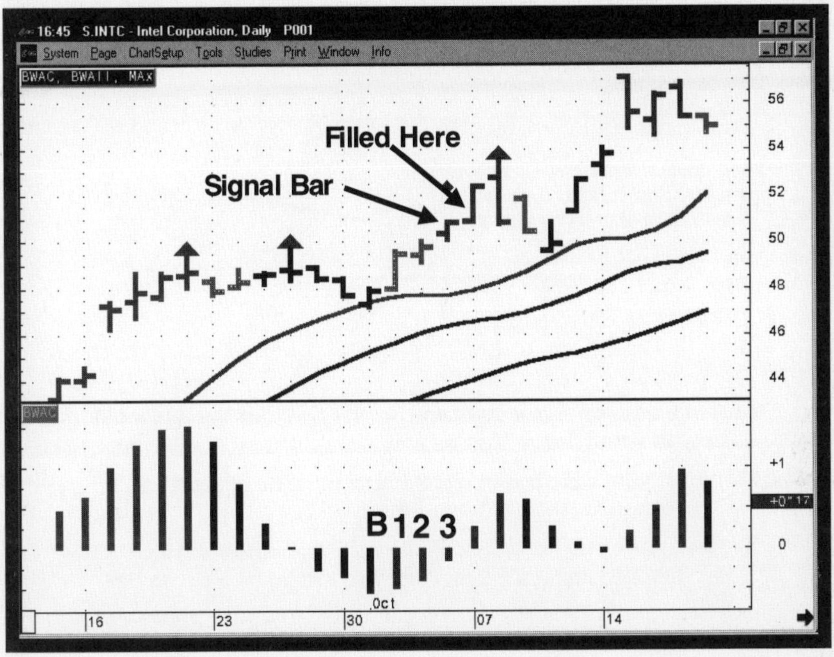

Figure 6–7 AC buy signal when the AC is below the zero line—Intel Corporation.

only have to count three green bars below the zero line and you have a signal.

This brings up two questions:

1. Is crossing the zero line on the AC a signal, as it is on the AO? Answer: No.
2. What effect does crossing the zero line have on the buy and sell signals?

These are the AC rules for buying when the histogram is "crossing" the zero line from below to above (negative to positive):

1. A buy signal is created if the AC histogram down peak is below the zero line and crosses the line on the second or third bar after the down peak. When that happens and the current "indicator" bar in the histogram is above the zero line, you need only *two* higher highs. (See Figure 6–8.)

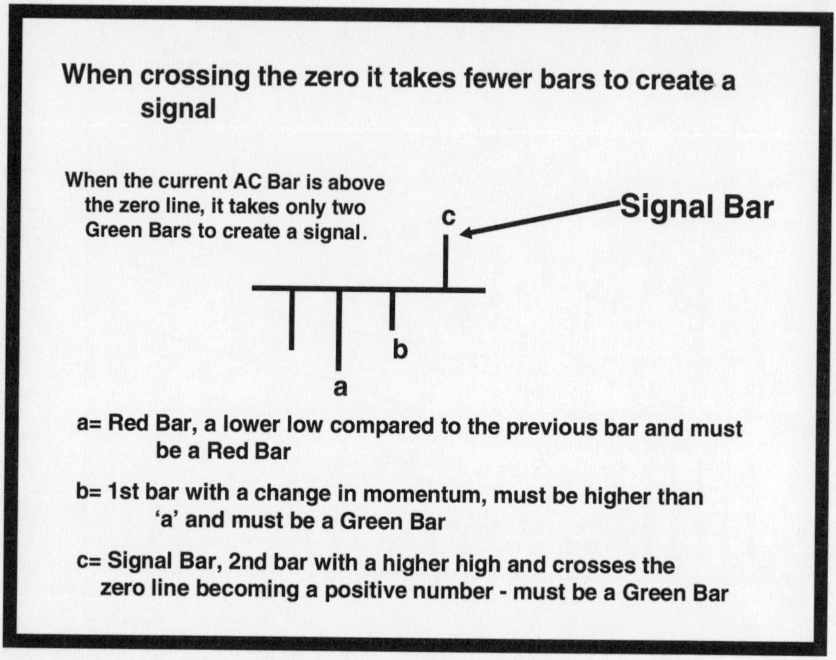

Figure 6–8 Buying when the histogram is "crossing" the zero line.

2. IT IS IMPORTANT TO UNDERSTAND THAT CROSSING THE ZERO LINE *IS NOT* A SIGNAL ON THE AC HISTOGRAM. (Crossing the zero line is a signal only on the AO chart.)
3. Crossing the zero line on the histogram chart only changes the *number* of green bars (higher highs) that you need for a buy signal. The reason behind reducing the number of histogram bars after crossing the zero line is that the momentum is now in your favor and you want to get in or add to your position as quickly as possible.

Figure 6–9 illustrates what happens when the AC crosses the zero line and how it affects the number of bars necessary to create a buy or sell signal. Crossing the zero line is not a signal. However, crossing the zero line may change the number of histogram bars needed to create a signal. Figure 6–9, we only need two higher highs because the second higher high is above the zero line. It does not matter where the other parts of the signal construction might be; what

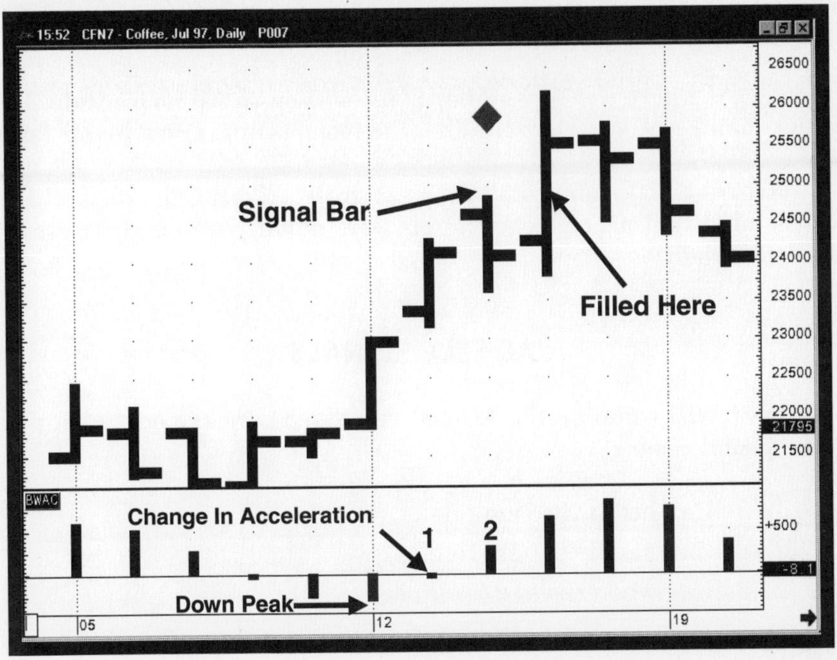

Figure 6–9 A special case: The AC histogram is crossing the zero line.

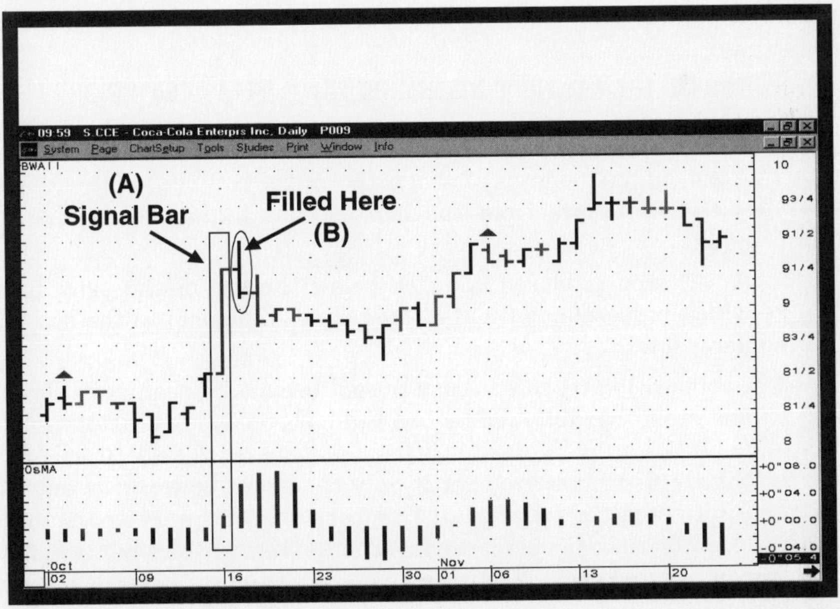

Figure 6–10 A special case: The AC histogram is crossing the zero line (Coca-Cola stock).

matters is where the *current* bar is in relation to the momentum. Because bar 2 is above the zero line, the momentum is now in our favor for a buy.

Figure 6–10 shows a similar setup in a Coca-Cola stock chart. Remember that all of these signals work equally well on both stocks and commodities.

AC SELL SIGNALS

Next, we will examine the AC sell signals. There are only two, plus one special case:

1. Selling below the zero line.
2. Selling above the zero line.
3. Selling when the histogram is crossing the zero line.

AC Sell below the Zero Line

Figure 6–11 shows a schematic of how the AC sell signal is created by the AC histogram's having two consecutive lower lows below the zero line.

These are the AC rules for selling when the histogram is below the zero line:

1. A sell signal is created when there are two consecutive bars with lower lows from the most recent highest high (an up peak).
2. A sell stop is placed one tick below the low of the price bar, which corresponds (in the same time sequence) to the second lower low.
3. In the software, this is easy to spot because it requires at least one green bar followed by two red bars on the AC histogram.

In Figure 6–12, we see that it only takes two lower lows on the histogram to create a sell signal. This is true because we are in tune with the momentum, as evidenced by the AC histogram's being below the histogram zero line. Figure 6–13 is a similar illustration for a stock chart.

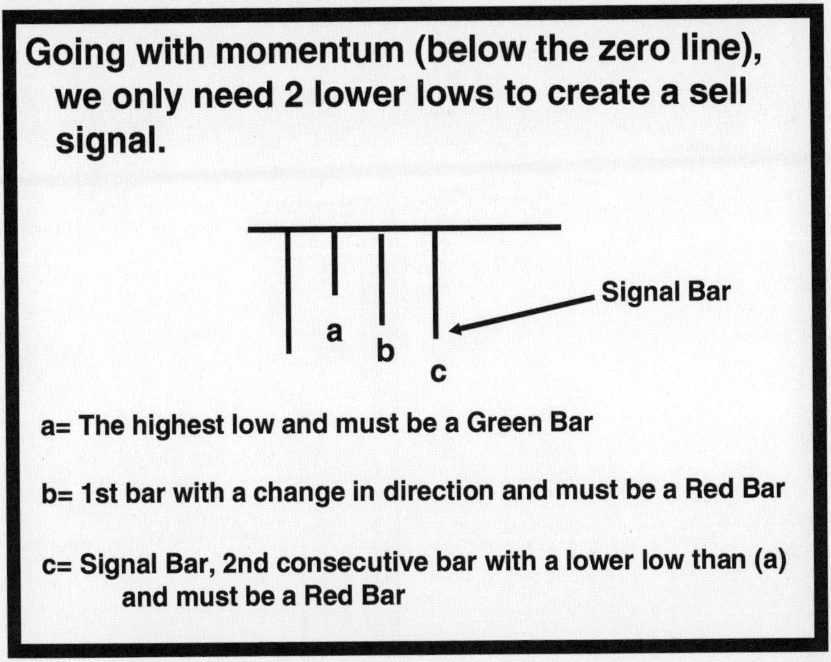

Figure 6–11 Selling when the AC is below the zero line.

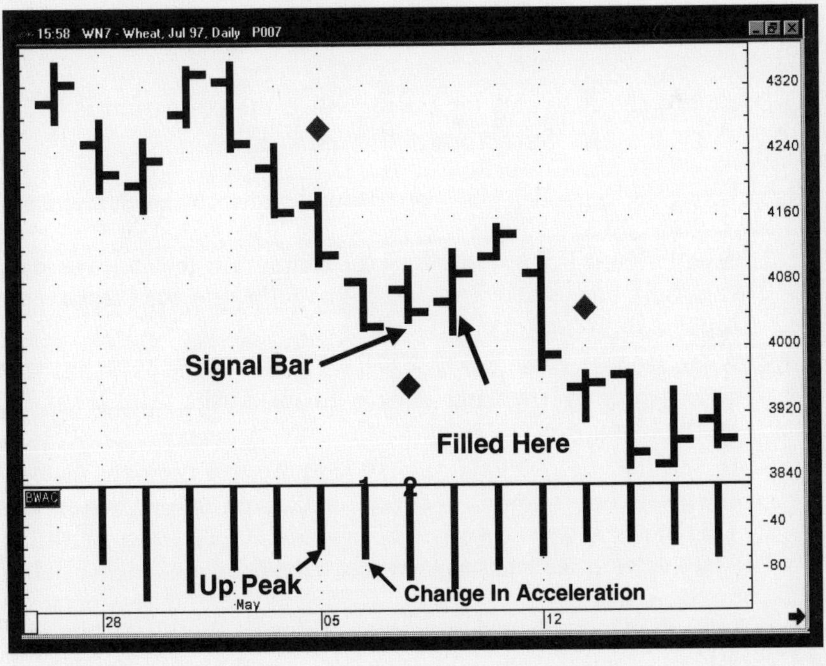

Figure 6–12 The AC sell signal below the zero line in wheat.

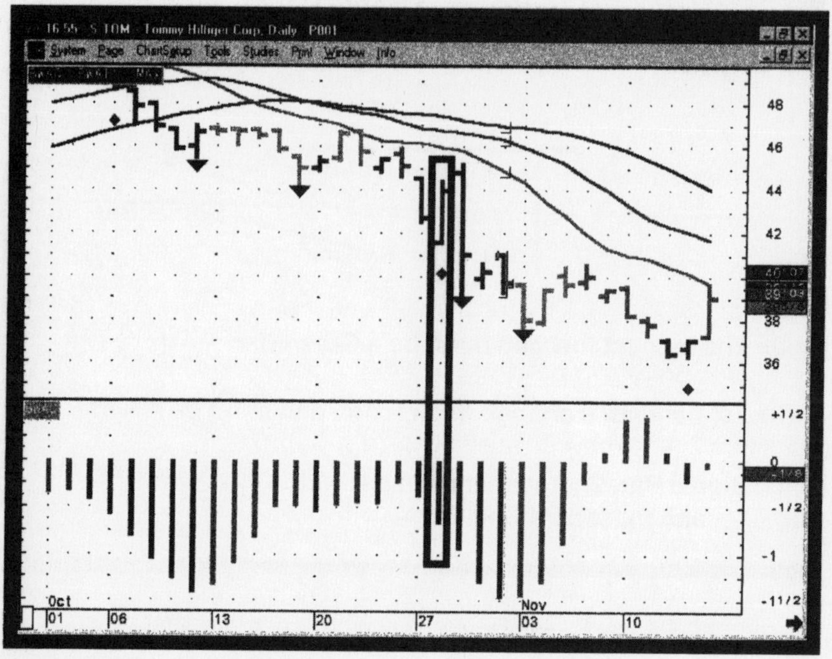

Figure 6–13 Sell signal when the histogram is below the zero line—Tommy Hilfiger Stock.

AC Sell above the Zero Line

The rules for selling when the histogram is above the zero line are:

1. A sell signal is created when the histogram forms three bars that have consecutively lower highs following the most recent highest high (an up peak).
2. A sell stop is placed one tick below the low of the price bar that corresponds (in the same time segment) to the third lower low on the histogram.
3. In the software, this is easy to spot since it requires at least one green bar followed by three red bars on the AC histogram. This same software will also indicate the sell stop with the exact order price on the price chart itself.

We will use Figure 6–14 to demonstrate this sell signal. A change in acceleration is required, as noted on bar 1, and that is followed by

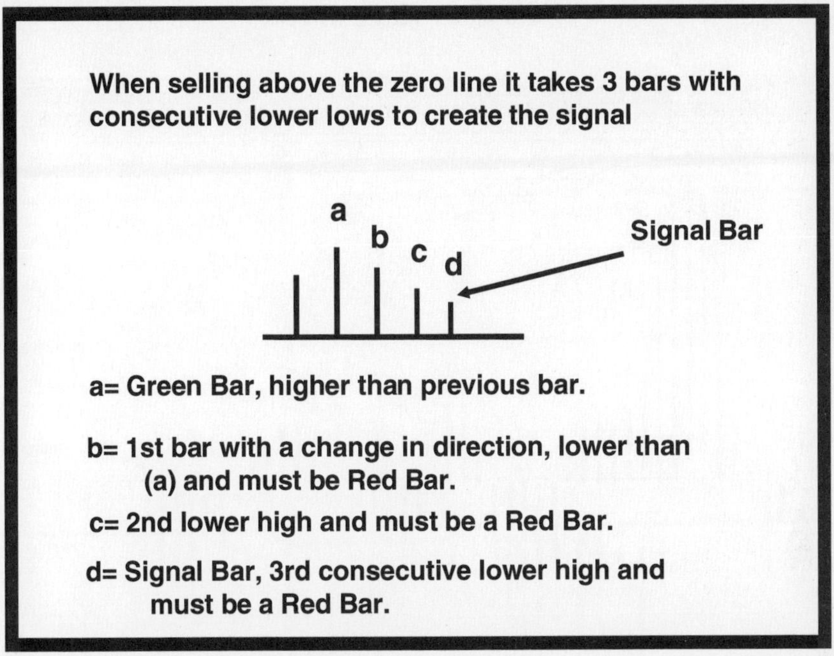

Figure 6–14 Selling when the AC histogram is above the zero line.

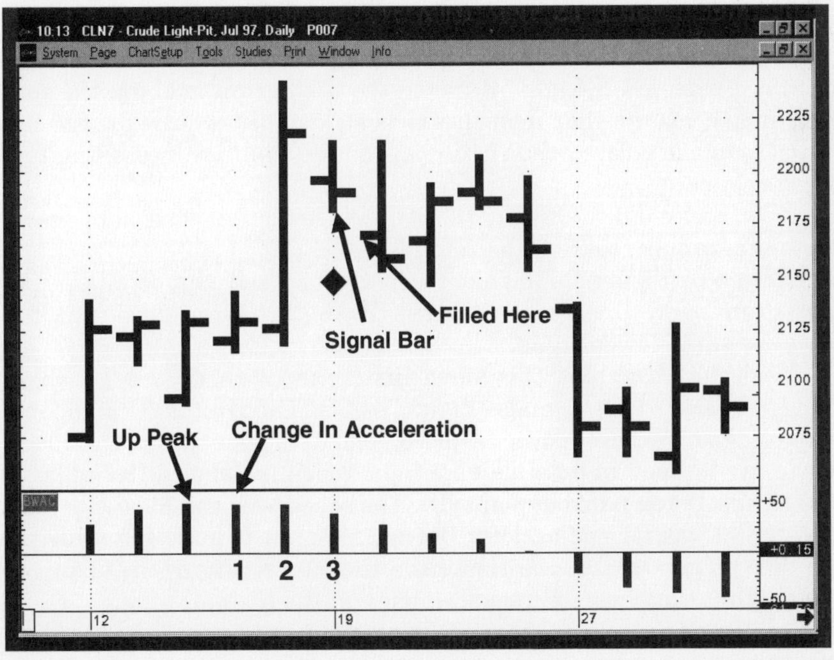

Figure 6–15 AC sell signal when the histogram is above the zero line.

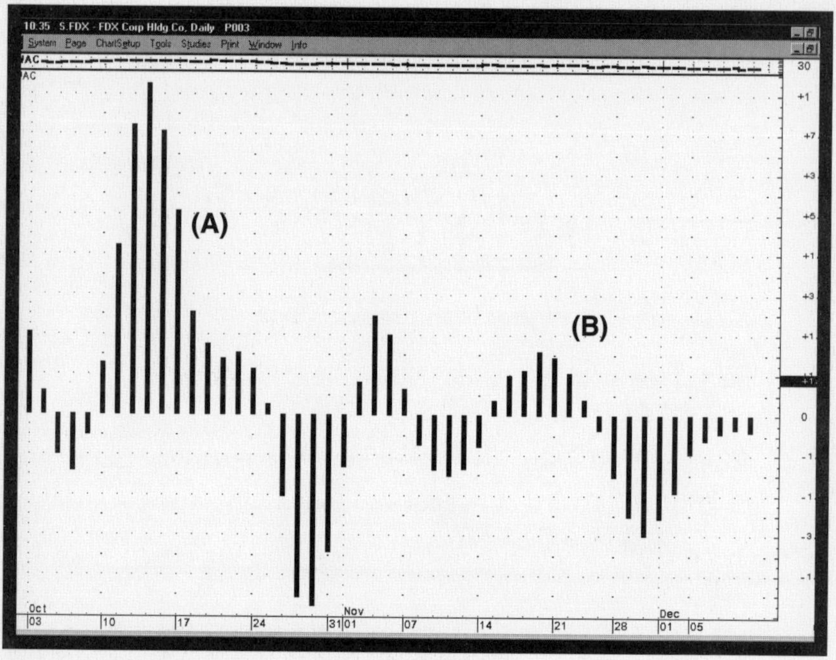

Figure 6–16 Histogram sell signals in FedEx stock.

two bars with lower highs. Because the histogram is above the zero line, which means that momentum is still up, it requires three red bars (bars are colored red if they are lower than the preceding histogram bar).

Now, as we did in the buy section, let's examine what happens as the histogram is crossing the zero line.

Notice in Figure 6–16 that there are two sell signals above the histogram's zero line. Points (A) and (B) require an upward peak followed by three lower highs.

Next, let's combine this same histogram with the FedEx chart that generated these signals (Figure 6–17). The first sell signal was not followed by lower lows in price, and the momentum continued down, giving us two possible blue light specials, labeled (B) and (C). The first sell was filled at point (D). The second AO sell above the zero line signal was formed at point (E) and filled at point (F). Because of the size of this chart, you may have to refer to Figure 6–16 to see clearly that there were three down bars on the histogram.

The rules for selling when the histogram is crossing the zero line from above to below (positive to negative) are:

1. A sell signal is created if the AC histogram up peak is above the zero line and crosses the line on the second or third bar after the up peak. When that happens and the current "indicator" bar in the histogram is below the zero line, you need only *two* lower lows (red bars). (See Figure 6–18).
2. IT IS IMPORTANT TO UNDERSTAND THAT CROSSING THE ZERO LINE *IS NOT* A SIGNAL ON THE AC HISTOGRAM. (Crossing the zero line is a signal only on the AO histogram.)
3. Crossing the zero line on the AC histogram only changes the number of red bars (lower lows) that you need for a sell signal. Again, the reason behind reducing the number of histogram bars after crossing the zero line is: Momentum is now in your favor, and you want to get in or add to your position as quickly as possible.

Figure 6–18 is a schematic of how crossing the zero line affects the AC sell signal.

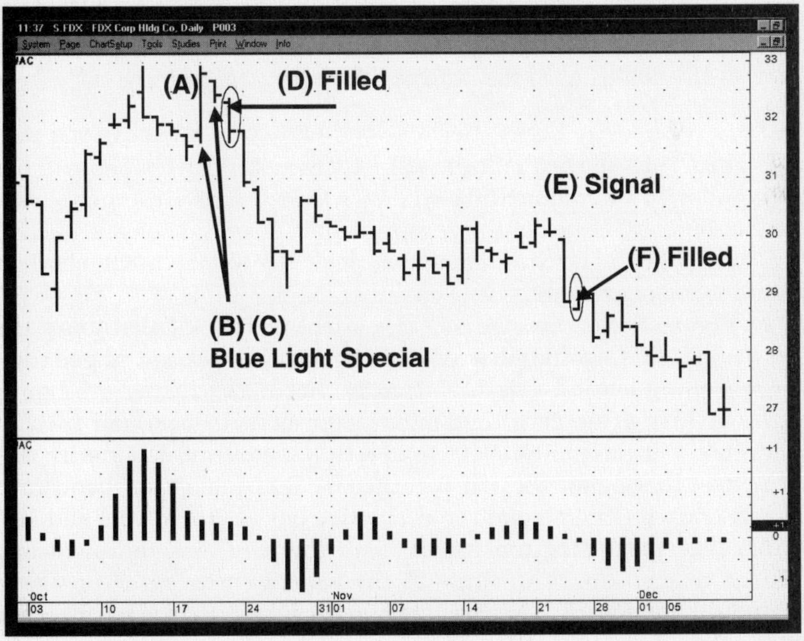

Figure 6–17 AC sell signals when the histogram is above the zero line—FedEx stock.

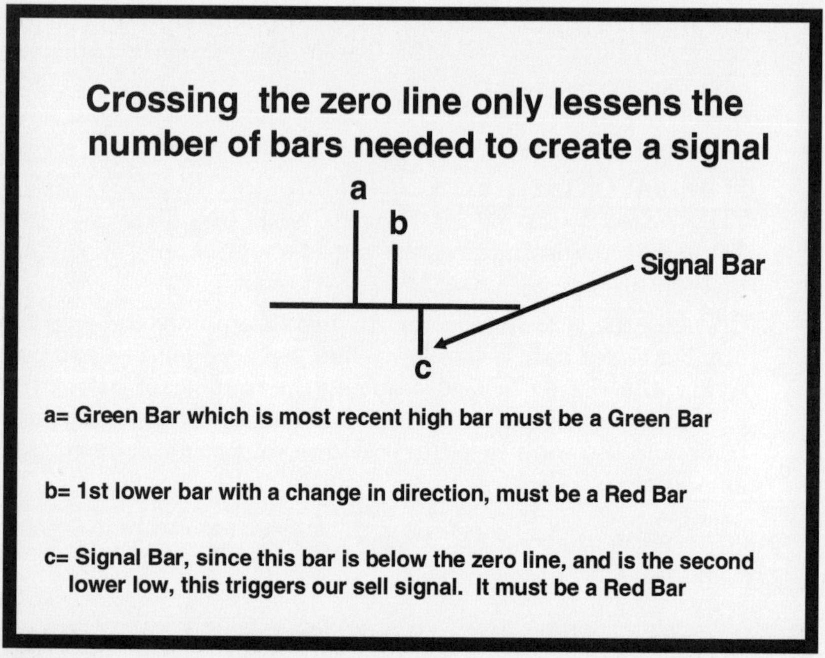

Figure 6–18 Selling when the histogram is crossing the zero line from above to below (positive to negative).

Figure 6–19 shows the highest histogram bar as "Up Peak." That bar is followed by the bar labeled "1," which is above the histogram zero line. Bar "2" is *below* the zero line and thus needs only a total of two lower highs after the histogram peak. In Figure 6–20, the histogram is enlarged so that it is easier to read.

In Figure 6–20, you can see the effect of the AC's crossing the zero line: it cuts the number of bars needed to create a sell signal. The reasoning behind this variation is that if the histogram bar is below the histogram zero line, momentum is now down and in your favor, so get in promptly. Next, place this histogram back with the price chart to see how they fit together for profitable opportunities.

In Figure 6–21, you can see that price bar (A) becomes a sell signal because the histogram has crossed the zero line, which means that the momentum is in favor of the sellers so we want to get in promptly. That now requires only two lower lows from the most recent peak. This signal was filled at point (B). Another similar signal on this chart, at point (C), was filled at point (D).

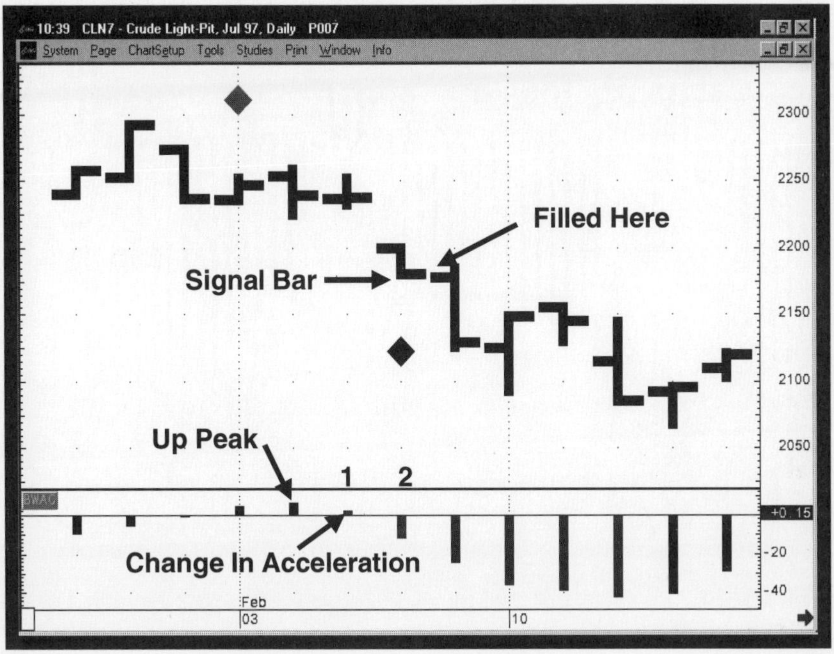

Figure 6–19 A special case: When the AC histogram is crossing the zero line—crude oil.

We have now covered the two buy signals and the two sell signals, and we have illustrated by a buy-and-sell special situation when the histogram bars are crossing the histogram zero line. For review purposes, they are all presented in Figure 6–22.

PRACTICE PAGES

This section contains charts for your practice in finding AC buys and sells. Each chart is followed by answer pages that show all the AC signals. Try your hand at demonstrating your understanding of the AC signals by marking the ones you see on the practice page and then checking the answer pages.

Figure 6–23 is for your practice in locating all the AC buy and sell signals.

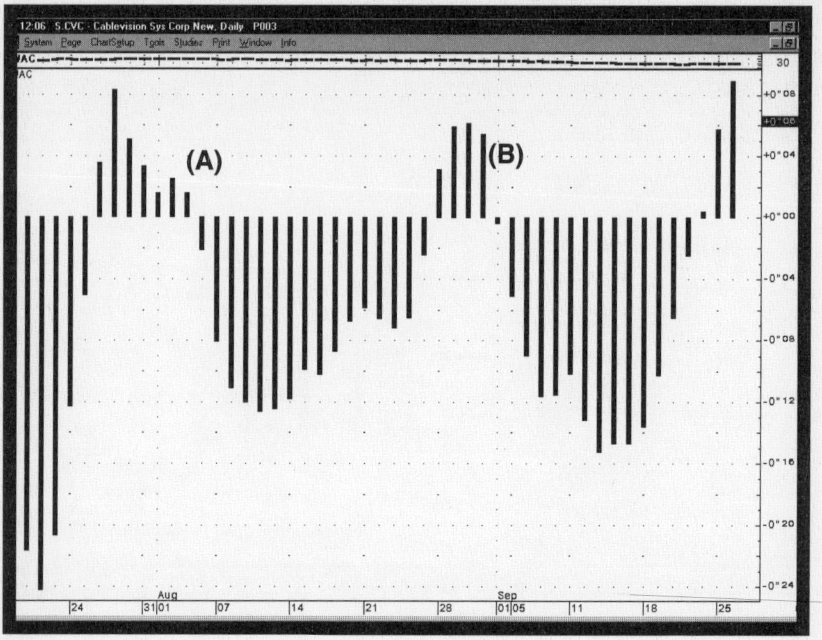

Figure 6–20 An enlargement of the AC histogram, demonstrating how crossing the zero line affects the placement of the sell signal.

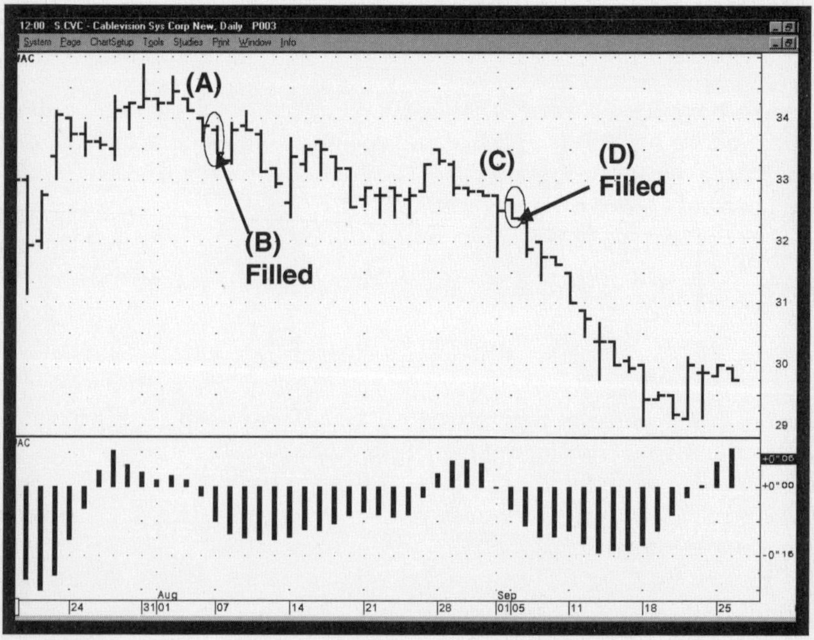

Figure 6–21 AC sell signals when crossing the histogram zero line.

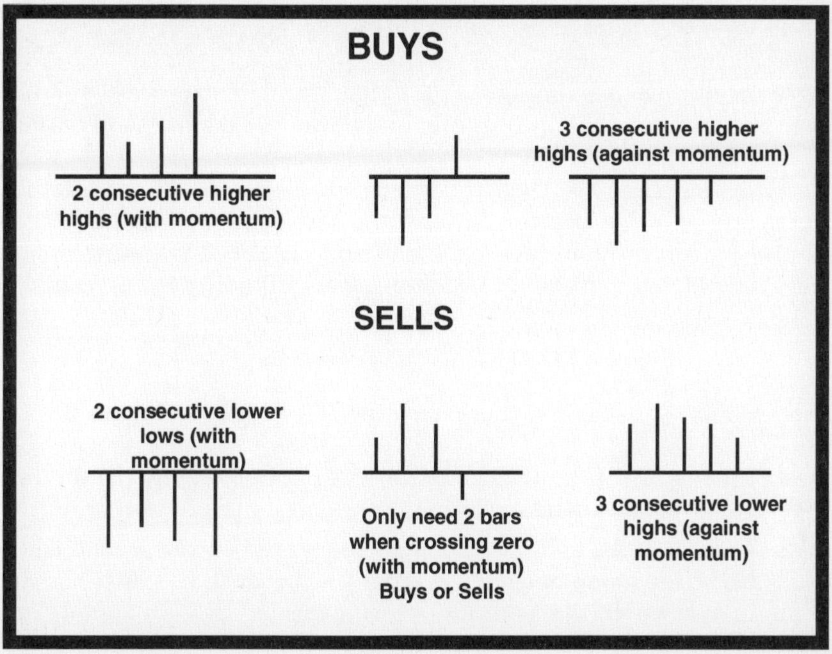

Figure 6–22 A review of the AC buy and sell signals.

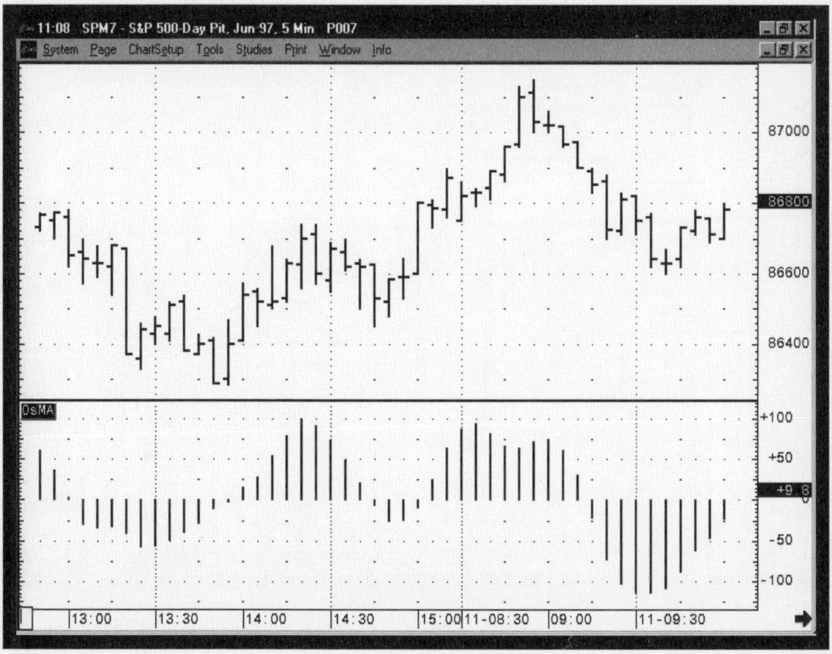

Figure 6–23 AC practice page, S&P.

We continue to strongly suggest that you do not proceed further with these signals until you really understand and can readily locate all the AC buy and sell signals without hesitation.

After you have finished practicing on Figure 6–23, go to other charts and practice locating AC buy and sell signals on them.

Only after you have accomplished and practiced the suggestions above should you move on to Chapter Seven, "Trading in the Zones."

Practice Page Answers

As shown in Figure 6–24, there are nine AC signals in Figure 6–23:

1. This is an AC sell. The signal was created on the third down bar after an up peak. The signal is hit on the following bar.
2. This is an AC sell. The signal was created on the second down bar after an up peak. The signal was never hit because the AC turned up on the next day, which canceled the sell signal. You cannot have a sell signal with a current green bar on the AO histogram.

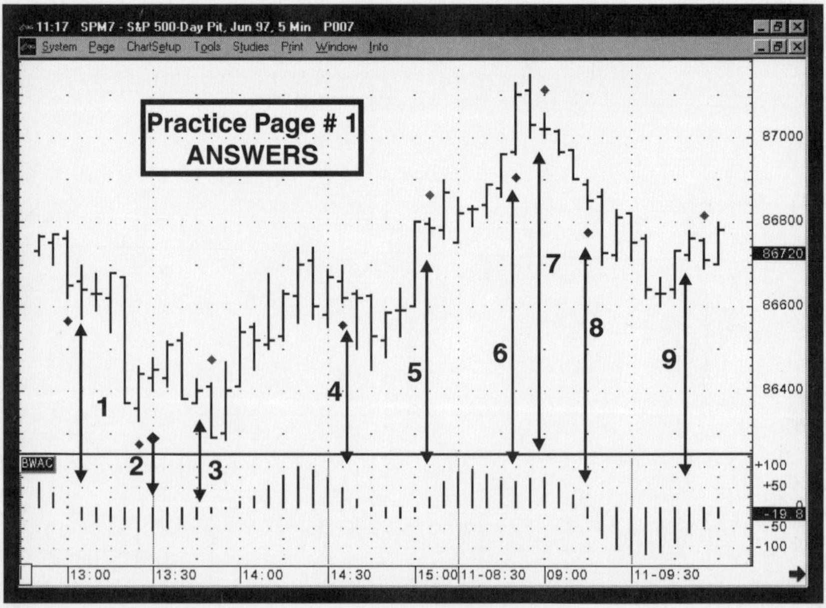

Figure 6–24 Answers to Figure 6–23—AC signals.

3. This is an AC buy. The signal was actually created two days before the bar marked. We continued to move the buy stop down until the buy stop was hit, because the AC continued up. This is a good example of a blue light special.
4. This is an AC sell. The signal was created on the third down bar after an up peak. The signal is hit on the following bar.
5. This is an AC buy. The signal was created on the third up bar after the down peak. The signal is hit on the following day.
6. This is an AC sell. This signal was created on the third down bar after the up peak. The signal was canceled on the following day because the AC turned up.
7. This is an AC buy. The signal was created on the second up bar after the down peak. This signal was canceled on the following day because the AC turned down.
8. This is an AC sell. This signal was created on the third down bar after the up peak. The signal was hit on the following day.
9. This is an AC buy. The signal was created on the third up bar after the down peak. The signal is hit on the following day.

Figure 6–25 is another practice chart for finding AC buy and sell signals. At this point, we are not taking into account the Alligator. Our purpose here is to be able to locate all the AC signals quickly and easily. Check your answers against Figure 6–26.

Figure 6–27 is a chart of Sears stock. See if you can find the valid buy and/or sell signals, taking into account the Alligator and the position of the AC histogram.

The answers to the practice chart (Figure 6–27) are listed below. How many of the signals indicated in Figure 6–28 did you find?

The Sears chart takes into account everything you have learned about using the Alligator and the first breakout fractal. In the first box on the left is an AC buy signal (two higher highs on the histogram after a base) that was triggered on the next price bar.

The second box from the left is an AC sell signal (a high in the histogram followed by three lower bars; it required three because the second one was still above the zero line). It also was triggered on the very next price bar.

The third box from the left is an AC buy signal that only required a low followed by two higher highs because the second higher high was *above* the zero line.

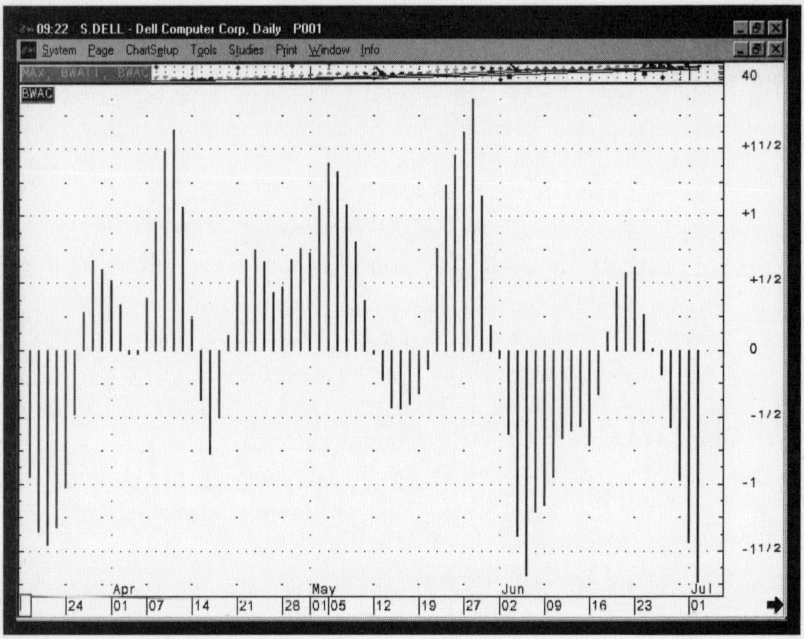

Figure 6–25 Practice page for finding AC buy and sell signals—Dell Computer stock.

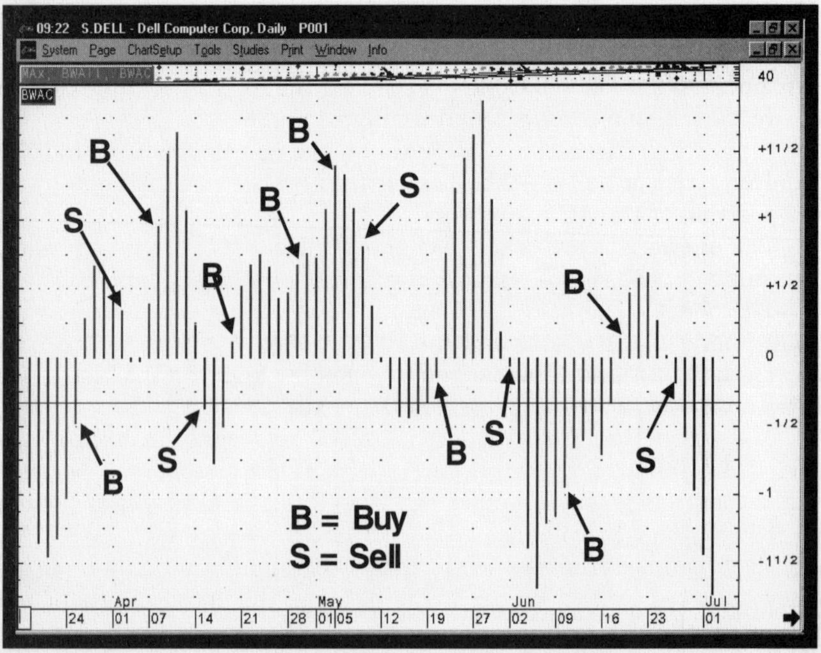

Figure 6–26 Answers to Figure 6–25—Dell Computer AC signals.

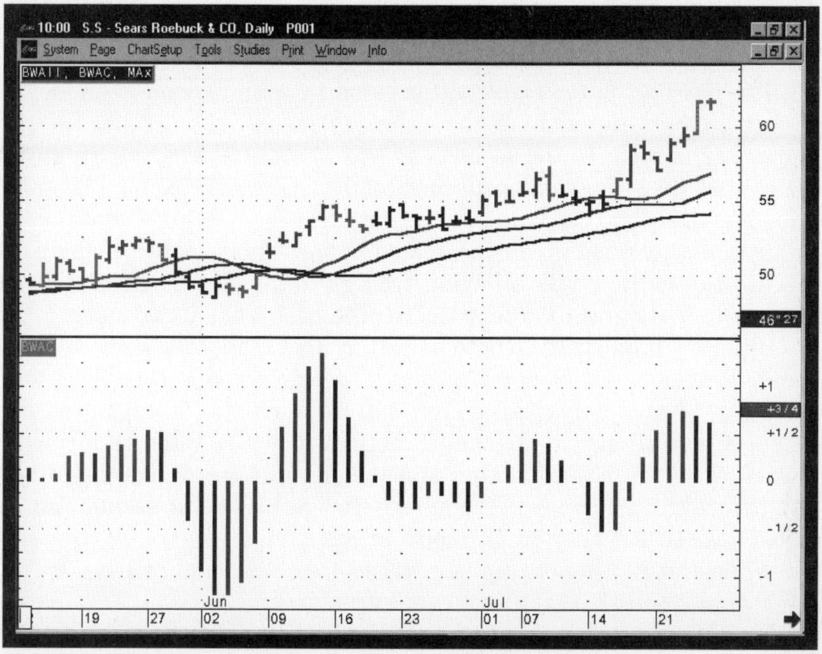

Figure 6–27 Practice chart for finding the valid buy/sell signals for Sears stock.

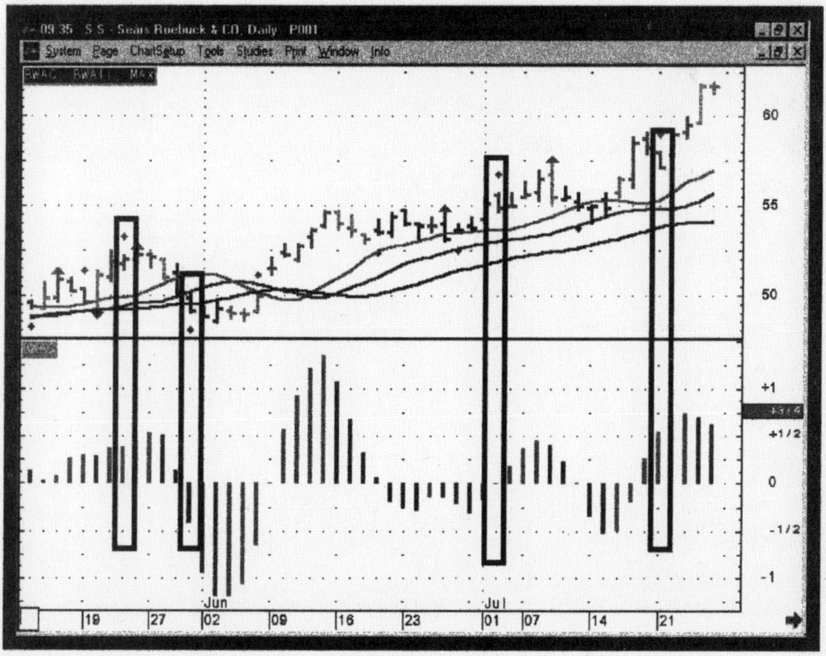

Figure 6–28 Valid signals in the Sears chart shown in Figure 6–27.

The box on the far right was created by a histogram low followed by two higher highs. Like the previous signal, it only needed two higher highs because the second one was above the zero line. However, notice that the signal was not triggered by the next price bar. The next price bar (the one that is inside the box) had a lower high, and the AC histogram continued up on the following bar. This created a blue light special; the market was allowing traders to buy the stock at a lower price than the signal. These are often the best trade locations.

It is very important to note here that all AC signals were not triggered. Remember that our first signal taken outside the Alligator's mouth is always a fractal. After that first fractal is triggered, we take any and all signals in that direction. It is also important to note that if an AC signal is created and the AC histogram changes direction before the price bar is triggered, that nullifies the signal and we do not take it. Another quick check is: you cannot have an AC buy signal when the AC histogram bar is red, and you cannot have an AC sell signal when the AC histogram bar is green.

The AC signal is our most sensitive indicator because it changes before the momentum, and the momentum changes before the price.

Figure 6–29 Actual trading examples of the S&P dailies.

ACTUAL TRADING EXAMPLES

Figure 6–29 shows actual trading signals beginning April 17 and ending on July 31—just over three months of trading the dailies. None of these trades was intraday, and only the AC signals are shown.

Note that not all the signals are numbered. The numbered signals indicate the ones that were actually hit and got us in on the long side. Those that were actually hit are listed in Table 6–1.

WHAT YOU SHOULD KNOW AT THIS POINT

You should now know . . .

1. What Chaos really is and how it gives us an advantage in the stock and commodity markets.
2. How to construct, recognize, and use the Alligator for both trade placement and asset allocation. We call the Alligator our odds maker.
3. How to recognize buy and sell fractals quickly and easily.
4. How the Awesome Oscillator (AO) is plotted and how to trade the momentum of the market as determined by the AO.
5. How to easily locate the three buy signals and the three sell signals, and how to identify Saucers, Twin Peaks, and crossing the zero line AO signals.
6. How to easily locate buy and sell signals above and below the zero line on the Accelerator/Decelerator (AC). You should also understand how crossing the zero line alters the bar count in buy and sell signals.

TABLE 6–1 Trading the S&P AC Signals.

#	Date	Signal	Date	Filled	P/L Points	P/L $	Cum. $
1	21-Apr	780.05	22-Apr	780.40	177.55	88,775.00	88,775.00
2	1-May	815.35	2-May	815.40	142.55	71,275.00	160,050.00
3	9-Jun	876.05	10-Jun	876.15	81.80	40,900.00	200,950.00
4	2-Jul	916.05	3-Jul	916.35	41.60	20,800.00	221,750.00
5	29-Jul	949.05	30-Jul	949.15	8.80	4,400.00	226,150.00
	Close	31-Jul		957.95	452.30	226,150.00	

CONCLUSION

If you have any problem with any of the statements above, please do not go further until you really understand all the signals to this point. You may want to review everything we have covered in these first six chapters. Every time you see a chart, try to find the signals. The key to successful trading is discretion, and the Alligator alerts us to *which signals* we should trade. Our job at this juncture is to thoroughly understand each of these signals.

We have two more dimensions (signals) to explore. The next one is especially designed to add on aggressively whenever your MAP (momentum, acceleration, and price) says you have everything going your way. We call it *trading in the zone.* It is also our MAP for maximizing profits when the market is going our way. It is not unusual to double your profits by using my zone trading techniques. Athletes talk about playing in the zone; we will be trading in our zone. Enjoy!

In the next chapter, you will learn how to increase your profits substantially in any trend run.

You should now know how to recognize and trade:

- **The <u>Alligator</u>**
- **The <u>Fractal</u>**
- **The <u>Awesome Oscillator</u>**
- **<u>Acceleration/Deceleration</u>**

7

TRADING IN THE ZONES

INTRODUCTION

We are now at a point where we want to start being aggressive so that we can maximize our return on investment (ROI). This is the point that separates the real traders from the wanna-bes. We want to invest to our limits, but only when *everything* is going our way. Once we know we are in that position, we want to "go for it."

Everything is going our way whenever the *Momentum* is in the same direction as our trade *and* the Momentum is *Accelerating* in our direction. The final confirmation comes when the traders take the *Price* in our direction. In other words, we have the Momentum in our favor, it is Accelerating in our direction, and the Price is closing in our direction. This gives us an absolute MAP for profits. MAP stands for Momentum, Acceleration, and Price. This is the best of all worlds and not the time to be faint-hearted. This chapter shows how we put this favorable combination into actual practice.

In Figure 7–1, we have condensed the explanation and the rules for creating a Zone. The Zone is created from a combination of the AO and the AC charts. Remember that the AO is the Momentum and the AC is the Acceleration. When both of these are up, which can easily be seen (the software paints the bars green if they are higher than the immediately preceding bar), we are in the Green Zone. When both the AO and the AC bars are red, we are in the Red Zone. If one of the bars is red and one is green, we are in the Gray Zone.

The Green Zone indicates a very bullish market, the Red Zone indicates a very bearish market, and the Gray Zone indicates a market that is in transition. In verbal communication,we say we are green

The Zone is shown on the bar chart. The Zone is determined by the AO and the AC. If the Momentum and Acceleration are in the same direction then we are in a either the Green Zone or the Red Zone. However, if they are not in sync then we are in the Gray zone.

The Zone does three things for us:

1) Allows us to get aggressive at the market.
2) Gives us a great profit taking technique.
3) Adjust the Balance Line Signal in the different Zones.

The philosophy behind Zone Trading is that whenever you are in the "ZONE" you want to be very aggressive in adding to your current position.

Figure 7–1 The Zone trading philosophy.

(in a buy zone), red (in a sell zone), or gray (in a transition/be careful zone). In Chapter 9, we will demonstrate how these zones give us an extremely good technique for getting out of the market and squeezing the profit in our favor.

CREATING A GREEN ZONE

Set up your computer so that (1) when both the AO and the AC are higher than their immediately preceding bars, the corresponding *price bar* will be colored *green,* and (2) if both the AO and the AC are lower than their immediately preceding bars, the corresponding *price bar* will be colored *red.* If the AO and the AC are different colors, set up the price bar to be gray. You can then read the zone color directly on the price bar. (If you have problems doing this, contact your vendor or call our office and we will walk you through the process.)

Figure 7–2 shows how the price bars are colored, depending on their relationship to the immediately preceding bar. It also demonstrates how

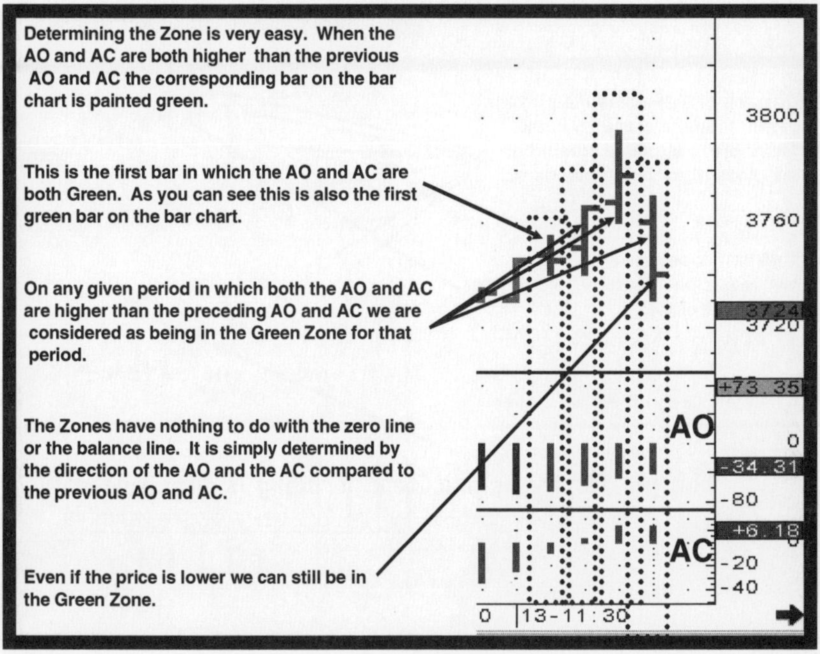

Figure 7–2 Creating the Green Zone.

the price can pull back but not necessarily affect the color of the price bar. The market, like you and me, has to breathe. These bars show the continual in-and-out breathing of the market. We also use the zones to help us allocate our resources in trading so that we get the biggest bang possible per buck of trading.

In Figure 7–3, the first bar on the left is a gray bar. The second bar from the left is a green bar. The third bar from the left is also green and fulfills the three requirements for an "add-on" buy: (1) The Momentum is still going up, (2) the Accelerator is moving up, and (3) the Price is closing higher. We have fulfilled the requirements to buy on the close of the third bar. It does not matter what time period we are using nor whether we are trading stocks or commodities. If we are trading dailies, we can use a Stop Close Only order. If we are trading intraday, we must watch the market and put in a market order at the end of whatever time period we are trading. If the following bars continue to give us the MAP (Momentum, Acceleration, and Price) signals, we add on the close of each consecutive bar until

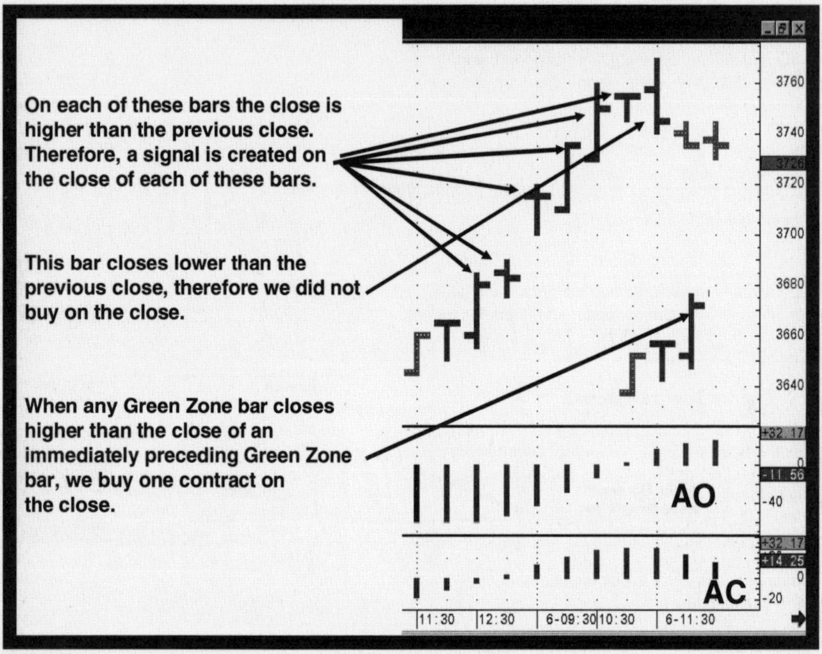

Figure 7–3 Trading in the Green Zone.

the price bar changes color, which signifies a change in either/both Momentum and Acceleration.

MORE EXAMPLES OF ZONE TRADING

Figure 7–4 gives some various configurations that will affect the trading of the zone signals.

WHEN TO STOP ADDING INSIDE THE ZONES

There is one exception that we often use when adding on to the zones. Remember that the market must always breathe and it is unusual for the market to have more than six to eight bars of the same color. Therefore, we use this information to help us maximize our profits. After the fifth red or green bar, we stop adding on based on the

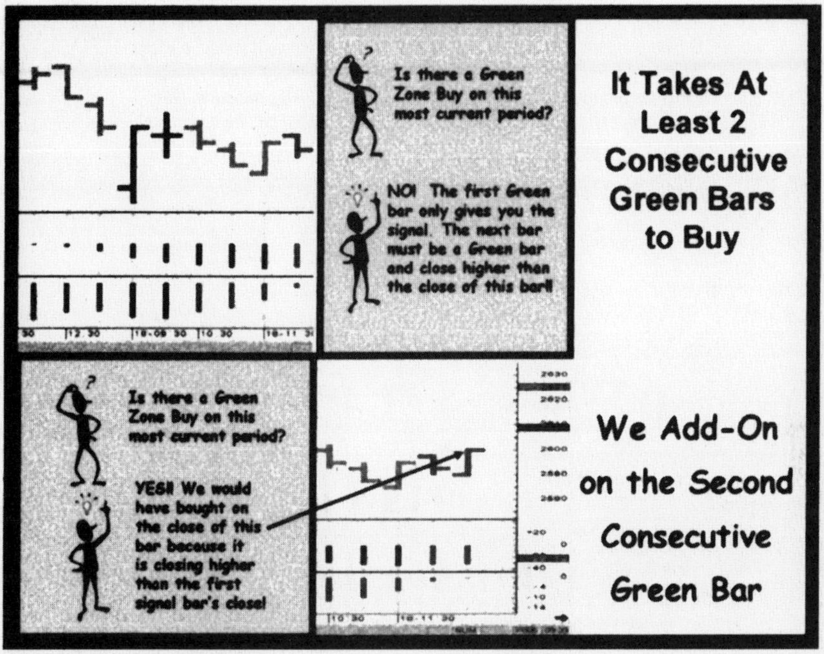

Figure 7–4 More on trading the zones.

zones. We still take any other signals in that direction. The reason is: we know from experience that it is rare to continue to get over six to eight bars of the same color. This means that after several of the same-color bars, the market is going to transition into either gray or the opposite of the current bar color. If you follow a few charts, you will see how this enhances our profits and cuts our potential losses.

TAKING PROFITS IN THE GREEN ZONE

Let me restate for emphasis: the markets, like you and me, must breathe regularly. Observing the color of the price bars can easily monitor this breathing. We turn this characteristic into a profit-squeezing technique to take more money to the bank on our trades.

Here is the approach. After you have five consecutive bars of the same color, you raise (or lower, in a down trend) your stop to one tick below the low of the fifth green bar. This would be the high plus one tick above the high of the fifth red bar in a down trend. After this

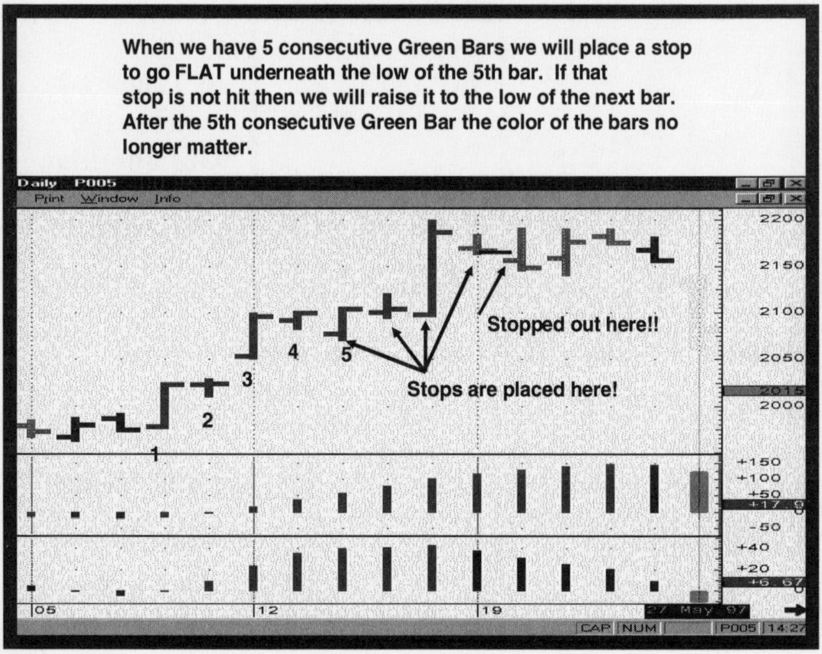

Figure 7–5 Taking profit in the Green Zone.

initial zone stop, if the price bars continue in the same direction, you would raise (lower in a down market) your stop to the next higher low (lower high) and keep doing that until you are stopped out. (See Figure 7–5.)

USING ZONES IN A DOWN MARKET

Creating a Red Zone

Figure 7–6 explains the details for creating a Red Zone on your price chart. This can be done with almost any charting service (or automatically with our Investor's Dream software). After you have created the zones on your chart, the next task is to understand how to trade these zones for the maximum ROI. As emphasized elsewhere in this book, these zones work equally well for stocks, commodities, and spread trading.

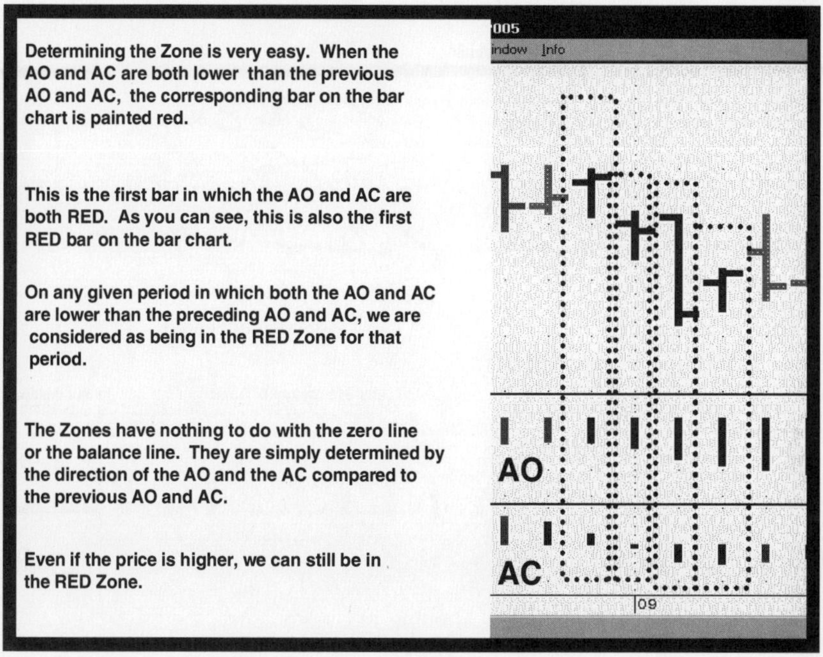

Figure 7–6 Creating a Red Zone.

Trading in the Red Zone

Trading in the Red Zone is just the opposite of trading in the Green Zone (see Figure 7–7). Whenever you have a red price bar that is preceded by a red bar, you add on at the close if the close is lower than the close of the previous bar. In other words, you must have a MAP to profit. The Momentum must be lower (red AO bar), the Acceleration must be increasing in a downward direction (red AC bar), and, finally, the Price must close lower than the previous bar's close.

You add on until you have five consecutive red bars. After the fifth consecutive red bar, you stop adding on based on the zone signals.

Let's look at some examples to see if you have grasped this idea.

Figure 7–8 demonstrates that you sell on the close of a red price bar if it meets the following requirements:

1. It must be preceded by a red bar, indicating both the AO and the AC are lower.

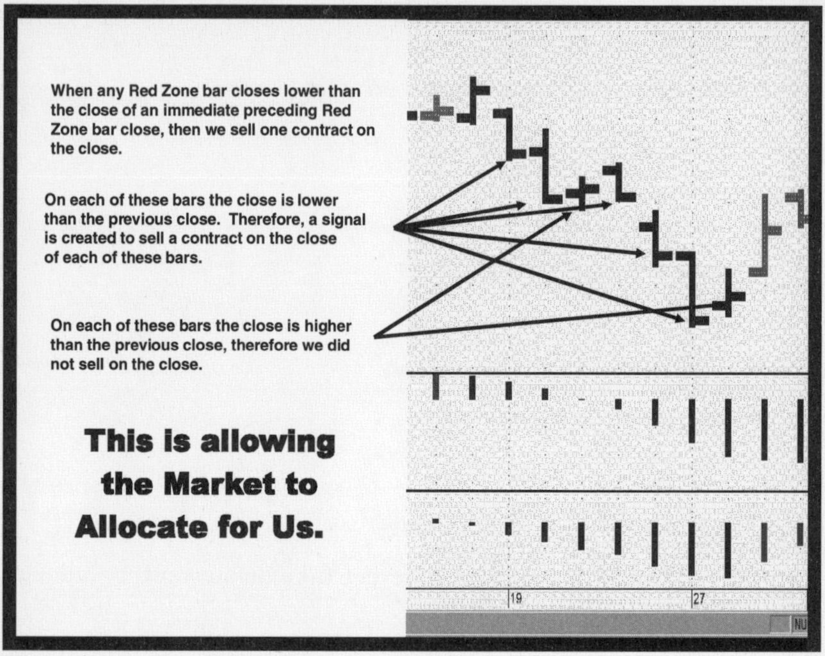

Figure 7–7 Trading in the Red Zone.

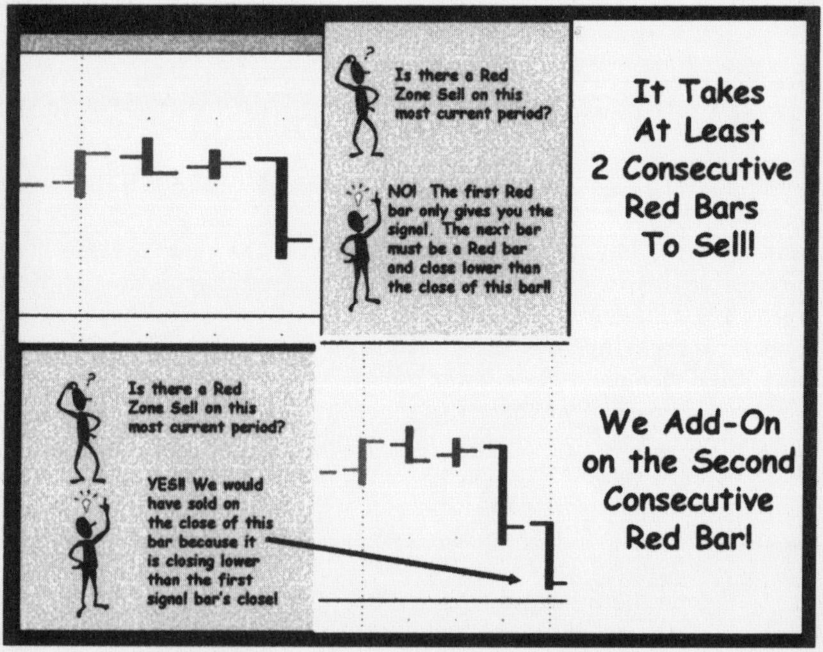

Figure 7–8 Examples of selling in the Red Zone.

2. It must close lower than the previous bar.
3. The add-on sell on close is canceled if there are more than five previous consecutive red bars.

Now let's determine how to use the sequential red bars as a profit-taking enhancement (Figure 7–9).

Taking Profits in the Red Zone

Remembering once more that the breathing cycle of any market can be traced by observing the red, green, and gray price bars, we want to use that knowledge to enhance our ROI. We have found that the optimum strategy for doing this is to exit our short position after five consecutive red bars. The specific technique is to place a protective stop (not a stop and reverse) one tick above the high of the fifth consecutive red bar. If the market does not take us out on the following

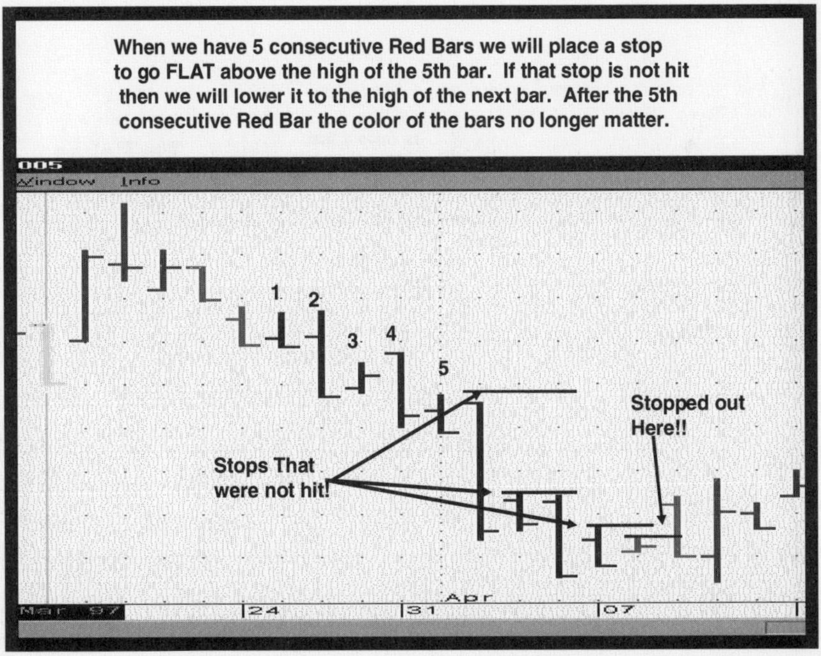

Figure 7–9 Taking profits in the Red Zone.

bar and it has a lower high, we move our stop down to one tick above the new lower high.

AN IMPORTANT POINT: After the fifth red bar, we continue to lower our stop to just above the high of the current bar—NO MATTER WHAT COLOR THE CURRENT BAR IS—until we are stopped out.

Now that we know how to trade the red and green bars, let's consider the gray transition bars. Gray bars indicate that the Momentum is in one direction and the Acceleration is in the opposite direction. This could indicate (1) the approaching end of a trend of some degree or (2) that the market is simply taking a breather. What is actually happening is: the market is temporarily losing interest in the direction in which it was going. It is running low on either buyers or sellers.

How the zones affect our fifth dimensional signal is the subject of the next chapter. The important points to remember here are that we do not add on, based on the zone signals, if the current price bar is gray. When using the five consecutive bars of either green or red, we

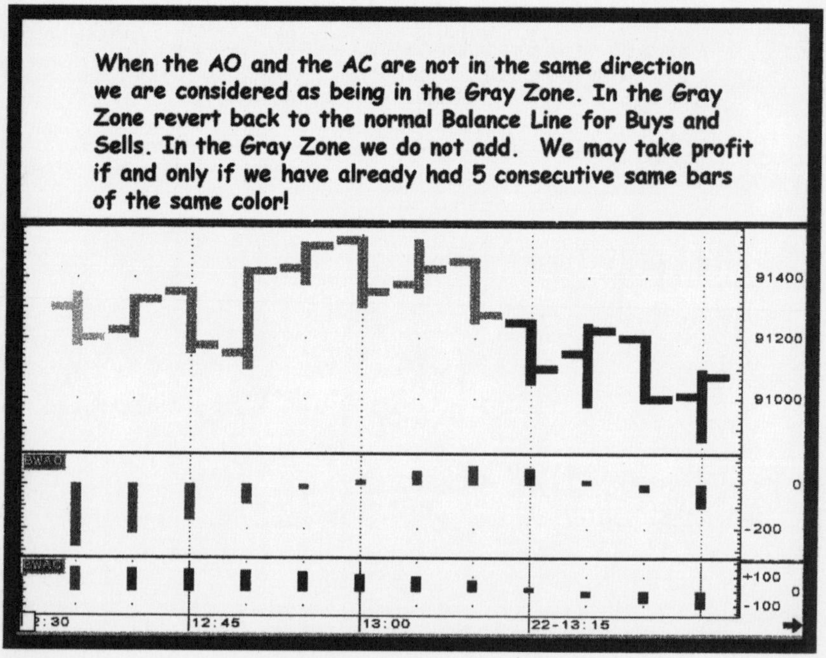

Figure 7–10 The Gray Zone.

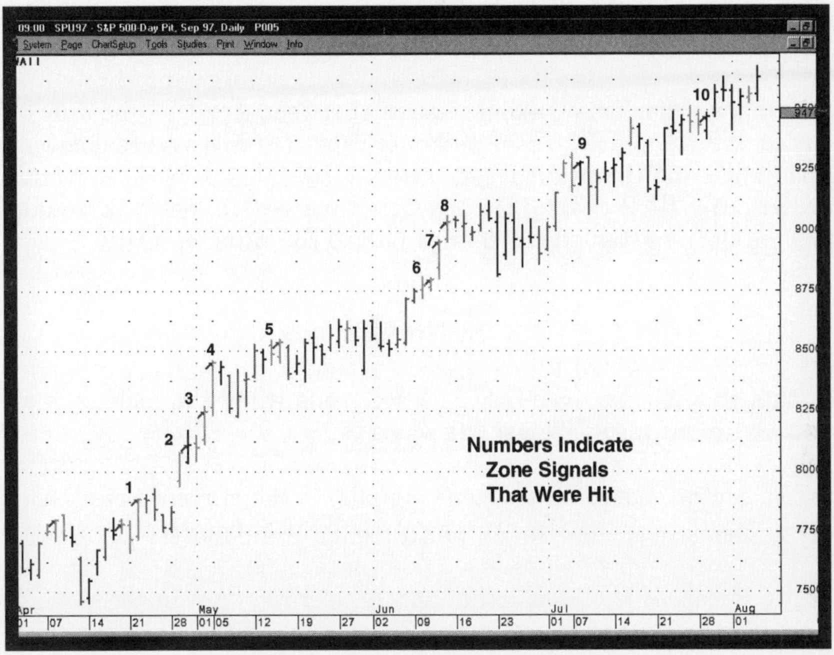

Figure 7–11 Trading the zone signals.

TABLE 7–1 Results of Zone Add-On Trades between April 17 and July 31.

	Date	Signal	Date	Filled	P/L Points	P/L $	Cum. $
1	21-Apr	771.90	22-Apr	788.60	169.35	84,675.00	84,675.00
2	29-Apr	807.80	30-Apr	810.80	147.15	73,575.00	158,250.00
3	1-May	810.00	2-May	824.65	133.30	66,650.00	224,900.00
4	2-May	842.65	3-May	845.05	112.90	56,450.00	281,350.00
5	14-May	848.60	15-May	853.45	104.50	52,250.00	333,600.00
6	10-Jun	877.60	11-Jun	879.40	78.55	39,275.00	372,875.00
7	11-Jun	879.40	12-Jun	895.10	62.85	31,425.00	404,300.00
8	12-Jun	895.10	13-Jun	903.45	54.50	27,250.00	431,550.00
9	7-Jul	918.35	8-Jul	927.80	30.15	15,075.00	446,625.00
10	28-Jul	943.65	29-Jul	947.00	10.95	5,475.00	452,100.00
	Close	7-31		957.95	904.20	452,100.00	

do continue to trail our stop behind the current high or low, no matter what color the current bar happens to be.

Figure 7–11 is the S&P chart that we are following through all five dimensions. This trading occurred between April 17 and July 31; notice that there are 10 zone add-ons. Table 7–1 gives a breakdown of each trade and the profit it generated during just over three months in the daily S&P charts. During this time period, one tick equaled $5.00. Shortly after, the Exchange halved the value of a tick.

SUMMARY

In this chapter, we examined how we trade when the market is absolutely in our favor. We use the zones to:

1. Add on aggressively.
2. Squeeze the maximum profit from a trend move.

To Recap: If the Momentum and Acceleration are in the same direction, then we are in either the Green Zone or the Red Zone. However, if one is up and the other is down when compared to the immediately previous bar, the price bar is colored gray to represent that we are in a transition or a Gray Zone.

The Zone concept does three things for us:

1. Allows us to get aggressive toward the market.
2. Adjusts the Balance Line signal in the different zones.
3. Gives us a great profit-taking technique.

In the next chapter, we will examine the Balance Line signal, which is our fifth dimension. After understanding the Balance Line, we will put all the dimensions into a tradable form to use in trading any market.

8

THE BALANCE LINE TRADES

THE FIFTH DIMENSION

We have now arrived at our fifth and final trading dimension. At first, this dimension may seem a bit more complicated, but it really isn't. In our earlier book, *Trading Chaos,* we described a signal we labeled the "thumb trade," which was basically a counter fractal signal. Its purpose was to get us into a trade before the fractal breakout signal. This has been profitable throughout the years we have used it, but we have now refined this signal to be even more effective, yielding greater profits and fewer whiplashes.

The basics behind this signal are what we label the Balance Line. This line was arrived at through the use of supercomputers (mainframes) and was determined mathematically. The mainframe computers then went through more than five million iterations to find a way to accurately estimate the placement of the Balance Line using a personal computer. We will describe the specifics shortly, but first let's get a picture of what is actually represented.

The Balance Line is where the price would be if there was *no new incoming information (Chaos)* affecting the market at the present time (Figure 8–1). This is where the price would be without incoming information, so we can judge the effect that new information is having in the market by how far away the current price is from the Balance Line. In our research, we constructed a histogram to measure this distance but found that it was almost the same as our 5/34 Awesome Oscillator and proved to be redundant when using the AO.

One way to think of the Balance Line is to imagine that it is the Continental Divide. When rain falls on the east side of the Continental

The Balance Line is that place where the current price would be if there were no

NEW INCOMING INFORMATION

CHAOS

Figure 8–1 What is the Balance Line?

Divide, the water will run downhill toward the Gulf of Mexico because gravity is a Strange Attractor. This will happen unless a strong east wind blows the raindrops over to the west side of the divide. If that happens, the windblown rain drops will run down toward the Pacific Ocean rather than the Gulf of Mexico. The wind, in this case, is the new information that changes behavior. A change in behavior is a fractal. In the markets, new information creates fractals (changes in behavior). There will always be a fractal at the end of any trend. When you decided to read this chapter rather than doing something else, that was a behavioral fractal.

The Balance Line could also be labeled the Saddle Point, which is the place where a small change in initial conditions produces results that are much stronger than the cause. One of the casualties produced by the new sciences of quantum physics and Chaos is the destruction of our old classical Newtonian idea that for every action there is an equal and opposite reaction. They have also done away with the global theory of entropy, which stated that eventually everything will go down the drain. We now know that there is Neg-entropy which has the capability to produce something from nothing.

Think of the Balance Line as the top of the mountain. Whenever new information comes into the market, the price will move *away from* the Balance Line more easily (it takes less energy, in the form of new information) than it will move *toward* the Balance Line. A simple way to say this is: "It is easier to go downhill than uphill." In Chaos theory, this is described as the "path of least resistance" (Figure 8–2).

Let's take a couple of very simple examples of how the Balance Line operates in any market—stocks, commodities, indexes, spreads, or options. The Balance Line shows us the direction of the current path of least resistance in markets.

Figure 8–3 is a caricature showing that going downhill (away from the Balance Line) is easier than going uphill. In a similar way, it is easier (takes less energy) for the price to move away from the Balance Line than to move toward the Balance Line. This can be demonstrated by simply examining a chart such as Figure 8–4.

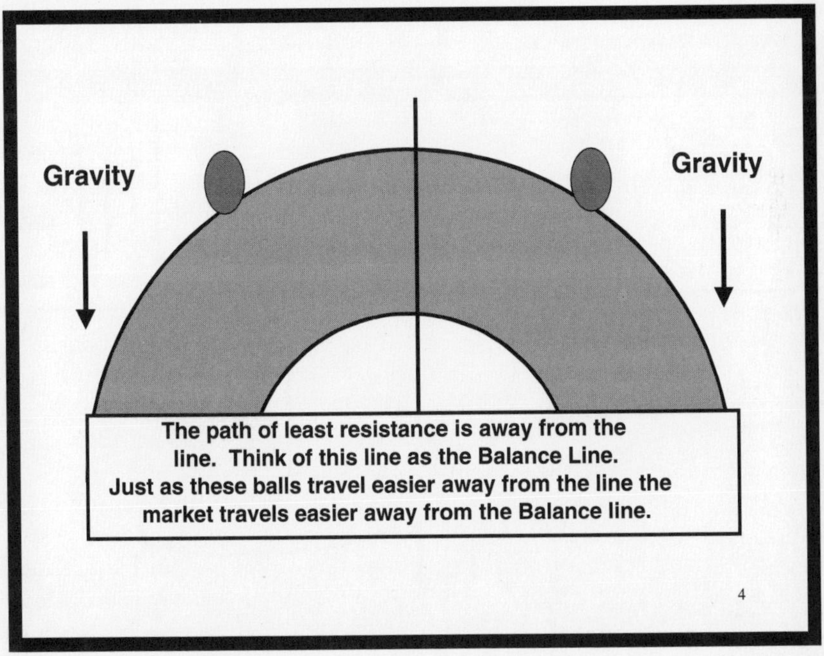

Figure 8–2 The path of least resistance.

Figure 8–3 Which one is using more energy?

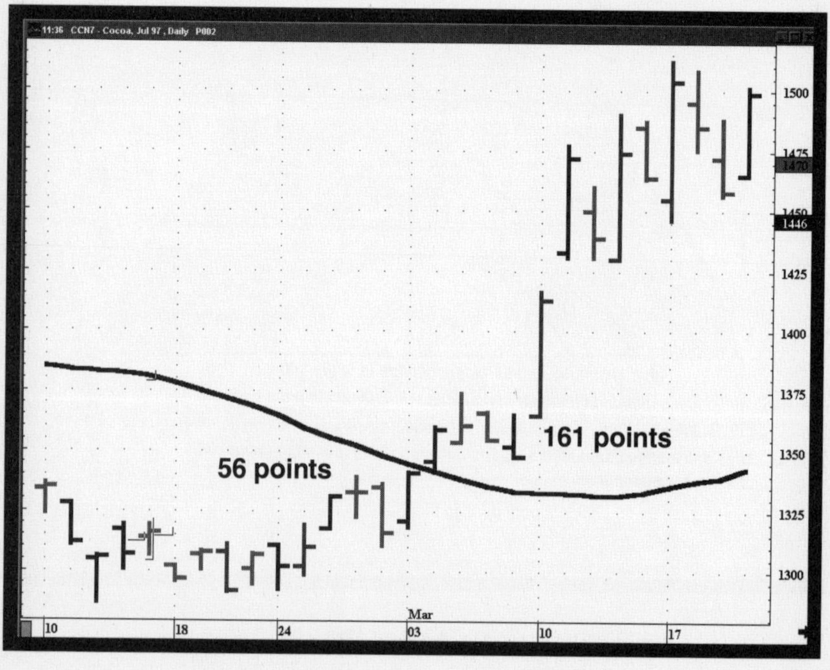

Figure 8–4 The path of least resistance.

Notice that the thirteen bars in the box on the left side of Figure 8–4 moved 56 points and were going toward the Balance Line, which is similar to walking uphill. Also notice that the thirteen bars in the next box were going away from the Balance Line. The thirteen bars on the right side covered 161 points because the price was moving downhill. In this illustration, downhill means the price was moving higher. Remember that the Balance Line is the top of the mountain, and it is easier for the price to move away from the Balance Line than to move toward the Balance Line.

Figure 8–5 basically repeats the two earlier illustrations, again showing that movement away from the Balance Line is easier (requires less new information) than moving toward the Balance Line.

Figure 8–6 illustrates the basic way of finding new information from the Balance Line signal. The current price high is lower than the previous high. When we interpret that, we must include the concept that, in any market, there is always a struggle between the buyers and the sellers. The buyers were obviously stronger in the first time period

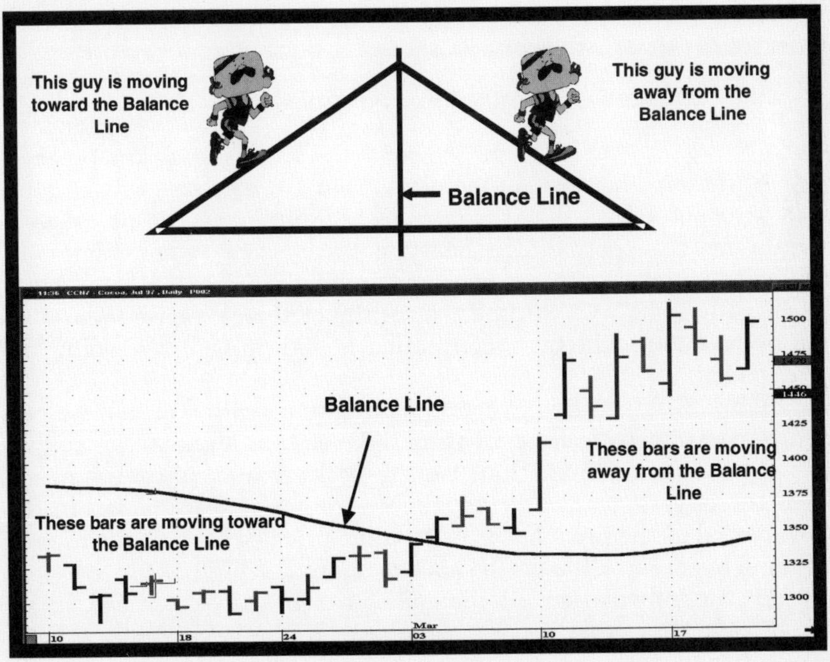

Figure 8–5 Two views of the Balance Line.

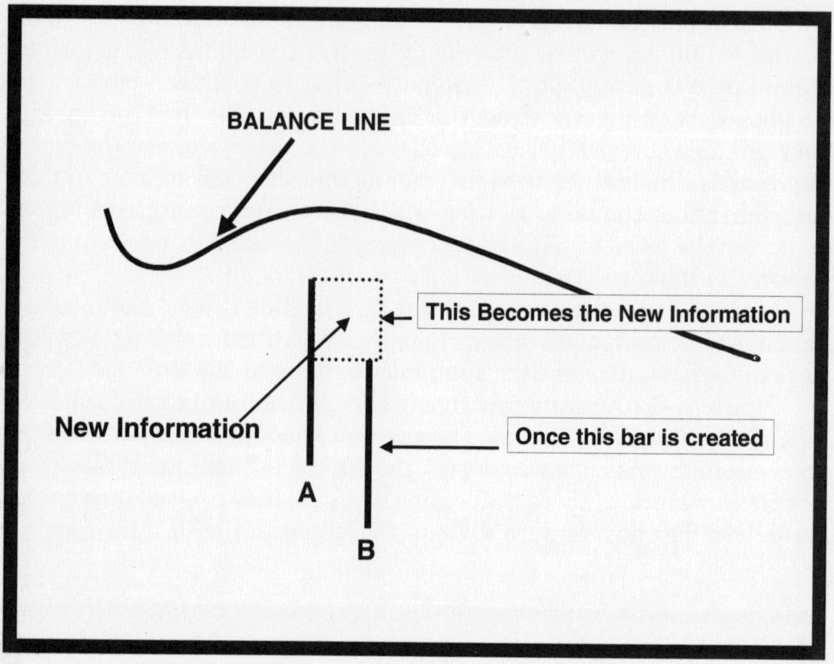

Figure 8–6 Locating new information on the chart.

(bar A) than in the second time period (bar B). We know this because they were not able to take the price as high in the second period as it was in the first period. The question can also be asked: Who is in charge and what are they doing? Fortunately, we do not have to know specifically "who"; we can see the results of the collective "who's" by the price action. The new information is determined by reading the price chart.

Figure 8–6 is quite important as a demonstration of how we recognize new information for creating Balance Line signals. Notice that bar B has a lower high than bar A. Looking at this configuration from the buyers' point of view, they were not strong enough in the time period of the price bar B to keep the price as high as the high of bar A. This creates the dotted square above the high of bar B as potential new information. At the end of bar B, the sellers had forced the buyers away from the dotted square. If the buyers regain their strength and move the market up above the top of bar A, a significant change in behavior will occur, giving us a signal to watch for a

Balance Line buy opportunity. Study this chart carefully; this concept is sometimes difficult to grasp in a first observation. We will go through several examples to make this clear.

Once we can understand where to look for the new information, we can filter in other fractal geometry concepts to create profitable signals. We take two different factors into consideration to get our most reliable Balance Line signal.

The first factor is: Where is the signal in relation to the Balance Line? We know that moving toward the Balance Line is more difficult than moving away from the Balance Line. The second factor is the number of new highs or lows needed to create a signal. Like the market, we want to take the path of least resistance (Figure 8–7).

Figure 8–8 contains the rules for our basic Balance Line strategy. Our purpose is to make it easier to get into a directional move when the movement is away from the Balance Line (similar to going downhill) versus toward the Balance Line (uphill). If we are going toward the Balance Line, we place our signal at base ± two higher

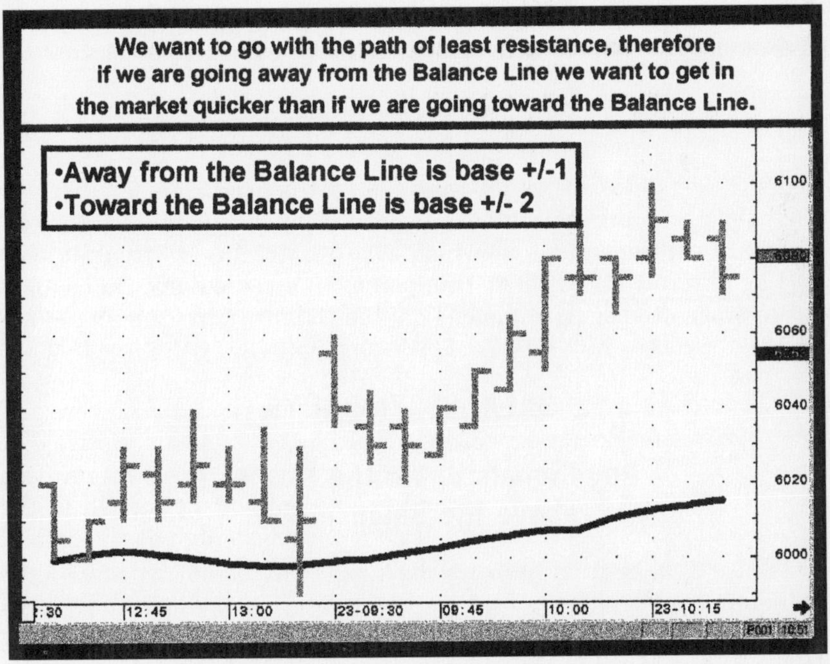

Figure 8–7 Basic Balance Line signal formation.

BALANCE LINE

- **Always read from right to left.**
- **Look at the highs *only* when looking for a buy signal.**
- **Look at the lows *only* when looking for a sell signal.**
- **Establish base bar first.**
  - **Base bar is the starting point.**
  - **To find the base when looking for buy signals, look at the current bar or the bar with the lowest high.**
  - **To Find the base when looking for sell signals, look at the current bar or the bar with the highest low.**
- **Once you have established your base bar**
  - **For a buy you need one new high if you are going away from the Balance Line and two new highs if you are going toward the Balance Line.**
  - **For a sell you need one new low if you are going away from the Balance Line and two new lows if you are going toward the Balance Line.**

Figure 8–8 Rules for the Balance Line signals.

highs (lower lows). If we are going away from the Balance Line, we use base ± one higher high (lower low). That is our basic approach. We modify it depending on which zone we are in—a situation that will be covered later on. At this point, let's review and summarize our approach to the fifth dimension, the Balance Line.

BALANCE LINE BUYS

Buy Signals When the Market Is above the Balance Line

In Figure 8–9, Section A shows the simple buy signal created by the base bar B and a higher high on bar 1. Section B illustrates that a higher high, which follows a base bar, does not create a new signal. The base bar is either the current bar *or the most recent lowest high.* Section C demonstrates a blue light special. The original buy was at

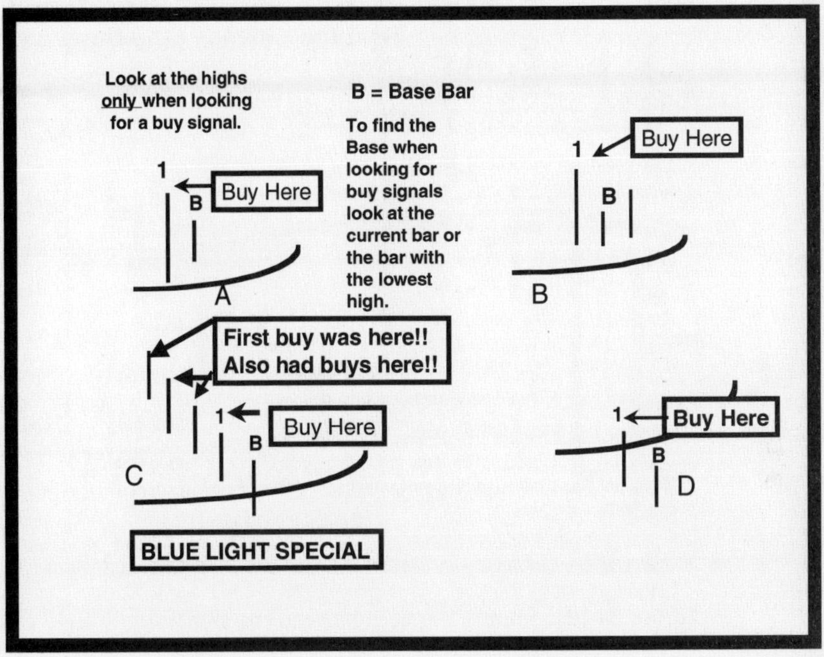

Figure 8–9 Buying above the Balance Line.

the leftmost bar. When a lower high was formed, the buy moved down one bar. When bar B was formed with another lower high, the buy moved down to bar 1. Section D illustrates that if the signal bar is above the Balance Line, we only need the base plus one higher high. As long as the signal bar itself is above the Balance Line, we act as if the entire formation were above the Balance Line. Make sure that you understand these three scenarios so that you can easily find a buy signal above the Balance Line on other charts.

Figures 8–10 and 8–11 are examples of how, once the base bar is established for a buy and that pattern is followed by bars with higher highs that do not trigger the buy stop, the buy stop is not affected. The buy stop stays in place unless (a) it is triggered or (b) another bar with a lower high is formed, creating a different base bar. The last three bars on the right side of Figure 8–10 and the last two bars on the right side of Figure 8–11 do not affect the placement of the Balance Line buy signal.

Now let's try a trick question (Figure 8–12).

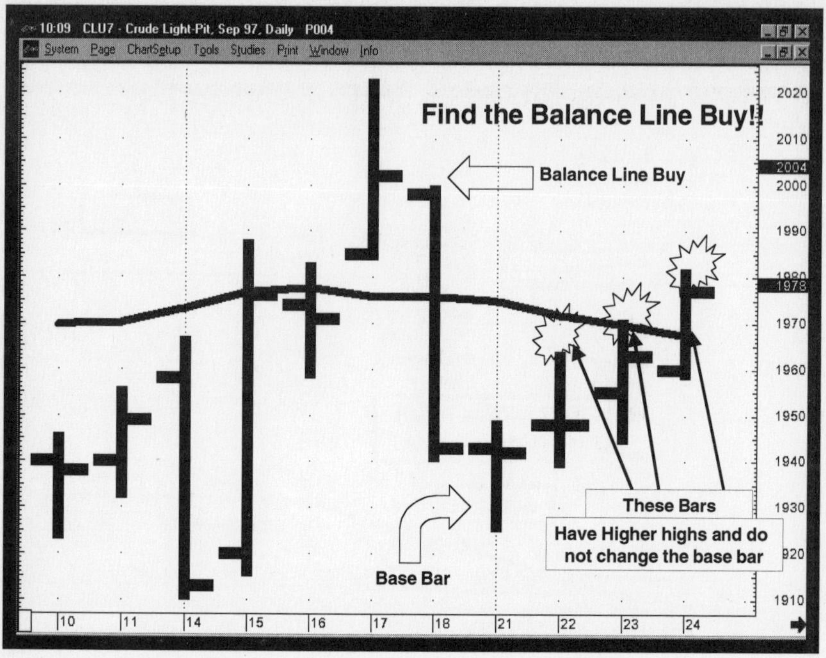

Figure 8–10 Finding the base bar and the signal bar.

Figure 8–11 Another example of locating the Balance Line buy signal.

Figure 8–12 Balance Line trick question.

Here is a tip to speed up your analysis. When the market is making new highs, you cannot have either a Balance Line or a fractal buy signal formation. The market must pull back and create a lower high before a new Balance Line or Fractal signal can be formed.

Buy Signals When the Market Is below the Balance Line

We know that going away from the Balance Line is easier (takes less energy) than going toward the Balance Line. Because the market always follows the path of least resistance, good strategy dictates that we do the same. (We did that in the previous section.) Now, we are buying below the Balance Line. We will require more energy because we are going uphill. We are going uphill because we are buying below the Balance Line.

Figure 8–13, B signifies the base bar. In section (A), we have the typical Balance Line buy signal. We require base plus *two higher highs* because we are below the Balance Line and therefore are plodding uphill to change the market's energy pattern. Section (B) illustrates that

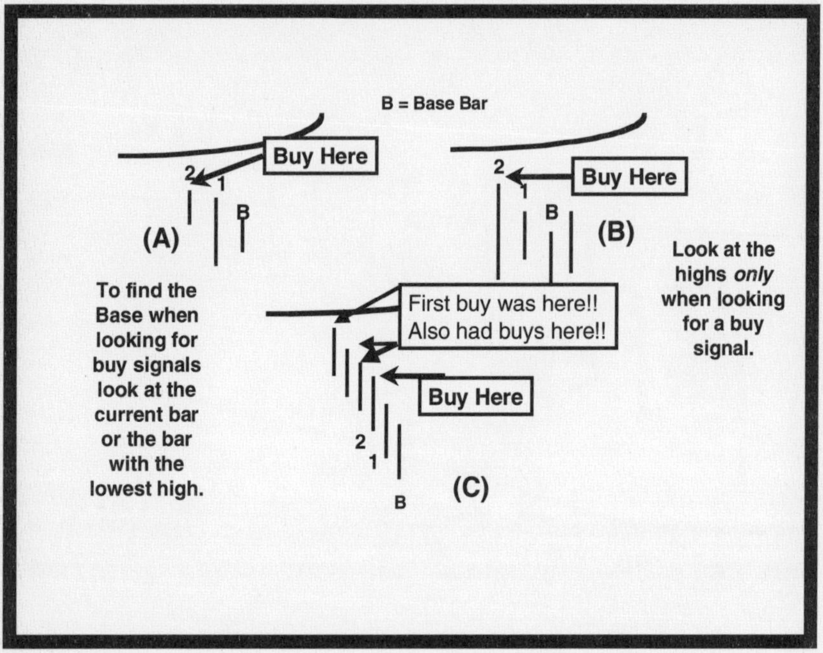

Figure 8–13 Buying below the Balance Line.

a current bar whose high is higher than the previous bar does not affect the Balance Line buy because it does not create a lower base bar. Section (C) illustrates a blue light special. Note the first buy. It was followed by a lower high, which moved the signal down. The market is giving us a chance to buy lower.

Let's look at the practice charts in Figures 8–14 and 8–15.

In Figure 8–15, the highs are circled because highs are all you are interested in when looking for a buy, and lows are all you check when looking for a sell.

BALANCE LINE SELLS

Sell Signals When the Market Is above the Balance Line

Figure 8–16 illustrates the typical Balance Line selling signals when the market is above the Balance Line. Section (A) shows the typical

Figure 8–14 Finding a buy signal below the Balance Line.

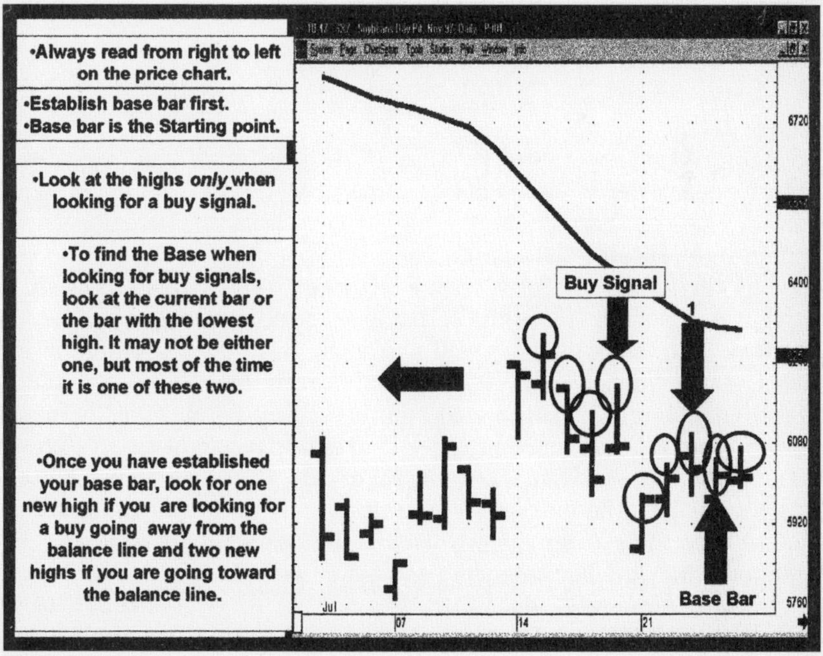

Figure 8–15 More practice in finding Balance Line buys below the Balance Line.

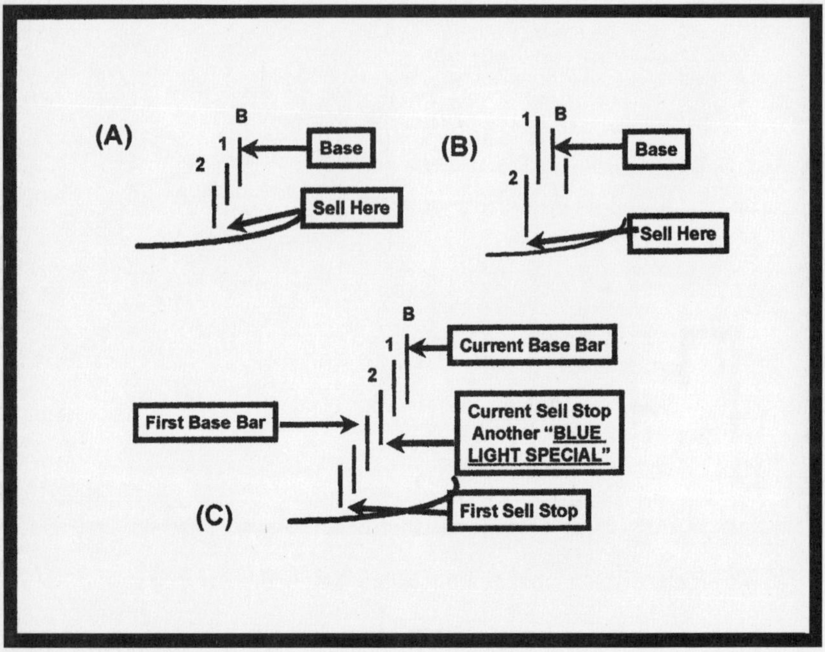

Figure 8–16 Sell signals above the Balance Line.

base minus two lower lows. Section (B) demonstrates that once a base is formed, a lower low does not create a new signal. A new sell signal can only be created by having a higher low. Section (C) demonstrates a blue light special sell signal. Note that the first sell signal is created by the first three bars on the left side. That is followed by three higher lows, which raises the sell stop up each time a new higher low appears. The current sell is well above the first sale, and the market has given us another blue light special. Again, make sure you understand this chart (Figure 8–16) before reading further. To help you understand, let's do a few practice charts and schematics, in Figures 8–17 through 8–19. Especially in Figure 8–20, we see four different possibilities for the market's creating Balance Line sell signals. Section (A) has the straightforward sell signal. You only need a base bar and one lower low because you are below the Balance Line and gravity is going your way—downhill. Section (B) illustrates that a lower low than the base bar does not alter the signal at this point. Section (C) illustrates a blue light special sell; the market is giving us a

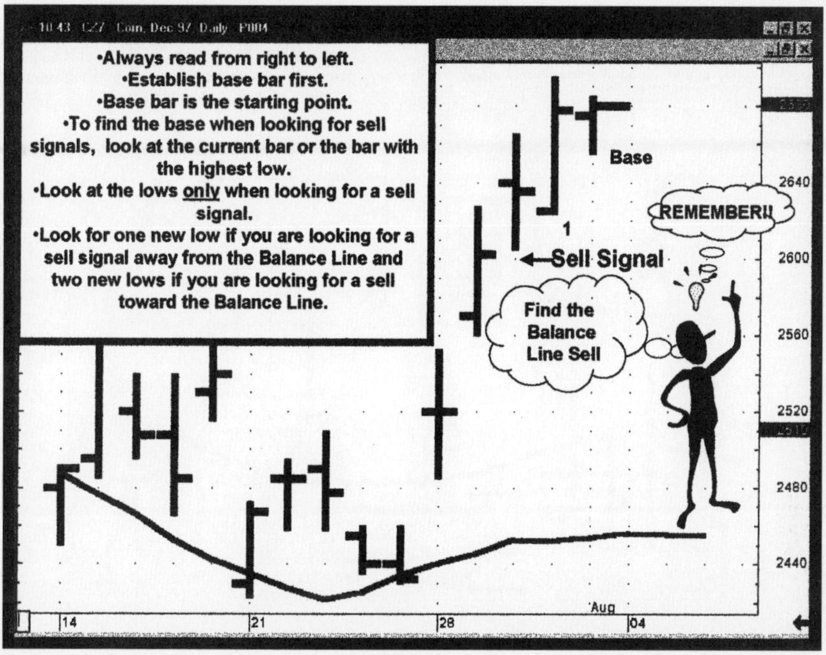

Figure 8–17 Practice chart—selling above the Balance Line.

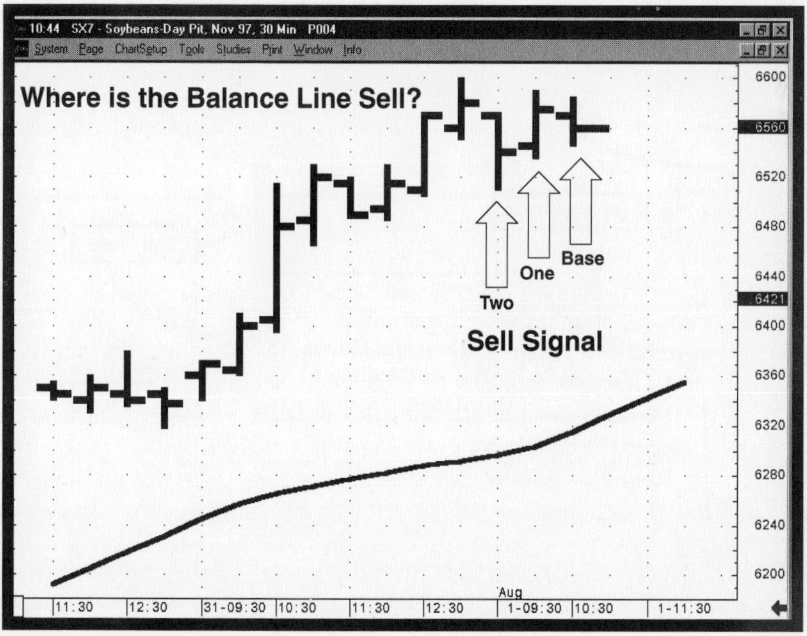

Figure 8–18 Another practice chart.

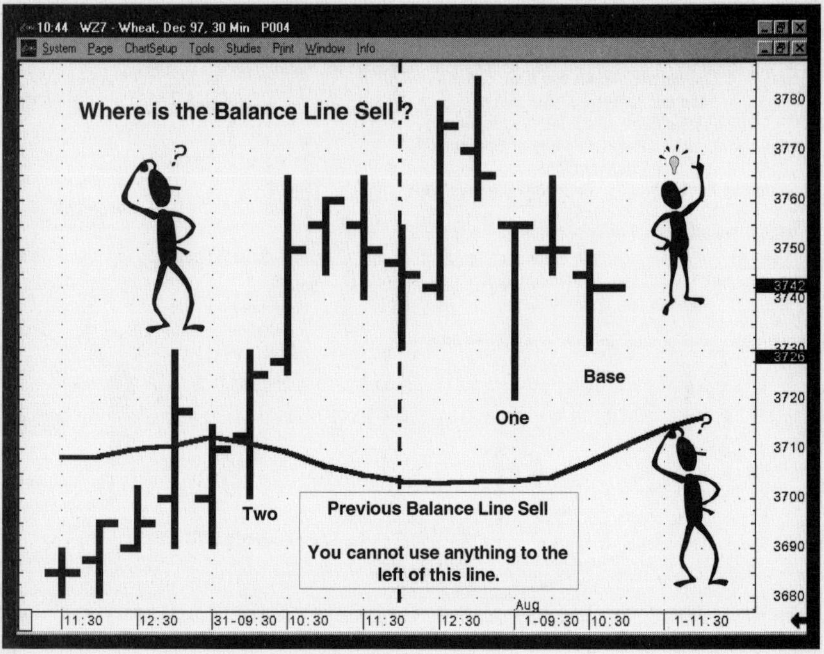

Figure 8–19 Trick question.

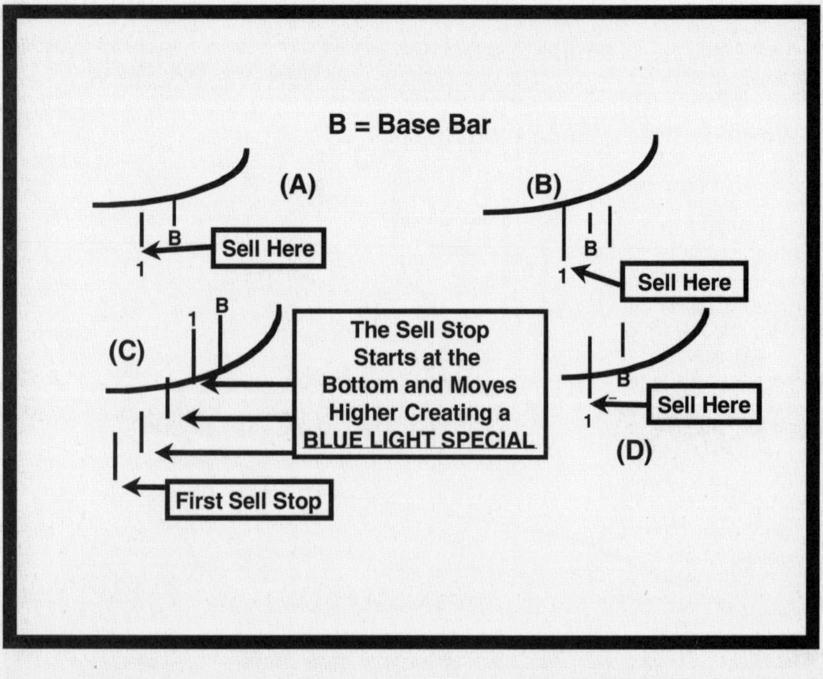

Figure 8–20 Selling when the market is below the Balance Line.

chance to sell at a higher price than the one we originally targeted. Section (D) illustrates that if the signal bar is below the Balance Line, we only need a base and one bar with a lower low, regardless of which side of the Balance Line the base bar is on.

PRACTICE PAGES

Figure 8–21 is a quite simple illustration of buying below the Balance Line. The price is below the Balance Line and going downhill (moving away from the line when reading from right to left), so you only need a base and one lower low.

Figure 8–22 poses another trick question: Is there a Balance Line sell? Why or why not?

Again, just as on the buy side illustrated earlier in this chapter, there is no sell here. Remember that for either a fractal or a Balance Line signal, the market must first retrace its move to create lower

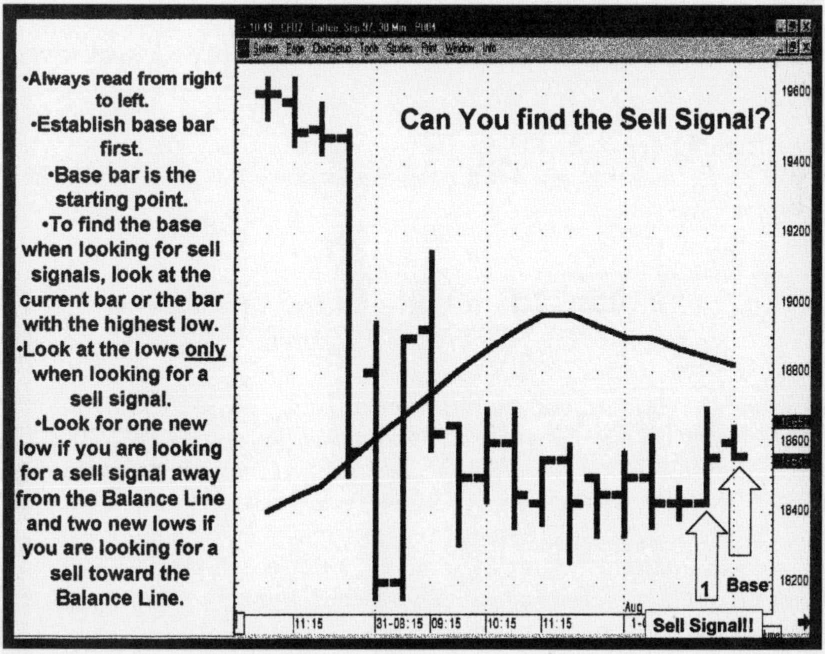

Figure 8–21 Practice page for finding the sell signal below the Balance Line.

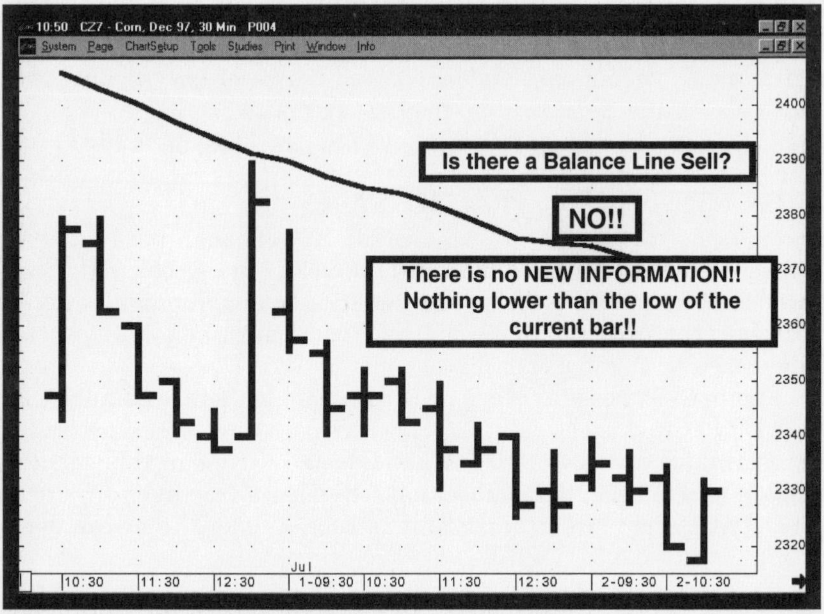

Figure 8–22 Is there a Balance Line sell?

lows that, in turn, will create a sell signal. Whenever the current price bar is making new lows, you cannot have either a fractal or a Balance Line sell.

TRADING THE BALANCE LINE SIGNALS IN THE VARIOUS ZONES

Now we are going to add factors that at first may seem confounding but they pay off extremely well in increased profits. We call them filters. They direct us toward the most profit-producing signals. The first filter is the Alligator. We know from earlier chapters that, no matter what signal is created, we only want to trade a signal that is outside the Alligator's mouth and is going in a direction that will keep us outside of the mouth. The second limiting condition is the zone the *current* price is in.

If you are attempting to buy in the Red Zone, you know that you are buying even though the Momentum is down and is accelerating to the downside. That doesn't appear to be to your best advantage. Therefore, our strategy is to make it twice as difficult to buy in the Red Zone. If the current bar is red and we are above the blue Balance Line and looking for buy signals, it would require a base bar and TWO higher highs (rather than one higher high, as in the Green or the Gray Zone).

Likewise, if we are above the Balance Line and in the Green Zone looking for a sell, we would normally require a base bar and two lower lows. However, being in the Green Zone tells us that the Momentum is up and accelerating upward, so we require twice as many lower lows (four rather than the usual two, as in the Green or Gray Zone).

Another way to express this is: You only double the requirements for a sell in the Green Zone, and you only double the requirements for a buy in the Red Zone. In any other situation, the number required would be the normal number of higher highs or lower lows.

Do not forget the other, extremely important filter: DO NOT FEED THE ALLIGATOR!

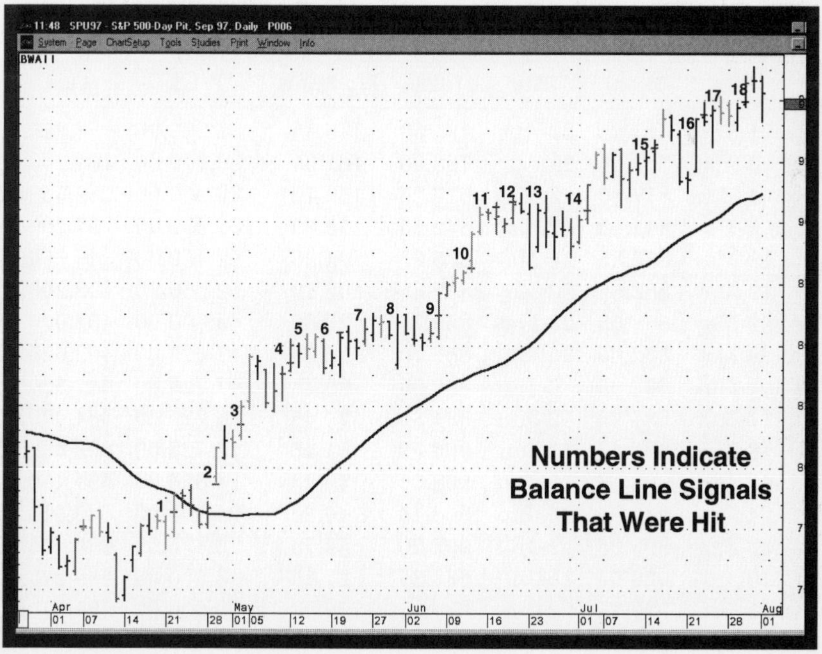

Figure 8–23 Trading the Balance Line signals in the daily S&P.

Real-Time Trading

In Figure 8–23 are the Balance Line trades you would have taken had you been following our trading method between April 17 and July 31, or just over three months.

An interesting point should be noted here. Whenever you have a long trend run such as the one in Figure 8–23, you will always have more Balance Line signals triggered than any of the other trading dimensions. The results from trading the Balance Line signals in a trend run can be quite impressive, as evidenced by Table 8–1, which is based on the same time frame as Figure 8–23.

RECAP AND SUMMARY OF BALANCE LINE TRADING

The Balance Line is that place where the current price would be if there was no new incoming information (Chaos).

TABLE 8–1 Results of Trading the Balance Line Signals in the S&P Contract between April 17 and July 31.

	Date	Signal	Date	Filled	P/L Points	P/L $	Cum. $
1	21-Apr	781.25	22-Apr	781.50	176.45	88,225.00	88,225.00
2	25-Apr	793.05	29-Apr	796.00	161.95	80,975.00	169,200.00
3	1-May	817.25	2-May	817.25	140.70	70,350.00	239,550.00
4	9-May	842.55	12-May	842.65	115.30	57,650.00	297,200.00
5	13-May	852.85	14-May	853.05	104.90	52,450.00	349,650.00
6	19-May	852.65	20-May	852.85	105.10	52,550.00	402,200.00
7	22-May	858.05	23-May	858.35	99.60	49,800.00	452,000.00
8	29-May	862.65	30-May	862.70	95.25	47,625.00	499,625.00
9	4-Jun	862.05	6-Jun	862.50	95.45	47,725.00	547,350.00
10	11-Jun	881.15	12-Jun	884.50	73.45	36,725.00	584,075.00
11	16-Jun	906.45	17-Jun	906.50	51.45	25,725.00	609,800.00
12	17-Jun	908.55	19-Jun	908.65	49.30	24,650.00	634,450.00
13	24-Jun	907.95	25-Jun	908.15	49.80	24,900.00	659,350.00
14	30-Jun	905.05	2-Jul	905.20	52.75	26,375.00	685,725.00
15	10-Jul	930.55	15-Jul	930.85	27.10	13,550.00	699,275.00
16	21-Jul	937.75	22-Jul	937.95	20.00	10,000.00	709,275.00
17	24-Jul	949.30	25-Jul	949.65	8.30	4,150.00	713,425.00
18	29-Jul	949.40	30-Jul	949.45	8.50	4,250.00	717,675.00
	Close	7-31		957.95	1,435.35	717,675.00	717,675.00

The Balance Line rules are:

Always read from right to left.

Look at the highs *only* when looking for a buy signal.

Look at the lows *only* when looking for a sell signal.

Establish the base bar first.

The base bar is the starting point.

To find the base when looking for buy signals, look at the current bar or the bar with the lowest high.

To find the base when looking for sell signals, look at the current bar or the bar with the highest low.

Once you have established your base bar:

1. For a buy, you need one new high if you are going away from the Balance Line, and two new highs if you are going toward the Balance Line.
2. For a sell, you need one new low if you are going away from the Balance Line, and two new lows if you are going toward the Balance Line.

The final two filters are:

1. You do not sell above the Alligator's mouth and you do not buy below the Alligator's mouth. If you do, you are feeding the Alligator, which can consume all your food (money).
2. If the current bar is in the Red Zone, you double the number of new higher highs to create a buy signal. If the current bar is in the Green Zone, you double the number of lower lows to create a sell signal.

We have now covered the five dimensions for entering a stock or commodity market. Most traders find it more difficult to get out of a trade than to enter a trade. Getting out is always an executive decision. However, four guidelines that I use in my own trading have been effective in maximizing the profits taken from the markets. We will explore these in the next chapter.

9

TECHNIQUES FOR TAKING PROFITS

Now that we know how to read the market, we want to devise some good strategies for squeezing the highest profit that is possible from our trades. Just as we listen for the market to tell us when and how much to invest, we can also expect the market to guide us in taking profits. Most traders experience much more difficulty in getting out of the market than they do in getting into the market.

Again, we want to emphasize that the answer is within you, and the reference is in the market. We said in the early chapters that we want to get in tune with the market and let Chaos work for us—or, using a better expression, *let us work with Chaos.* Figure 9–1 reminds us of the nature of Chaos.

TYING IT ALL TOGETHER

We have now covered all five dimensions of our Profitunity method of trading. We know how to get into the market by buying or selling:

1. The fractal.
2. The Momentum.
3. Acceleration.
4. The Zone (add-ons).
5. The Balance Line.

Figure 9–1 Chaos is freedom.

We also know that we never initiate a trade going against the Alligator. We want the Alligator to be on our side, and we want to stay out of his mouth. We also filter our entries, depending on which zone we happen to be in with the current bar. Now we are ready to develop our best profit-producing strategies for getting out of our trades. The name of the game is *taking money to the bank.*

At this point, we are approaching the fourth and fifth levels of trading, where educated intuition begins to pay off with profits. We have four market-generated indicators that aid in our executive decisions and allow us to get out of trades based on the market rather than on our wants and wishes. These four are:

1. Red line (Alligator's Teeth).
2. Five consecutive bars of the same color.
3. Green line (Alligator's Lips).
4. A signal in the opposite direction.

THE BEST OVERALL STOP WHEN YOU KNOW YOU ARE WITH THE TREND AND THE TREND IS NOT OVER

When you have evidence that you are still in a trending market, your best overall stop is the Red line. The Red line is the Alligator's Teeth. It is also where the current price would be if there were no new incoming information (Chaos) affecting the market. This is a Stop Close Only order, which can be put into most markets as either a Stop Close Only or a Market On Close order. If you are trading Intraday, you have to watch the market at the close of each period and get out with a market order if the close is below the Red line.

In Figure 9–2, you will see several penetrations of the Red line but no closes below the Red line. If you were trading this market and using the Red line as a stop, you would still be long this market. Let's look at another example.

In Figure 9–3, we see another example of the market touching and going below the Red line but closing above that line, negating getting out of the market there. The very rightmost bar did close below the Red line and we exited at that point.

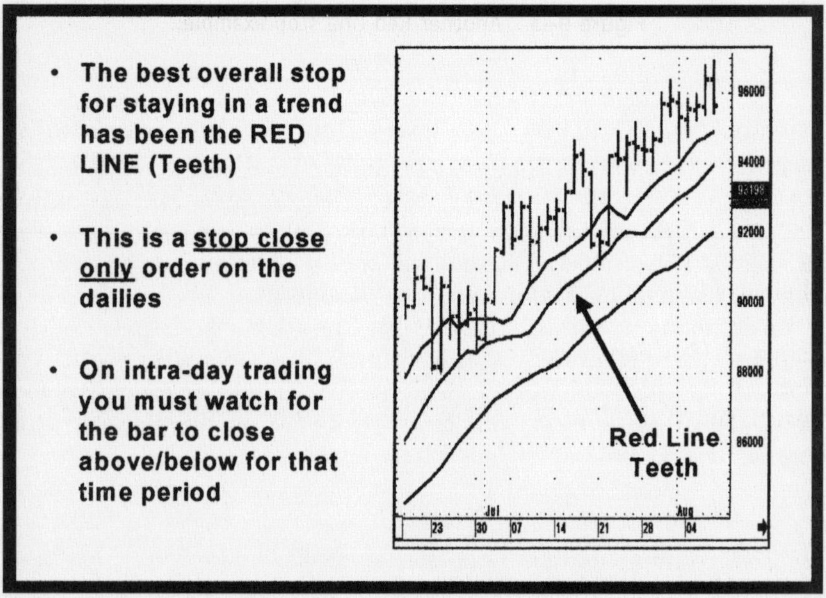

Figure 9–2 The best overall stop.

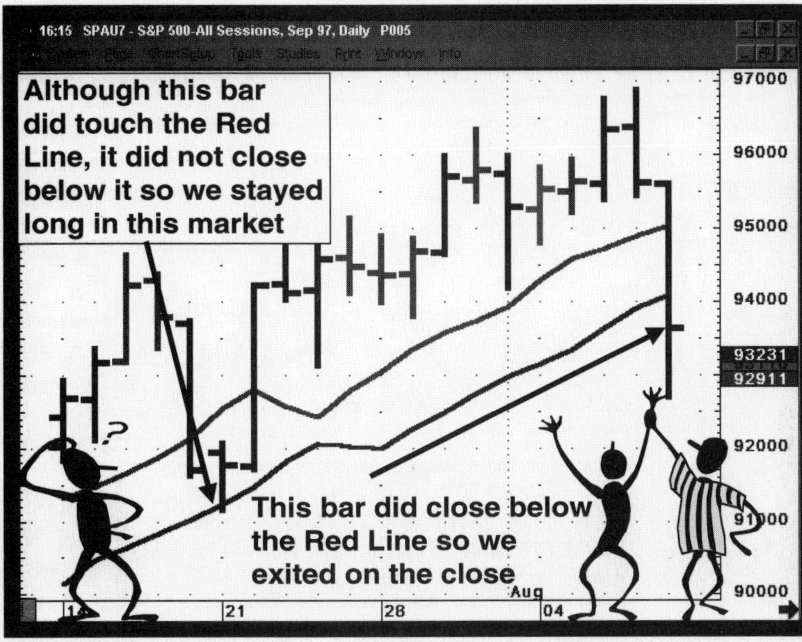

Figure 9–3 Another Red line stop example.

Figure 9–4 is an example of how the Red line stop keeps you in an extended trend. This is a daily chart of the S&P 500 from April 24 until July 31, just over three months. All of the relevant signals are marked on this chart. Had you taken all of the valid signals and used the Red line as your stop, you would have a profit of over $2,000,000 by trading one contract for each signal. This could have been accomplished starting with about a $50,000 account. Again, this type of trading opportunity opens up during every day the market is open. You will also note that had you used the Lips of the Alligator (the Green line, which is the Balance Line for two significant time frames lower), you would have been stopped out four different times.

THE FIVE CONSECUTIVE BARS OF THE SAME COLOR STOP

Probably our most used stop for squeezing profits is the FIVE CONSECUTIVE BARS OF THE SAME COLOR. This is a sort of

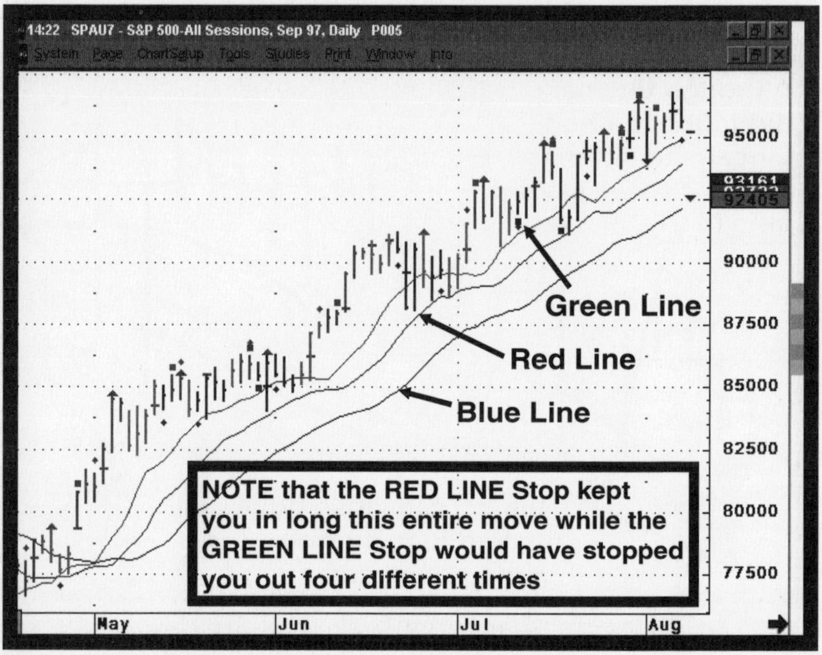

Figure 9–4 Another example of a Red line stop.

"Run-and-Gun" trading approach that allows you to place your assets (trading money) with markets that are moving. When a market starts to slow, you immediately move the assets to another market that is beginning to trade aggressively.

The technique is simple. Suppose you are in a long position and the market is moving up. You notice that there have been five consecutive green bars. You then place your stop one tick below the fifth green bar. If the market takes you out, you simply look for another good potential move. If the market continues to go in your direction, you raise the stop up to just below the most recently completed bar. You keep doing this until you are stopped out, no matter what color the bars are after that fifth green bar. You would use the same technique in a down market by placing your stop one tick above the fifth red bar.

Figure 9–5 illustrates this stop. The numbers 1 through 5 designate the first five red bars. The sixth and seventh bars are also red. Our first stop is placed one tick above the fifth bar. When the sixth bar has a lower high, we lower the stop to just above the high of the

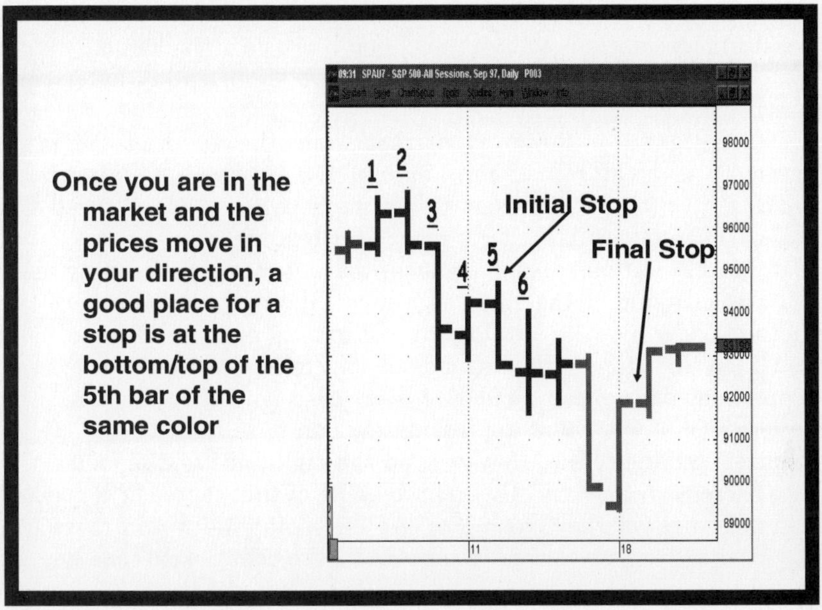

Figure 9–5 Five consecutive bars of the same color stop.

sixth bar. The seventh and eighth bars happen to be gray bars, meaning the Momentum is still down but the Acceleration is up. This is another way of saying that the Momentum to the downside is slowing. When that happens, we want to start looking for places to take profits. We then have a trailing stop, which usually gets us out of a down move on the lowest high and gets us out of an up move on the highest low. You can't get much better than that for profit taking.

Remember that once you have the five consecutive bars of the same color, you keep your trailing stop until you are stopped out, no matter what color the subsequent bars are.

You may have already thought of this question: What if you get stopped out with a profit and the market continues to move in your direction after you are out? The answer is: Reenter on any of the five dimensional signals going your way, provided the current price is still outside the Alligator's mouth.

What do you do with a Runaway market that does not have the five consecutive bars of the same color and has a Red line so far away from the present price that you are uncomfortable? You do not want to give up all the profit that the market has given you at this point. In a Runaway market, we use the Green line as a stop close only stop. The Green line is the Balance Line for two significantly lower time frames than we are trading.

We designate a Runaway market when the angle of the price movement is greater than the angle of the Green line. It indicates that some very powerful new information (Chaos) has entered the market, leaving the Alligator's mouth far behind.

Figure 9–6 illustrates a Runaway market versus a Trending market. The left side of the chart is a nice Trending market where the prices stay for a while outside the Alligator's mouth. Had you used the Green line stop on the left side of the chart, you would have been stopped out before the trend was over. Also note that the prices on the left side of the chart approximately run parallel with the Green (topmost) Balance Line. However, on the right side of the chart, the price increases dramatically and the angle of that increase is greater than the angle of the Green line. At this point, we would move our stop close only order to the Green line for the next period (one day, in

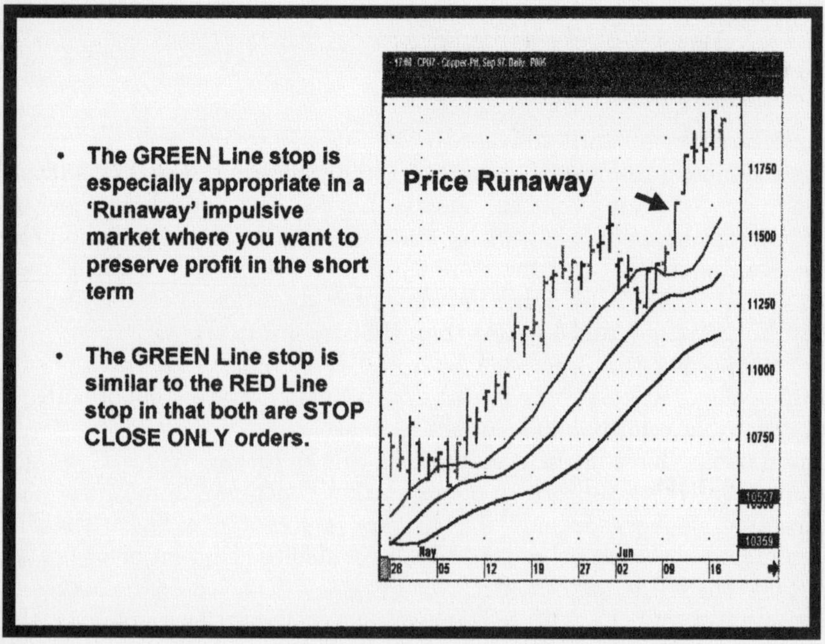

Figure 9–6 The Green line stop in a Runaway market.

this chart). You can see that the Green line is going to lock in more profit than the Red line (middle line) in Figure 9–6.

Remember: AT THE END OF THE CURRENT PERIOD, THE GREEN AND/OR RED LINE STOPS ARE PLACED AT THE GREEN OR RED LINE FOR THE NEXT PERIOD. For example, in Figure 9–6, the next day's stop will be on the Green line for the next day. Also remember that when using either the Green or the Red line stops, they are close only orders.

BUY OR SELL SIGNALS IN THE OPPOSITE DIRECTION

We now come to our final executive decision stop, which is a signal in the opposite direction (Figure 9–7). This is our least used and least desirable get-out signal. If you use this signal constantly, you will find that you are leaving too much profit on the table. Although it is a signal in the opposite direction, you would usually just exit rather than stop and reverse, because you should be on the proper side of the Alligator's mouth. In other words, if you are long and decide to exit on a sell signal, that signal would most likely be above the Alligator's mouth. The thing you definitely do *not* want to do is to feed the Alligator.

- A Buy or Sell Signal in the opposite direction means taking a signal
- GOING TOWARD THE ALLIGATOR'S MOUTH INSTEAD OF AWAY FROM THE MOUTH
- Using this indicator for Profit Protection will sometimes get you out too soon
- This will hinder you in accumulating large positions and staying in the market

Figure 9–7 Using buy/sell stops in the opposite direction to take profits.

Figure 9–8 summarizes the four executive decision possibilities for taking profits. Our decision process usually follows this path:

1. Any time we have five consecutive bars of the same color (red or green), we will place our stop one tick below the low of the most recently completed bar in an up move, and one tick above the high of the most recently completed bar in a down move.
2. If we believe we are in a continuing trend move, we will use a stop close only order just under the Red line, which is the Balance Line for one significant time frame lower than our trading time frame.
3. If we are in a Runaway market, as indicated when the angle of the current price move is greater than the angle of the Green Balance Line, we place a stop at the Green line to keep from giving back too much profit. We do the opposite in a sell situation.
4. We will use a buy/sell stop in the opposite direction from the current move.

Any time there is more than one choice for placing a stop, we usually prefer to use the five consecutive bars of the same color. Our least preferred and least used stop is an opposite buy/sell signal.

- **RED LINE—Usually the best for long-term appreciation**
- **Five Consecutive Bars of Same Color—Good at times where you do not want more risk**
- **GREEN LINE—Good for protecting profits in a Runaway market**
- **Signal in Opposite Direction—For use when you are scared. It tends to increase whiplashes and drains potential profits.**

Figure 9–8 Summary of profit-taking signals.

At this point, we have covered the Alligator decision maker and the five dimensional entry points for getting into any market. These are "grounded assessments," which do not change. In trading the markets, there are also times where the trader must make an executive decision about his or her trading strategy and especially about taking profits. Other more generalized factors can add to our confidence in trading and making profits. The most valuable information we can glean from a market is to know when one trend is ending and an opposite trend is beginning. All trends will end in a fractal, and one of the three top or bottom bars of that fractal will always be a squat bar. (See our earlier book, *Trading Chaos,* pages 133–151.)

Let's examine two characteristics of the markets that will give accurate early warning of the end of a trend and the beginning of a trend in the opposite direction. These characteristics are (1) Divergence and (2) the Profitunity five magic bullets that end a trend.

DIVERGENCE BETWEEN PRICE AND MOMENTUM

One of our very best tools to discover the underlying structure of the market is our 5/34 Awesome Oscillator (AO). Basically, it is a simple 34-bar moving average of the midpoints of the Price [(H – L)/2] that is subtracted from a 5-bar simple moving average of the Price bars' midpoints. If the short-term Momentum moves faster than the longer-term Momentum, the 5/34 oscillator will increase. This simple tool is the most effective technique we have found to measure the underlying Momentum of the market. This is not an "oversold/overbought" indicator because, as we pointed out early in this book, there is no such thing as oversold/overbought.

A divergence is created in an up move when the Price is higher than it was at the most recent Price peak and the Momentum (as measured by the 5/34 AO histogram) is lower than the Momentum peak that was at the last Price peak (Figure 9–9). In other words, the Price is higher and the Momentum is lower, and this is divergence between the Price and the Momentum (underlying structure).

Most markets tend to turn on a double divergence. A double divergence in an up market requires a Price peak followed by a higher Price peak (first divergence), and that higher peak is followed by a still higher Price peak. The Momentum is highest on the first Price peak, lower on the second Price peak, and still lower on the third Price peak. This is a double divergence, and most markets will turn at this point.

- **Most markets tend to turn on a Double Divergence between the Price and the AO [meaning for example, the Price is making a higher high but the Momentum is not]**
- **Periodically you will see a market turn on a Triple Divergence**
- **Only once in a great while will you see a Quadruple Divergence**

Figure 9–9 Noticing the divergence between Price and Momentum.

If the market doesn't turn on a double divergence, it will most likely turn on a triple divergence. Only perhaps once or twice a year will you see a quadruple divergence.

In Figure 9–10, we have one of those rare quadruple divergences. This happened in the daily S&P, and in the next few days after this fourth divergence, the market dropped over $38,000 per contract (Figure 9–11).

In Figure 9–10, notice that:

1. Point 1 is a higher Price than point zero. This is the first divergence.
2. Point 2 is a higher Price than point 1 but the Momentum is less. This is the second divergence.
3. Point 3 is a higher Price than point 2 but the Momentum is less than at point 2. This creates a triple divergence.
4. Point 4 is a higher Price than point 3 but the Momentum is less than at point 3. This creates a quadruple divergence. This is a rare occurrence. When it does happen, there is a very high probability that the market will move dramatically in the opposite direction.

Reviewing again, we know that Momentum always will turn before Price, and the speed of the Momentum will turn before the Momentum does. Thus, we can set up a procedure to monitor the end of

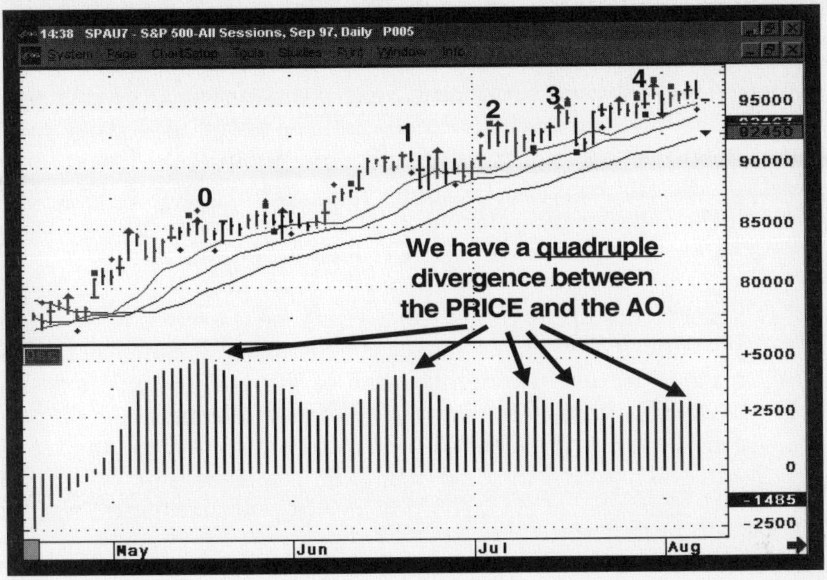

Figure 9–10 An unusual quadruple divergence between Price and Momentum.

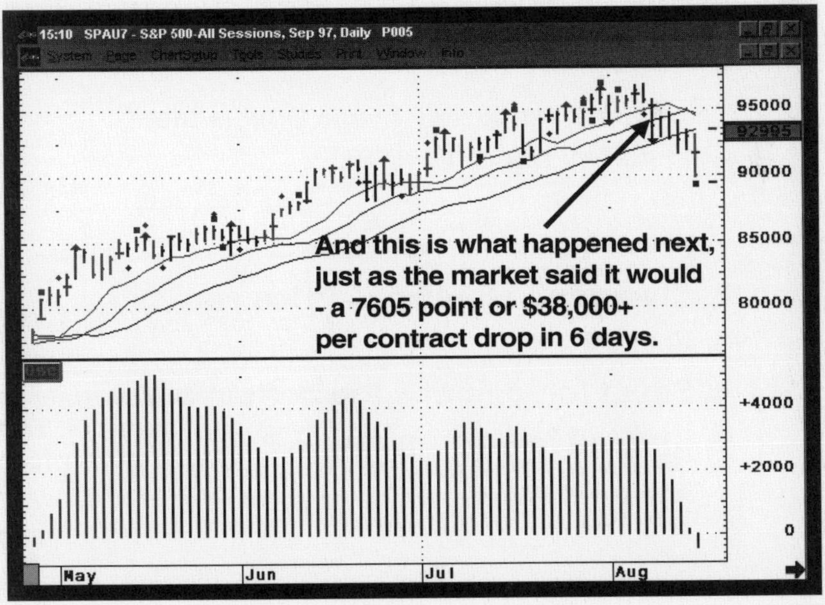

Figure 9–11 What happened after a quadruple divergence.

any trend. To aid us in being even more positive that a trend is ending, we have noticed that all trends will end only after they have been hit by what we refer to as the "five magic bullets"—five characteristics that any trend will exhibit before turning and setting up a trend in the opposite direction.

As shown in Figure 9–12, these five magic bullets are:

1. The Price is in the target zone. This zone is arrived at by using the Elliott Wave count, noting the distance between the beginning of Wave 1 through the end of Wave 3, and adding that price difference to the bottom of Wave 4. We then take 62 percent of that difference. Over 90 percent of the time, the trend will end between the 62 percent and 100 percent marks. (For a full discussion of this technique, see our earlier book, *Trading Chaos,* page 130.)
2. Divergence between Price and Momentum as measured by the 5/34 AO. This indicator becomes stronger if there is a double or possible triple divergence.

There are 5 Profitunity Magic Bullets that will end any trend. They are:

1. Price in the Target Zone
2. Divergence (between Price and Osc.)
3. Fractal
4. Squat (on one of 3 top/bottom bars)
5. Change in Momentum

Figure 9–12 The five magic bullets that will end any trend.

3. A fractal is created at the top/bottom.
4. There is a squat bar in one of the three top or bottom bars.
5. There is a change in the Momentum indicator.

SUMMARY

In this chapter, we have devoted our attention to finding the best possible exits to secure more profits and maximize our return on investment (ROI). We have gone through each of these executive decisions in the order that we have found to be most profitable. The most valuable commodity you will ever deal with is your own perspective, and whatever interferes with that should be dealt with immediately. That is one of the primary reasons I suggest that you DO NOT read the *Wall Street Journal,* listen to CNBC-FNN, read newsletters, or even read the news on your computer. Our best profit opportunities have consistently come when the players were just us and the market. Anything else is old news and not worth the cost of cluttering your mind.

Once you know all these signals and how to place them, everything else is psychological. We will focus our attention on the psychological aspects of trading in the last chapter of this book. We will explore some of the more important aspects of using our own personal psychology to increase both our profits and the fun of "playing" in the markets. In the next chapter, we will tie together everything we have covered in this and the previous chapters, to make sure you understand how to implement these profit-making techniques in both the stock and commodity markets.

10

TYING IT ALL TOGETHER

So far, we have taken apart the entire Profitunity approach to taking profits from the stock and commodity markets. In this chapter, we are going to review those techniques and put everything together into a composite whole, just the way we trade in our trading rooms.

GOALS

We are often asked what one can expect from trading these techniques. That question is absolutely impossible to answer because it depends on so many "unknowable" variables about each trader. Remember that we all trade our own personal belief systems, which are our biggest limiting factors. However, to give some sort of verifiable answer, I believe an achievable target to strive for is about a 10 percent average per month. Many traders have tripled that average, but we are talking here about an achievable goal. I also want to emphasize that I am talking about an *average*. You will not make 10 percent every month, and there will be months where you make several times that much.

How much is 10 percent per month? Well, it is almost 300 percent per year. A straight-line 10 percent per month compounded would take a $10,000 account to over a million dollars in a bit more than four years. Has that been done? Absolutely, and it is being done even as you read this. Why then do not all traders earn this percentage return? Mainly because they are not following the rules and they are letting their personal belief systems ruin their trading. In Figure 10–1, I have combined the Profitunity approach so that you can see

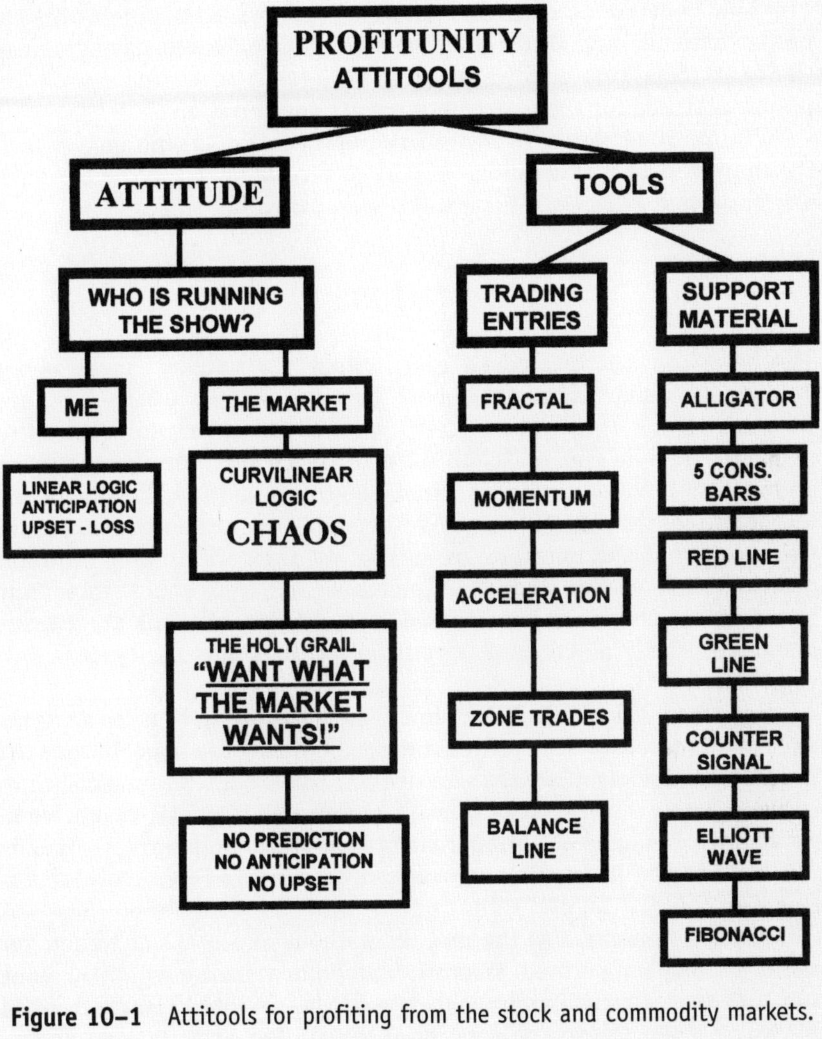

Figure 10–1 Attitools for profiting from the stock and commodity markets.

how it all ties together. This is the Science of trading. Once you learn, understand, and begin following this unambiguous approach you will, with experience, start developing the *ART* of trading, which cannot be put into book form nor taught to you by anyone except yourself. It is the end result of experiencing and reflecting and, from that reflecting, learning more about yourself and your interaction with the market.

Good continuous profitable trading is the result of combining the proper attitude and the right tools. The new sciences have given us the best tools yet, and we want to integrate those tools with the proper attitude for the ultimate winning combination.

Figure 10–1 sums up my entire approach for taking money from the markets. In this chapter, we will go through each of the blocks as a review and will then illustrate them on various charts.

ATTITUDE

The basic variant in traders' and investors' attitudes can be boiled down to: "Who is running the show?" Basically, we are all selfish and we want things to go just the way we imagine. Ask yourself at this moment: Who do you really think are the people running the show, and are they friends or foes? Ninety-eight percent of all traders and investors feel that there is a war going on between themselves and the markets—that the markets are out to get them. This very paranoid position leads to fear and loss. Remember Einstein's most important question: "Is the Universe a friendly place?" If you think the market is not a friendly place, that is your belief. It is not reality, it is only your belief.

Because most of us are extremely centered on the way *we want* the market to move, we set up expectations. When these expectations are not met, we are disappointed. We use our linear logic to predict behavior, and when that behavior doesn't match our predictions, we blame the behavior instead of our approach to the world and markets. (I refer you back to the illustration of the hydrogen and oxygen molecules in Chapter 2.)

What if you came to the market without expectations? Then you could not be disappointed. What if, instead of wanting what you want, you just gave that up and decided to WANT WHAT THE MARKET WANTS? Then there would be no disappointed expectations and no upsets. Can this be done? Absolutely, and it is a lonely job because you can only do it for yourself.

Remember that the market is always right and is always the perfect teacher. She will tell you exactly what you did wrong when you lose, and will also show you what you must do to correct your mistakes. Then there is no longer winning and losing, there is only winning and learning.

In sum, unless you are willing to give up your preconceived ideas about the market and how to make profit from it, there is little chance of your success being any greater than it already is. To repeat a statement I made earlier: IF THE THINGS YOU HAVE BEEN LOOKING FOR COULD BE FOUND IN THE PLACES YOU HAVE BEEN LOOKING, YOU WOULD NOT BE READING THIS. If you are really ready to give up your personal and petty outlook to join the larger molecule of the market, you are in for some of the highest highs available on this planet.

Having made the proper attitude adjustment, let's now review the science part of trading and put it all together.

TOOLS

Looking at the right side of Figure 10–1, you will notice the column labeled "TRADING ENTRIES" on the left and "SUPPORT MATERIAL" on the right. Using both of these columns, let's go through some typical trades. We will break this exercise down into six steps.

Step 1. Finding a Tradable Market

Assume now that you are *not* in the market but are looking for opportunities. You are not locked into any particular stock or commodity; you just want to set yourself up for incoming profits. You remember that, most of the time (70 to 85 percent), the markets are really going nowhere, and it is almost impossible to make significant profits from this type of market behavior. Therefore, we look to our first supporting mechanism: the Alligator. We are looking for a sleeping Alligator that has already been asleep for a while (the Jaw, Teeth, and Lip lines are close together or intertwining).

We then want to bracket this market with buy stops above and sell stops below the Alligator's mouth. Because we make money only when the market is moving and we don't know what kind of meat the Alligator is hungry for, we want to cover all possible alternatives. Remember, this is the spiderweb approach: we will take anything the market gives us, and, most important—WE DO NOT CARE WHICH WAY THE MARKET MOVES OR BREAKS OUT. By using this approach, we can look at the market and say honestly, "I don't care which way it goes."

In the left portion of Figure 10–2, you can see that the Alligator was closing his mouth and starting to take a nap. This is not the prime time to initiate trading. In the middle portion, notice that the Alligator is indeed taking a nap. This is the time to be ready to trade.

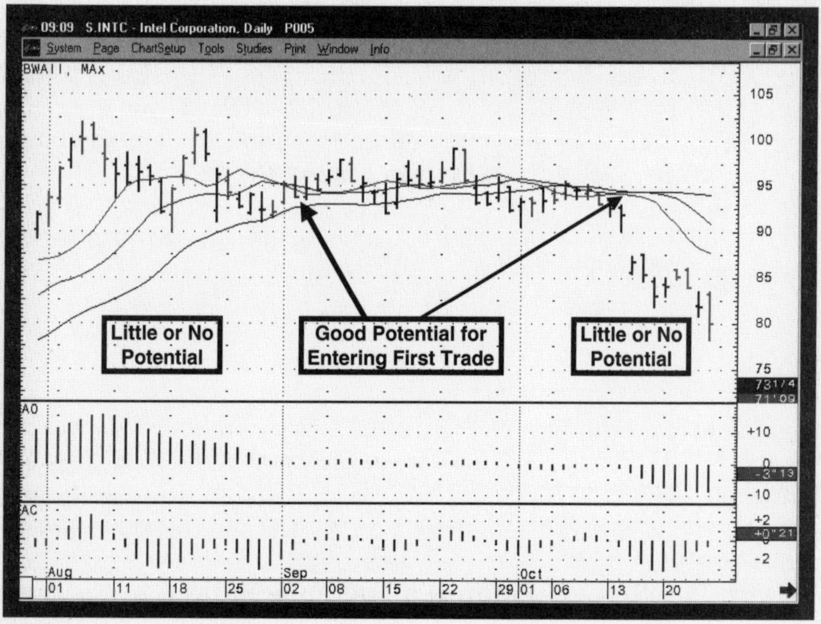

Figure 10–2 Using the Alligator to locate potential opportunities—Intel Corp.

It is a general rule of the market that the biggest moves tend to originate from the dullest markets. Therefore, the very time when it is most boring to follow the markets is when you should be at your sharpest. If you first looked at Figure 10–2 on the last day to the right, you realized that the price is already out of the Alligator's mouth and the best opportunity has already passed. You would then search for another more promising chart.

Another factor to monitor here is where the Momentum and Acceleration are while the Alligator is sleeping. In early October, there are three conditions that will almost always set up a good trade:

1. The Alligator is asleep.
2. The AO is near the zero line.
3. The AC is near the zero line.

In Figure 10–3, you will see a similar situation in crude oil. The sleeping Alligator gives us our best entry timing for initiating a new trading campaign.

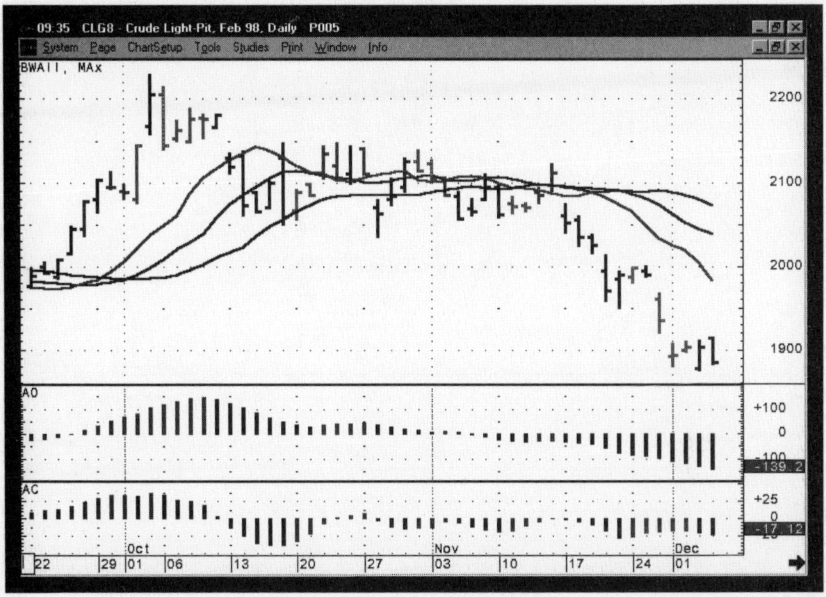

Figure 10–3 Looking for entry opportunities in crude oil.

The crude oil chart is similar to the Intel chart (Figure 10–2). The only possible signal from the middle of November on was on the short side. To review this first step: In entering any market, you should *start* from a sleeping Alligator. Once you have positioned yourself in a market, you can become very aggressive, but only after the first breakout entry, which is the next step.

Step 2. Taking the First Fractal Breakout

We have found the sleeping Alligator and we want our first entry to be a true breakout signal, which is the fractal. To qualify, the high of the fractal's middle bar must be above/below the Alligator's Teeth, which we color Red on the price charts. No matter how many other signals may be created, we do not take any of them until this first fractal out of the mouth has been hit.

Figure 10–4 is a good illustration of getting into a market. Notice the fractals outside the closed mouth. The up fractal labeled "A" was triggered, and we bought just as the fractal labeled "B" was in the process of forming. A fractal sell signal was formed at point "D," and

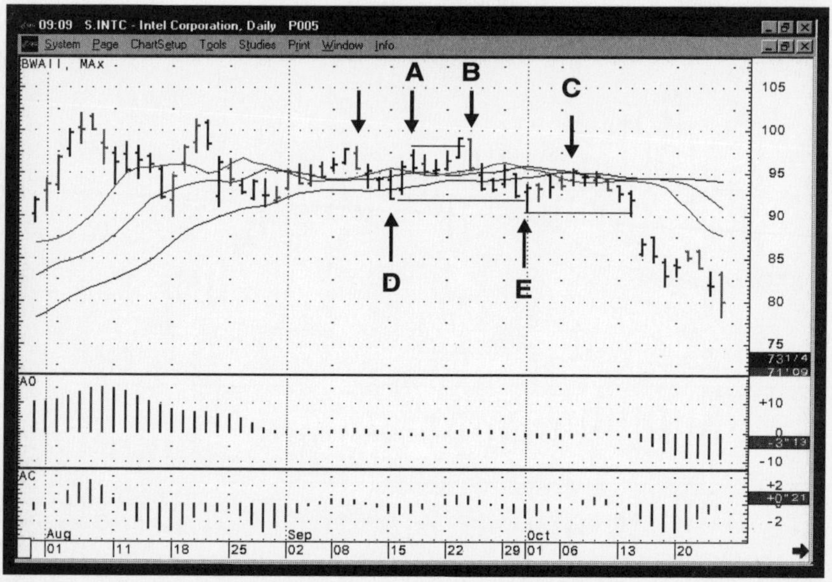

Figure 10–4 First fractal trades outside the Alligator's mouth—Intel Corp.

this reversed us to a net short position at point "E." Point "E" also formed a second fractal sell signal that was hit in mid-October. We went short on both fractals since we took every sell signal after the first fractal "D" was hit. Notice also that a buy fractal signal was created at point "C" but was never hit. Had the market moved above the high at point "C," that would have put us net long. Another fractal, formed near October 17, was also taken.

It is interesting to note that we were stopped and reversed with a small loss on the fractal buy signal at "A." We do not mind this, and we call this behavior playing in the "low-rent district." Our losses are generally very small, and there is great advantage in being in the market *before* a move as opposed to chasing a market that is already moving.

Figure 10–5 demonstrates again the proper initiation of a trading campaign out of the Alligator's mouth. Points "A," "D," and "E" are all valid fractal signals, but they became invalid when more recent fractals were formed that were closer to the then-current price. Remember that we always take the most recent signal. The buy fractal at point "B" was hit at point "C." This turned out to be a small loss

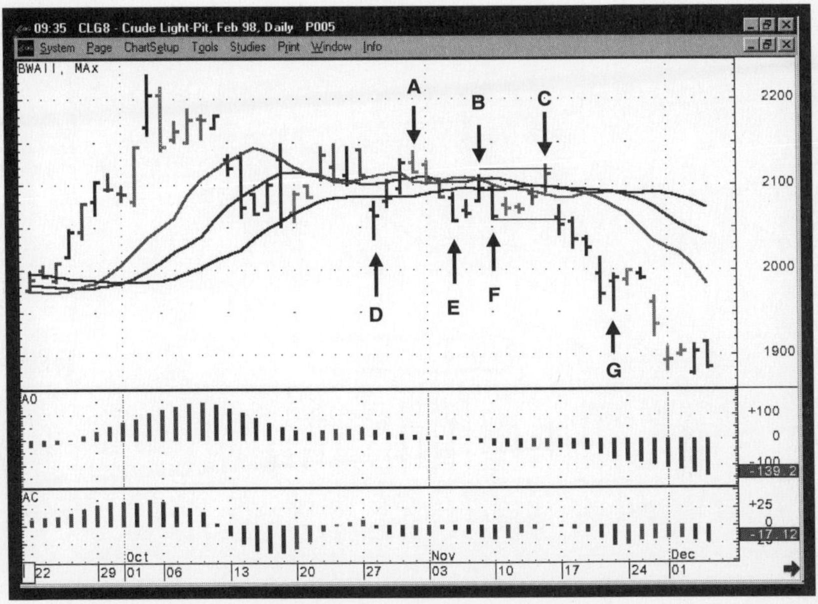

Figure 10–5 First fractal outside the Alligator's mouth—crude oil.

when we were stopped and reversed at the fractal sell signal at point "F." As stated above, we consider this to be trading in the low-rent district. After the fractal sell signal is triggered, we become aggressive and take each and every sell signal that is outside the Alligator's mouth, including the fractal sell signal at point "G." Note that only fractal signals are marked on this chart. Next, we'll look at a chart with fractal signals that are not outside the Alligator's mouth.

Figure 10–6 points out an invalid fractal sell signal. It is invalid because the price was not out of the Alligator's mouth when it was triggered. (To review how an invalid fractal becomes a valid signal, see Figures 4–16 and 4–17.)

Step 3. Adding on Aggressively

Once this first fractal signal has been hit, we take any and all signals in that direction. At this point, we want to be very aggressive traders. Usually we will have everything going our way, including the Momentum and Acceleration, but even if we do not, we will still take the signals once that first fractal has been hit. We now know that one

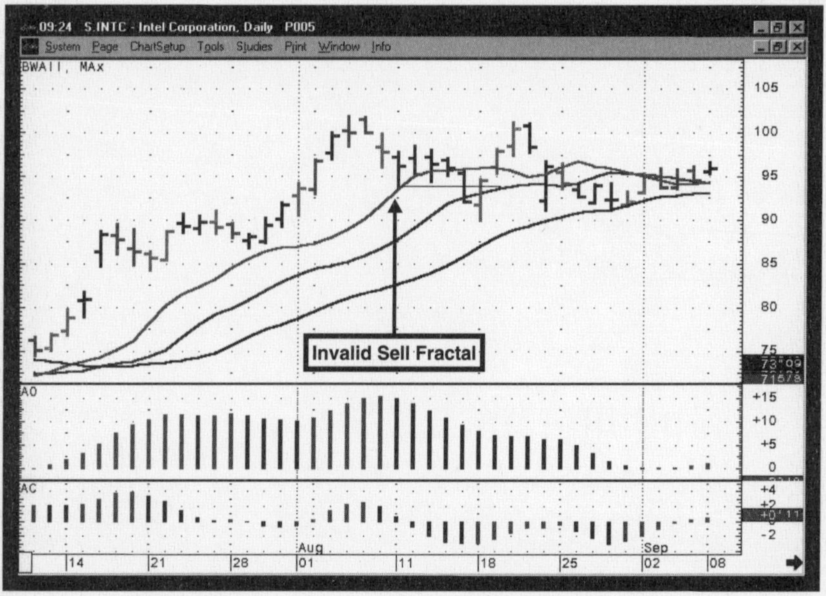

Figure 10–6 An invalid fractal sell signal—Intel Corp.

of two things will happen: we will make a profit or we won't. If we do, fine. If we don't, let's have a close protective stop.

In the Dell Computer chart shown in Figure 10–7, the first signal taken was a buy signal at point "A." When that signal was hit, our strategy was to add on aggressively, using any and all of the five different dimensional signals. Between this first entry and the top of the chart, there were 18 different add-on signals that should have been taken. Of these 18 signals, 14 turned out to be winners and the last 4 were relatively small losers. Typically, this strategy allows us to take three to five times the amount in a trend run. For example, this trade campaign lasted for approximately one month and covered approximately a $25 increase in price per share. We would normally expect to profit $75 to $125 per share from this move, multiplied by the number of shares placed on each signal.

Figure 10–8 is another example of using all signals after the first fractal entry is triggered. The first sell fractal was hit during late November, and the market continued down outside the Alligator's mouth for about six weeks. There were 23 add-on signals after the first fractal sell entry. Because this was approximately a $3.50 move, we would expect our profit to be approximately three to five times that move.

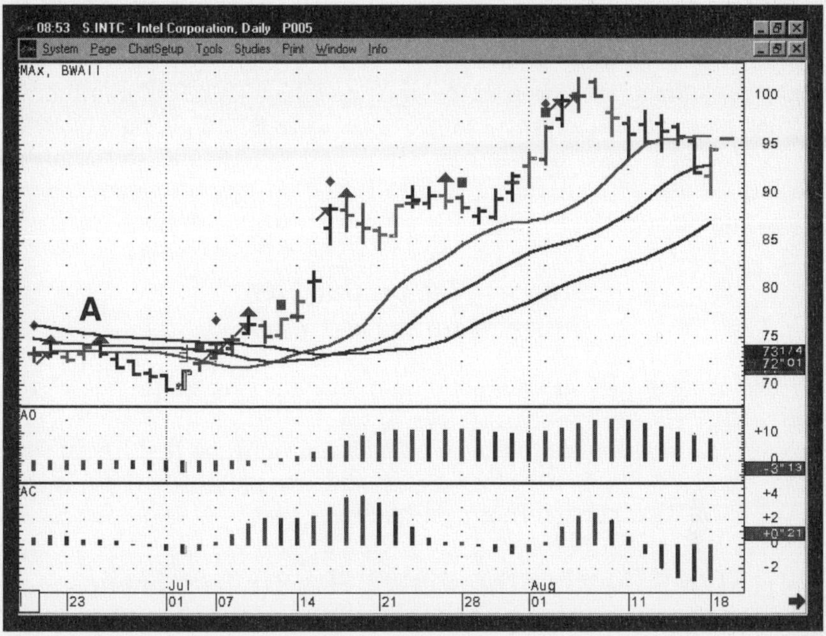

Figure 10–7 Adding on aggressively in Dell Computer.

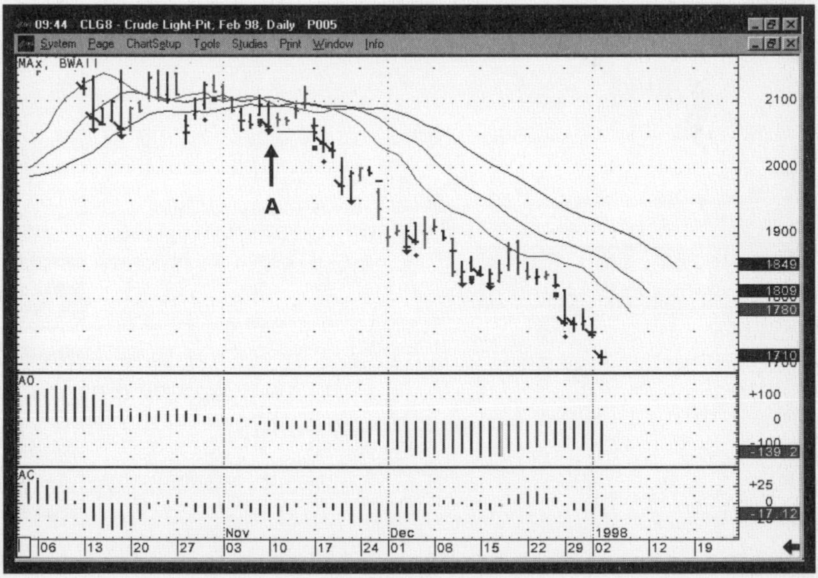

Figure 10–8 Aggressive selling in crude oil.

This move on a one-contract basis would have been approximately $3,500, so we would expect a profit of between $10,500 and $17,500.

Next, let's examine Figures 10–9 and 10–10 and formulate a method to extract maximum profits based on market-generated information as opposed to our wallet or bank account needs.

Step 4. Placing Our First Protection against Loss

My choice generally at this point is to place a stop to get out of the market (go flat) on the first close above the Alligator's Teeth (Red line). If the mouth does not open immediately and the Red line stop is closer than I want, I will place a stop and reverse at the first fractal in the opposite direction that is outside the Teeth.

Step 5. Letting the Market Play Its Own Music

We are letting the market run its own show, so we do not place any targets to get out. This would be wanting what *we* want rather than

Figure 10–9 Using the Red line (Alligator's Teeth) for a profit-protecting stop—crude oil.

Figure 10–10 Using five consecutive bars of the same color for a stop—crude oil.

what *the market* wants. We continue to add on aggressively and, as the profits accumulate, we start looking for the market to tell us how and when to take profits.

Step 6. Taking the Money to the Bank

Now we are in a trade; it is making profits, and we want to make sure we stay in tune with Mother Market. The name of the game *is* taking money out of the market. At this point, we must make an executive decision as to which one of the four profit-taking strategies best suits our current circumstances. They are, in rank order of total profits over a period of time:

1. *A close above (below in an up market) the Alligator's Teeth—the Red line* (Figure 10–9). This is the best profit-making close over time. However, there will be times when the market has moved in your direction and the Red line stop would give up

much of your accumulated profits. If that is a concern, you may want to use the next strategy.

2. *Five consecutive bars of the same color* (Figure 10–10). For example, you are in a bearish market and have had five red price bars in a row. You might decide to squeeze the stop up to just above the high of the fifth red bar. If you use this technique, you should trail your stop to just above each new lower high until you are stopped out. In Figure 10–10, there were two occasions (marked inside the boxes) where there were five consecutive red bars. Once you are out, use this profit-taking technique. If the market continues in the original direction, you would get back in on any sell signal that is outside the Alligator's mouth.

3. *Green line (Lips) stop.* There will be cases when the market simply takes off in your direction, such as in an Elliott Wave 3, and you will want to take advantage of this generous gift the market is giving you. You may then choose to use the Alligator's Lips or the Green line, which would be closer to the current price. This will often give you much less profit than if you had the courage to stay with the Red line, but immediate circumstances may dictate that this is the better choice for you at this time.

   Figure 10–11 is an example of a breakaway market to the down side in Intel Corp. We define a breakaway market when the Price angle is greater than the angle of the Alligator's Lips (Green line). This indicates that the price is moving rapidly and, when the market starts to breathe, the Price will come back toward your entry. Stops based on the Red or Green line are always stop close only stops. The market must not only penetrate the line, it must also close above (below) the line.

   The last of the four profit-taking methods is shown in Figure 10–12.

4. *A signal in the opposite direction.* This is our least used strategy. It is reserved for those times when you are just very scared and want to get out. You are not maximizing your profits but rather protecting your perspective. Remember that the most valuable commodity you will ever deal with is your own perspective, and anything that disrupts it must be avoided at all costs.

Figure 10–11 Using the Green line stop in a breakaway market—Intel Corp.

Figure 10–12 A signal in the opposite direction—Intel Corp.

Step 7. Enjoying Your Profits

At this point, it is very important that you reward yourself for doing what most people can't or won't do. You are a winner on your own, and you owe no allegiance or obligation to anyone. You did it yourself in a relatively free market and there is no necessity to be politically correct. Enjoy your freedom, your unlimited possibilities, and your profits. And then get ready to do it again.

This simple formula can put you in the top 1 percent of all traders and investors in the world and can give you an almost unlimited income. You will find, by following these steps, that you will grow not only financially but also as a self-aware and self-confident person.

MORE EXAMPLES

Now let's look at some longer-term examples to see how this technique works in stock and commodity markets. We will look at the April and June contracts for Gold and then look at Dell Corp. Figure 10–13 is the chart for the April Gold contract from mid-November until late February (about three months).

Figure 10–13 Daily April gold contract with all signals marked.

In Figure 10–13, you can see how Gold was generally bearish, as evidenced by the Price's staying below the Alligator's mouth. Table 10–1 gives the actual sell signals and the results you would have achieved by following this technique.

As you can see from Table 10–1, trading with the Alligator and using these techniques can be quite rewarding. Let's go further with

TABLE 10–1 Trade by Trade in April Gold.

Date	Signal	Date	Filled	P/L Points	P/L $	Cum. $
8-Nov	FRAC	9-Nov	382.4	33.1	3,310.00	3,310.00
19-Nov	BL	21-Nov	381.9	32.6	3,260.00	6,570.00
21-Nov	ZT	21-Nov	380.5	31.2	3,120.00	9,690.00
21-Nov	BL	25-Nov	379.7	30.4	3,040.00	12,730.00
2-Dec	ZT	2-Dec	372.9	23.6	2,360.00	15,090.00
2-Dec	AC	3-Dec	372.8	23.5	2,350.00	17,440.00
9-Dec	FRAC	16-Dec	371.4	22.1	2,210.00	19,650.00
12-Dec	BL	16-Dec	371.8	22.5	2,250.00	21,900.00
24-Dec	FRAC	31-Dec	372.2	22.9	2,290.00	24,190.00
24-Dec	BL	31-Dec	372.2	22.9	2,290.00	26,480.00
3-Jan	ZT	3-Jan	364.0	14.7	1,470.00	27,950.00
6-Jan	ZT	6-Jan	360.5	11.2	1,120.00	29,070.00
6-Jan	BL	8-Jan	359.4	10.1	1,010.00	30,080.00
7-Jan	ZT	7-Jan	358.5	9.2	920.00	31,000.00
9-Jan	BL	14-Jan	357.3	8.0	800.00	31,800.00
15-Jan	FRAC	22-Jan	354.0	4.7	470.00	32,270.00
16-Jan	BL	21-Jan	355.8	6.5	650.00	32,920.00
8-Jan	FRAC	14-Jan	356.9	7.6	760.00	33,680.00
17-Jan	AO	20-Jan	356.9	7.6	760.00	34,440.00
20-Jan	AC	21-Jan	355.2	5.9	590.00	35,030.00
20-Jan	ZT	20-Jan	356.2	6.9	690.00	35,720.00
23-Jan	FRAC	30-Jan	348.9	−0.4	(40.00)	35,680.00
23-Jan	BL	30-Jan	348.9	−0.4	(40.00)	35,640.00
31-Jan	FRAC	6-Feb	345.3	−4.0	(400.00)	35,240.00
3-Feb	BL	6-Feb	345.5	−3.8	(380.00)	34,860.00
4-Feb	AO	5-Feb	346.0	−3.3	(330.00)	34,530.00
4-Feb	AC	5-Feb	346.0	−3.3	(330.00)	34,200.00
7-Feb	FRAC	12-Feb	339.9	−9.4	(940.00)	33,260.00
7-Feb	BL	12-Feb	339.9	−9.4	(940.00)	32,320.00
11-Feb	AO	12-Feb	340.2	−9.1	(910.00)	31,410.00
Totals			349.3	314.1		31,410.00

Gold by switching to the June contract and continuing with the exact same techniques.

Figure 10–14 continues where Figure 10–13 left off. You will notice that the price took a bounce upward and then settled back down below the Alligator's mouth from March through May. Table 10–2 details the trading of Gold during this time, based on taking one contract for each signal. Note that there was less profit than in the April contract (in Table 10–1) because this market was not trending as much as it was during the previous three months. However, it was still quite profitable, and there were fourteen winners and only four losers.

At this point, let's compare this same trading approach in the stock markets. Figure 10–15 shows a campaign for trading Dell Corp. stock.

In Figure 10–15 you see fourteen days of actual trading of the Dell Corp. stock, with all the signals marked on the price chart. Notice that only buy signals were taken because the price was above the Alligator's mouth. Our goal, as stated before, is to take from three to five times the trend move in profits. In this instance, we were able to take

Figure 10–14 June Gold with all the five dimensional signals marked.

TABLE 10–2 Trade by Trade in June Gold.

Date	Signal	Date	Filled	P/L Points	P/L $	Cum. $
4-Feb	FRAC	20-Feb	351.6	0.3	30.00	30.00
21-Feb	BL	25-Feb	358.8	–6.9	(690.00)	(660.00)
25-Feb	AO	26-Feb	359.1	–7.2	(720.00)	(1,380.00)
7-Mar	RL	7-Mar	351.9			(1,380.00)
7-Mar	FRAC	17-Mar	351.0	6.2	620.00	620.00
17-Mar	AO	18-Mar	349.9	5.1	510.00	1,130.00
18-Mar	FRAC	26-Mar	348.5	3.7	370.00	1,500.00
20-Mar	ZT	20-Mar	354.6	9.8	980.00	2,480.00
21-Mar	AC	24-Mar	353.9	9.1	910.00	3,390.00
20-Mar	BL	24-Mar	353.6	8.8	880.00	4,270.00
1-Apr	AO	2-Apr	352.1	7.3	730.00	5,000.00
31-Mar	BL	3-Apr	350.9	6.1	610.00	5,610.00
7-Apr	ZT	7-Apr	351.1	6.3	630.00	6,240.00
7-Apr	FRAC	11-Apr	349.3	4.5	450.00	6,690.00
7-Apr	BL	11-Apr	349.3	4.5	450.00	7,140.00
9-Apr	ZT	9-Apr	350.4	5.6	560.00	7,700.00
8-Apr	AC	9-Apr	350.5	5.7	570.00	8,270.00
16-Apr	ZT	16-Apr	343.3	–1.5	(150.00)	8,120.00
17-Apr	BL	24-Apr	342.0	–2.8	(280.00)	7,840.00
Totals			344.8	78.4		7,840.00

seven times the trend move. Table 10–3 gives the signal-by-signal recap of this trading, based on buying 100 shares for each signal.

Figure 10–16 shows more trading in Dell Corp. and it again illustrates the power of concentrating only on prices and direction that are outside the Alligator's mouth. This particular trade campaign was three months long from entry to exit. Table 10–4 shows the action during this time, which produced over eleven times the actual move itself. Remember that our goal is three to five times the move, and sometimes you get rewarded in a large way, as here.

In Table 10–4, you see the results of using the five Profitunity dimensional signals in trading a stock for approximately three months. Again, the key is to let the Alligator filter your perspective. When you find you are in tune with the market, become aggressive with your investments.

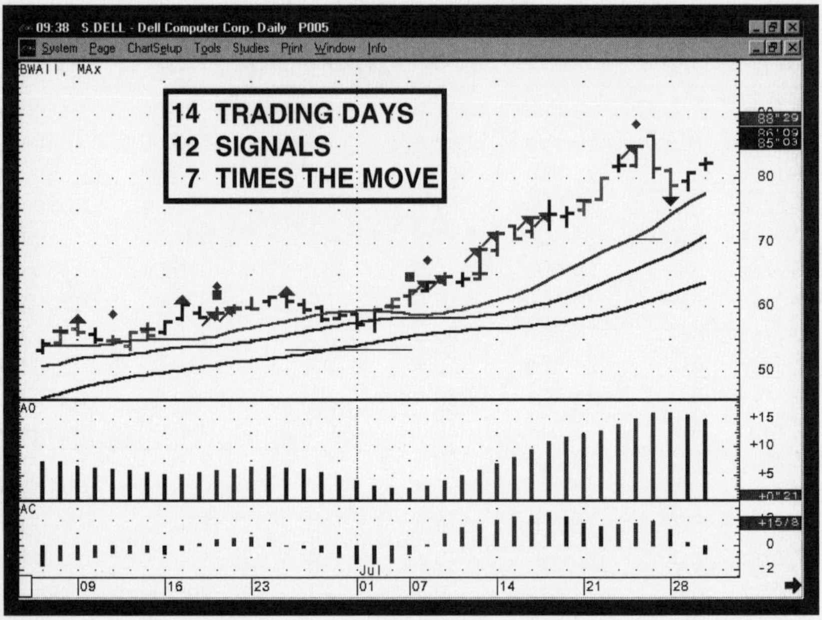

Figure 10–15 Fourteen trading days in Dell Corp. stock.

TABLE 10–3 Fourteen Days of Trading Dell Corp.

Date	Signal	Filled	Date	P/L Points	P/L $	Cum. $
25-Jun	FRAC	62.00	7-Jul	22.75	2,275.00	2,275.00
7-Jul	AO	62.50	8-Jul	22.25	2,225.00	4,500.00
8-Jul	AC	63.50	9-Jul	21.25	2,125.00	6,625.00
8-Jul	ZT	63.75	8-Jul	21.00	2,100.00	8,725.00
9-Jul	ZT	64.75	9-Jul	20.00	2,000.00	10,725.00
9-Jul	BL	65.50	11-Jul	19.25	1,925.00	12,650.00
11-Jul	ZT	69.00	11-Jul	15.75	1,575.00	14,225.00
14-Jul	ZT	71.25	14-Jul	13.50	1,350.00	15,575.00
16-Jul	ZT	73.50	16-Jul	11.25	1,125.00	16,700.00
17-Jul	BL	76.75	22-Jul	8.00	800.00	17,500.00
24-Jul	ZT	85.00	24-Jul	–0.25	(25.00)	17,475.00
24-Jul	AC	85.25	25-Jul	–0.50	(50.00)	17,425.00
Totals	STOP	84.75		174.25		17,425.00

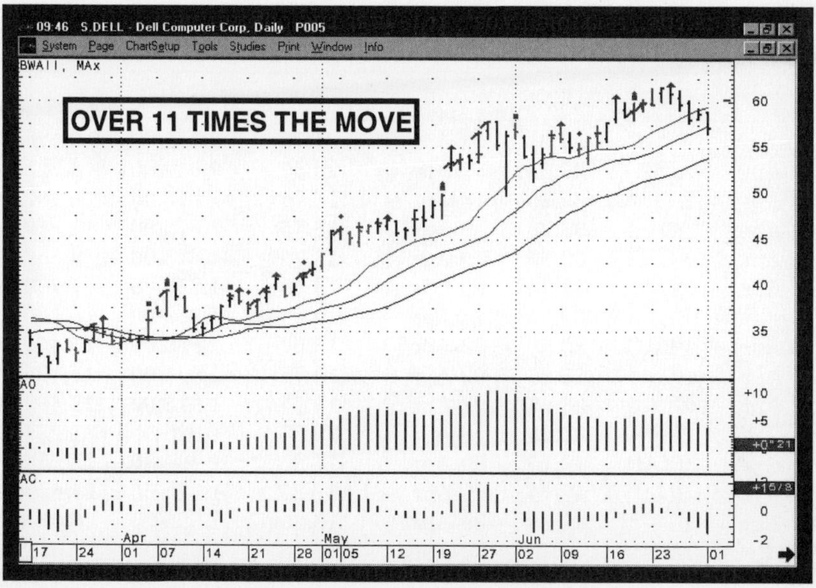

Figure 10–16 More trading of Dell Corp. stock.

MAKING SUCCESS "AUTOMAGIC"

After trading and learning for over four decades, we have been able to put our approach onto computer software. Through the assistance of programmers from literally around the world, we have developed the Investor's Dream.™ All the strategies have been programmed so that the indicators can be automatic and easy to find. In fact, Investor's Dream will even tell you exactly what words to use to place the order with your broker. I strongly suggest you download the fully functioning demo of this program for serious study and practice. It is programmed so that you can go through any chart one bar at a time, and it will list all the possibilities available.

Then all you need do is decide which strategy is best suited for your personality and your goals. This demo version is free. If you wish more information, you may contact our office or visit our Web site at:

www.profitunity.com

TABLE 10–4 Three Months of Trading Dell Corp. Using the Alligator Techniques.

Date	Signal	Filled	Date	P/L Points	P/L $	Cum. $
27-Mar	FRAC	36.25	4-Apr	21.75	2,175.00	2,175.00
4-Apr	AO	37.50	7-Apr	20.50	2,050.00	4,225.00
8-Apr	ZT	39.25	8-Apr	18.75	1,875.00	6,100.00
8-Apr	AO	39.25	9-Apr	18.75	1,875.00	7,975.00
8-Apr	AC	39.25	9-Apr	18.75	1,875.00	9,850.00
17-Apr	AO	39.50	18-Apr	18.50	1,850.00	11,700.00
10-Apr	BL	39.00	17-Apr	19.00	1,900.00	13,600.00
18-Apr	FRAC	39.50	23-Apr	18.50	1,850.00	15,450.00
21-Apr	AC	38.25	22-Apr	19.75	1,975.00	17,425.00
22-Apr	ZT	38.25	22-Apr	19.75	1,975.00	19,400.00
23-Apr	ZT	39.75	23-Apr	18.25	1,825.00	21,225.00
24-Apr	FRAC	40.75	29-Apr	17.25	1,725.00	22,950.00
24-Apr	BL	40.75	29-Apr	17.25	1,725.00	24,675.00
29-Apr	ZT	41.75	29-Apr	16.25	1,625.00	26,300.00
29-Apr	AC	41.50	30-Apr	16.50	1,650.00	27,950.00
5-May	ZT	46.25	5-May	11.75	1,175.00	29,125.00
5-May	BL	46.50	7-May	11.50	1,150.00	30,275.00
7-May	BL	47.00	9-May	11.00	1,100.00	31,375.00
12-May	FRAC	47.50	15-May	10.50	1,050.00	32,425.00
12-May	BL	47.50	15-May	10.50	1,050.00	33,475.00
20-May	AO	52.75	21-May	5.25	525.00	34,000.00
20-May	AC	52.75	21-May	5.25	525.00	34,525.00
21-May	ZT	53.25	21-May	4.75	475.00	35,000.00
21-May	FRAC	55.00	27-May	3.00	300.00	35,300.00
22-May	BL	54.25	27-May	3.75	375.00	35,675.00
27-May	ZT	56.75	27-May	1.25	125.00	35,800.00
28-May	ZT	57.75	28-May	0.25	25.00	35,825.00
3-Jun	BL	56.25	6-Jun	1.75	175.00	36,000.00
9-Jun	FRAC	57.75	16-Jun	0.25	25.00	36,025.00
10-Jun	BL	57.00	13-Jun	1.00	100.00	36,125.00
11-Jun	AC	55.75	12-Jun	2.25	225.00	36,350.00
17-Jun	FRAC	60.50	24-Jun	–2.50	(250.00)	36,100.00
18-Jun	BL	60.25	20-Jun	–2.25	(225.00)	35,875.00
19-Jun	AO	60.00	20-Jun	–2.00	(200.00)	35,675.00
19-Jun	AC	60.00	20-Jun	–2.00	(200.00)	35,475.00
19-Jun	ZT	59.25	19-Jun	–1.25	(125.00)	35,350.00
20-Jun	ZT	59.75	20-Jun	–1.75	(175.00)	35,175.00
Totals		58	27-Jun	351.75		35,175.00

Figures 10–17 and 10–18 are charts from Investor's Dream. They illustrate how this works automagically, using your personal computer. It is important to note that this program is quite flexible and is not a "black box" system. All the parameters are fully disclosed, and you may choose the combinations that best fit your personality and your goals.

In the topmost portion of Figure 10–17, you see the Alligator (while this is in black and white, on the computer everything is color-coded for easy recognition) with the current valid signals displayed just to the right of the prices. The ^'s and the v's point out the fractals. The two arrows between the current signal display the market's current momentum and acceleration. These two arrows are both down, indicating that even though the Price is rising, the Momentum

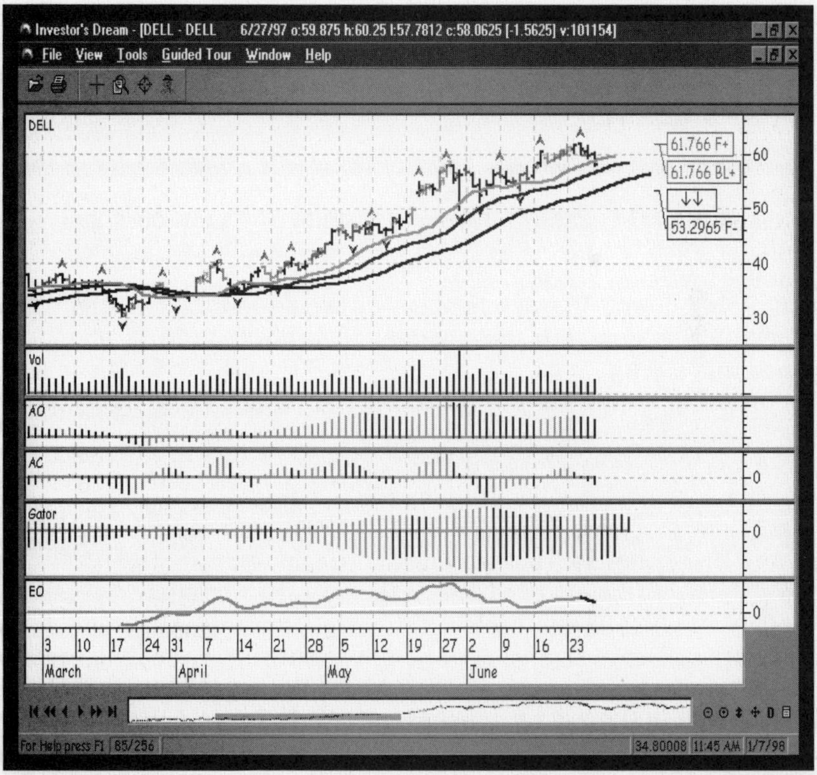

Figure 10–17 Dell Corp. stock as displayed using Investor's Dream.

DELL COMPUTER

Tuesday, April 29

4/28/97 o:39.25 h:40.1875 l:38.9375 c:39.4688 [+.5938] v:81409

- **Enter long 1 unit if close is 39.4848 or higher. (Zone+)**
- **Place a buy stop to enter long 2 units if price rises to 48.9535 or higher. (F+BL+)**
- **Green Line Long Exit Strategy: Close all long positions on close if price falls to 38.1395 or lower. (Below the Green Balance Line)**
- **Red Line Long Exit Strategy: Close all long positions on close if close falls to 36.7955 or lower. (Below the Red Balance Line)**
- **Place a sell stop to enter short 1 unit if price falls to 36.609 or lower. (F+)**
- **Place a sell stop to enter short 1 unit if price falls to 35.7965 or lower.(BL-)**
- **Green Line Short Exit Strategy: close all short positions on close if price rises to 38.9375 or higher. (Above the Green Balance Line. Take the Red Balance Line here because it is below the Green Balance Line)**

Figure 10–18 Broker's instruction from Investor's Dream software.

is not only down, it is accelerating in the downward direction. This normally is a sure sign that the market is about to turn around. (It did in this stock.)

The next horizontal portion shows the volume. The charts can be displayed in any manner you choose, or you can select for display only those you wish to look at on a regular basis.

The AO histogram is a display of the current Momentum, bar by bar. Remember that Momentum will always change well in advance of any Price change, thus giving you ample warning to either take profits and/or initiate positions in the opposite direction.

The AC histogram displays the Acceleration/deceleration of the Momentum. Repeating what was pointed out in earlier chapters, the AO is like reading tomorrow's *Wall Street Journal* today, and the AC is like reading the day after tomorrow's *Wall Street Journal*.

The Gator histogram displays exactly what the Alligator's Lips, Teeth, and Jaw are doing, and their relationship to each other. This display makes it extremely simple to visualize the exact current behavior of the Alligator. Notice also that the Gator looks into the future for eight bars, giving you a glance at what is to come.

The chart labeled EO is our proprietary method of counting the Elliott Wave. Because we are only interested in going with impulsive waves and staying out of reactive waves, this chart shows each on a simple line that changes color. In the chart above, there is a color change on the last few bars. This is another indication to stay long, as long as the impulsive color does not change. When the color does change, that is an Elliott Wave warning of a change in trend in the immediate future. Using this chart, it is quite easy to trade the Elliott Wave without bothering to know what wave you are in.

Another advantage of Investor's Dream is that the pull-down menu labeled "Broker's Instructions" will give you the exact wording of what to tell your broker when you place the various orders. Figure 10–18 shows an example.

Modern electronics, when combined with good research based on valid scientific assumptions, can produce the greatest potential in trading and investing in the twenty-first century. I again strongly urge you to download this software and practice all the examples given in this book. I am sure you will be amazed and pleased.

SUMMARY

The goal of this chapter has been to tie together everything we have discussed about trading using the Profitunity techniques. The entire approach is encapsulated on page 187, which shows both sides of the trading/investing coin including the *attitude* and the *tools,* which we combined into ATTITOOLS.

We devoted relatively little space to attitude in this chapter, but we will examine it more closely in the next chapter.

Under the heading of Tools, we outlined a six-step procedure to tie these techniques together in a usable and profitable approach. These steps were:

1. Finding a tradable market using the Alligator.
2. Taking the first signal, which should always be a fractal breakout.
3. Adding on aggressively after the first fractal is hit.
4. Immediately placing protection for your new position.

5. Letting the market play its own music.
6. Taking money to the bank after using one of four executive decisions for profit taking.

A final step should then be: Enjoying your profits.

These steps were followed by more examples demonstrating actual market action and trading in both stocks and commodities. These are typical Profitunity type trades where our goal is to take three to five times the amount of any trend move from the markets.

We ended with illustrations from our own proprietary software, which we believe to be unique in this industry. We also included a Web site address where you can download this software for practicing everything we have discussed in this book. If you would like to enable this software for real-time trading in both the stock and commodity markets, contact our office and we will make it available to you.

11

HOW TO BE A MASTER TRADER

NOW AND ZEN—STAYING IN THE ZONE

Ask any traders with experience and they will tell you that profiting from trading is 90 percent mental. And that remark is true. The question is: What is that 90 percent all about? You need to learn about this from a trader and not a psychologist or some "mental practitioner" who has never traded profitably, much less made a good living at trading over a period of time. You must find out what this mental part is all about.

This book is about getting into and trading from what athletes call the "zone." In a recent NBA playoff game, Michael Jordan made an astounding 55 points. In the interview immediately after the game, he was asked to explain his amazing performance. His answer was: "I was in the zone and couldn't get out." Michael often refers to the zone as his "fourth gear." What a problem! In this chapter, we are going to engineer a technique for not only getting into the zone, but staying in it by flowing (surfing) while trading and—probably most important of all—getting back into it when you fall out of it.

Professor Mihaly Csikszentmihalyi, the former chairman of the Department of Psychology at the University of Chicago, calls what happened to Michael Jordan, and others, *flow*. In fact he has written a book with that as its title. He says flow occurs when an individual reaches a state of concentration that is so intense it amounts to an absolute absorption in a particular activity, which may be in the context of sports, business, trading, or life.

I am greatly indebted to Dr. J. Mitchell Perry and Steve Jamison, who pointed out that this process can be generated and that it works and gets results. In their research, they have taken much from athletics and applied it successfully to business. We are going to make it specific to trading and investing, which can be even more important in giving you the kind of lifestyle that you want.

The state of flow so absorbs a person that it precludes doubt, anxiety, and fear. All distractions seem to fall away, and optimum winning performances happen "auto-magically." It is a state of mind that can be characterized by the terms:

1. Self-trust.
2. Engrossing enjoyment.
3. Focused relaxation.

Flowing in the zone is elusive. Most of us experience a great deal of frustration attempting to get into and/or staying in this state for any period of time. Our inability to remain in this state frustrates our ability to get desired results and/or compels us to use our primary defensive mechanism, *procrastination.* Just as a runny nose is a symptom of a cold, procrastination and not getting desired results are symptoms of being *out* of the zone.

Our most formidable opponent is none other than ourselves. As Pogo so truthfully put it, "We have met the enemy and it is us." It is our misused mental technology that beats us to the ground. This misuse often discourages us so much that we consider simply giving up and leading a "regular/normal/average" life. Our goal is to get in the zone and flow while using the same techniques to "automagically" take the stress from success.

RIGHT-BRAIN TRADING FOR LEFT-BRAIN PEOPLE

Our current educational system is heavily loaded with left-brain learning and neglects our right-brain zone. About the only activity that really teaches how to get into the zone is athletics. Most of our teachers neglect the "coaching" aspects of their job and substitute the inferior standardization of rote learning. There is too much math (left brain) and not enough music (right brain), and that hampers our success and enjoyment of living and winning.

What we know for sure is that the standard way of thinking that we learned in school (including especially business schools) is not very rewarding and produces many more life failures than successes. In commodity trading, for example, over 90 percent of all traders lose money consistently. The reason is that the common mode of thinking is not productive in the naturalistic world of the markets, and losing rather consistently produces a diminishing enjoyment of our tasks.

We will examine the power of logical trading based on the proper use of our mental equipment rather than the bipolar thinking of win/lose. By moving from left hemispheric (digital) thinking to right hemispheric (analog) thinking, we will gain financial and worry-free peace. We find that Chaos gives us choice, and by right choosing we create everything we value. We learn that the markets work just like our minds, and by understanding our minds we can use the markets in any fashion that suits us.

We must get to know our opponent, whom we will name Joe Gremlin ("Joe G"). The concept of *gremlins* became popular during World War II. They were blamed for anything that did not perform as it was designed to do. Joe G is the product of bipolar thinking and is our biggest roadblock to flowing in the zone.

In this chapter, we will examine what advantages and attributes we can bring to bear on this problem of enjoying maximum performance and winning consistently. We will formulate a procedure of getting into this flow auto-magically whenever we choose. We will look inside our brain/mind to see how we trap ourselves by the *thoughts* we think and the *words* we use.

Finally, using equipment we already have, we will devise a game plan to use in our trading and in our lives. We will tune up our motor to qualify for any race we choose. Our own best speed will bring victory, prizes, good feeling, and a joy of living unknown to most people. Let me welcome you now to the portals of your own personal zone. You are going to love it!

THE NEXT WAVE

The Key Rule: "Be-aware"

I use the term "be-a-ware" in the hyphenated form to remind us to not only be aware but also "beware" by getting to know your own greatest opponent to success in the markets and in life (Joe G). Once you go through this material and use these techniques, YOU WILL NEVER LOOK AT A BAR CHART THE SAME WAY AGAIN.

THE PARADOX OF PROFITS

One of the most interesting paradoxes in our world is how we have screwed around the whole concept of producing results and getting outstanding performance from ourselves in any activity. It is obvious that our current educational system is not producing consistently successful traders. Government employees and people on welfare and entitlements now outnumber the productive people in the United States. And our government seems to be in a war with the creative and rich, producing a prejudice against anyone who makes a great deal of money. This prejudice is just as injurious as and much more insidious than the more publicly debated gender, racial, or religious prejudice that we supposedly spend so much time fighting.

Why don't we spend more time enjoying producing as we flow through the waves of our own zone? Mainly, because we don't know how to distinguish or move between work and play. The highest paid group of individuals in this country is the professional sports stars. They make much more than most CEOs of large Fortune 500 companies. The CEOs are generally paid because of the performance of thousands of employees; the sports stars are paid for their "individual" performance. We are most interested here in our own individual performance in trading and investing. We do not want to be dependent on other people.

Let's go deeper into this difference and notice the words used to describe these two very different worlds. The CEO goes to WORK in the OFFICE. The athlete goes to PLAY on the PLAYING FIELD. Is there a hint here? Much more than a hint. The answer lies precisely in that distinction. Playing and flowing in the zone come from the right hemisphere of the brain. Working and toiling are always initiated and continued only in the left hemisphere.

When the playing field becomes the workplace, the athlete knows that it is time to get out. The 1997 Houston Rockets (my home team) included some of the world's best-ever players, including three of the all-time fifty best: Hakeem Olajuwon, Charles Barkley, and Clyde Drexler. In the playoff round against a much younger Utah Jazz team, the press kept pointing out how much older the Rockets were. Some were playing in the NBA when their younger opponents were still in grammar school. Most of the team had championship rings, and in 1997 their age didn't defeat them. Basketball had become a *profession,* and they had lost the joy of *playing.* After losing the first two games to the Jazz, Eddie Johnson, who had played for 15 years, came off the bench and made 34 points in 26 minutes. The crowd started yelling "EDDIE, EDDIE." Johnson's face lit up, and it was obvious to the entire basketball world that, this night, Eddie was in the zone and couldn't get out. He was *playing* his heart out. The smile on his face on the front page of the *Houston Chronicle* told the entire story. Sports at this level is not work—it is "hands off" play. It is the same feeling that you had when you first learned to balance a bicycle without your hand on the handlebars. Remember shouting, "Look, Mom, no hands." That is the feeling Eddie Johnson had that night in May 1997. He came off the bench and was worshipped by the Houston basketball fans. The team caught Eddie's fire; they started playing and smothered the Jazz. The first string of the Rockets were all standing, leading the chant "EDDIE, EDDIE." The Houston newspaper's headline summed it up with the headline—"They all *played* well tonight."

The only way to reach that particular level of play is to get into the zone and the flow. The paradox of this whole endeavor is that we were taught all the wrong ways of getting into the zone and few or none of the right ones.

THE DIFFERENCE BETWEEN WORKING AND PLAYING IS HOW YOU HANDLE CHAOS

The Science of Chaos has given us the most powerful and innovative tool of the past 2,500 years. Unfortunately, even the term *Chaos* carries a connotation of "complex, difficult to understand, unwieldy," when in fact it is almost the opposite. Chaos is not disorder, but rather a *much higher form of order.* To get a handle on understanding this new science, simply substitute the term "NEW INFORMATION" in place of "Chaos." Let's examine very closely how this relates to winning or losing. Whenever we encounter new information (Chaos), we have two choices. The one we almost always choose is to fit that new information into old categories: "Isn't that like . . ." or "It reminds me of. . . ." This seems a natural response—linking something new to something we are accustomed to doing. We are attempting to "organize" this new incoming information in order to give it familiar meaning. Familiarity lets us feel less risk and more predictability; we feel we have some control, and the more control we have the less *fear* we have. This is the key. We compulsively organize new incoming information to ward off fear. "I don't know what this younger generation is coming to; we were never like that." Translation: "This new incoming information from this younger generation does not fit my old categories and it really scares the hell out of me."

In the market, we attempt to compare this year's action with last year's or the most recent crash or whatever we can drag up to talk about. The problem with organizing anything is that as soon as it becomes organized it takes on a life of its own and its primary motivation is to *survive*. Everything from junior proms to political parties wants to ensure its own survival. Four organizing forces move more money around than any country on earth:

1. War.
2. Medicine.
3. Insurance.
4. Religion.

No nation has as much economic clout as any one of these four. Ask yourself: What do they have in common? Exactly what every organization in the world has, including your brain structure: *survival*.

1. War breaks things and kills people.
2. Medicine patches up those who weren't killed and makes them available to fight again.
3. Insurance takes care, financially, of the supporters and kin of those who were killed.
4. Religion takes care of those who are killed.

The common thread is *survival*. An old country and western song lyric points out that everyone wants to go to heaven but no one wants to die. Survival is the motivation that keeps organizations together. And all four of the above organizations tap into our own personal desire to live rather than die. More than anything, we want this organization we call "ourselves" to go on surviving and not die.

In the market, when trends go on longer than we expect, we call it market mania. Range-bound markets also seem to go on longer than we expect. The usual way an organization attempts to survive is by fitting new information into old categories (Figure 11–1). We will distort this new information in whatever way is necessary to keep our old categories (organization) alive. We begin learning this around two years old when we first decide, "I want it my way." We often refer to this era as the "terrible twos." It is just the beginning.

CHAOS Really Means *New Information*

The Most Important Question We Can Ask Is
HOW DO YOU HANDLE NEW INCOMING INFORMATION?

Your Two Choices Are:

- **(a)** Massage (distort) it to fit into OLD CATEGORIES (creates overwhelm and/or boredom) or you can
- **(b)** Let the New Information (Chaos) Organize itself (which means letting go = **RISK**).

Figure 11–1 Handling new information.

The question now arises: What other ways are there to deal with new incoming information? Actually, there is only one: Let the new incoming information organize itself. Scientifically, the new Science of Chaos, nonlinear dynamics, and/or fractal geometry are about the only approaches that emphasize allowing the new incoming information to organize itself. The new viewpoint says to deal with new information by letting it organize itself with as little interference from old categories as is humanly possible. In art and music, it is known as creativity or improvisation, and it is apparently generated and handled with our little used right hemisphere.

The simplest organization I can think of is a hydrogen atom. It contains one proton, made up of three quarks, and one electron. It just can't get much simpler than that. These two particles, the electron and the proton, come together to form this organization. In the room where you are now, trillions of these small organizations are floating around in the air. They are just doing their thing and following the path of least resistance. On this same playing field, there are some much more complex organizations we call oxygen atoms. The oxygen organization is about sixteen times larger than the smaller hydrogen organization, and, like the hydrogen, trillions of these atoms are floating around the room you are in now.

With that many atoms bouncing off each other, they are bound to come into each other's gravitational field. Atoms, like planets, have their own gravitational fields. In fact, one way to look at gravity is that it is the primary force that attempts to hold current organizations intact. When you get tired, you can literally feel the earth's gravitational pull trying to get you to join it. If you get tired enough, you will just "let go" and join more closely with the earth's larger field—you lie down. If everything else is working properly, this "giving up" will allow your organization to recoup, gather energy, and go on its way a bit stronger for the experience.

Back to the atoms. This feeling of the presence of another organization is new information, and here comes the most crucial decision any organization can make (Figure 11–2). That decision is whether to

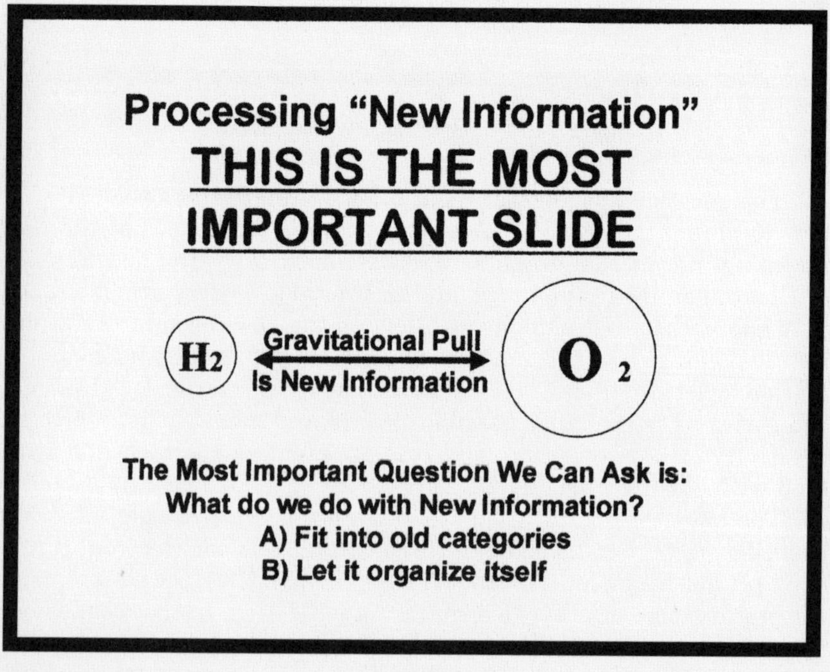

Figure 11–2 The most important concept: What do you do with new information?

"let go" of the current organization, or, more likely, to keep the current organization and "distort" the new incoming information into old categories. In fact, 99.99999 percent of the time, the hydrogen atom makes the choice to hold on to its current organization and remain a hydrogen atom. "After all," it might say, "ever since I can remember, I have been a hydrogen atom and I suppose that is what I should be and I further suppose that I will just remain that way—it has always been good enough." We do exactly the same thing in the markets, and that is what keeps us in our current trance of either losing or limiting our winnings.

But here is the kicker: About 0.00001 percent of the time, the hydrogen atom makes a different decision. It makes a "TRANCE-ENDING" decision to "let go" and just see what happens. Instead of distorting the incoming "new information" (Chaos), it *lets the new incoming information organize itself.* The difference is that instead of "solving the problem of new incoming information" (the gravitational pull), it allows *real creativity* to come in by letting the new information organize itself. The result is WATER, which is very different from either hydrogen or oxygen atoms. Basically, it has no characteristics of either of its components. It has literally "trance-ended" to a different and more complicated organization that also gives it more freedom. Now it has a choice of being not only a gas (steam) but also a liquid (water) or a solid (ice). With the higher levels of organization, more alternatives of behavior are created.

We know that the market is at least a five-dimensional animal, so it is no surprise that trading a two-dimensional chart (price and time) leaves a lot of room for improvement. The entire basis of the Profitunity approach is to tap into these higher and somewhat more complicated levels to "trance-end" our losing behavior and create more profits. One specific part of our organization that does more to defeat us than any other part is our "belief system." All belief systems create a trance of one level or another.

When the hydrogen atom decides to give up and let the new information organize itself, it is necessary that it be in a playful mood. It is, in human terms, in the alpha brain wave pattern; it feels secure, focused, and relaxed. We must share that same space to create trading at a higher level. So there is ample justification for studying the comparison between work and play, and how world-class athletes get into their own zones.

When we think about sports, we picture them being played on a *playing* field. We ask: "Who is *playing* this weekend?" "Do you know the score of the *game?"* On the other side of this equation is the obvious fact that WORK IS WORK.

When you go to work, you work. You don't go to work to play. Most people can't even imagine that concept. You spend some of the money you make at work to pay to see others *play.* Now there is an interesting concept. There seems little to connect your working and their playing, but they all are the same game. We just "play" it in a different manner. While we all want to perform in an optimum manner, we (the workers) and we (the players) go at it in very opposite ways.

> **I'm a firm believer in the theory that people only do their best at things they truly enjoy. It is difficult to excel at something you don't enjoy.**
>
> **—Jack Nicklaus**

According to Jack Nicklaus, you do your best only when you are really enjoying what you are doing. You are so focused on the *process* of what you are doing that extraneous thoughts are not present—you have no anxiety, you are relaxed, you trust yourself, and you have a high level of confidence in your abilities. *Any goal is exponentially more difficult to accomplish if you dislike the experience.* When you are on a roll, it is effortless, smooth, and fun. In other words, you are in the zone and flowing with the experience. You are letting the new incoming information create your life and your experience.

Perry and Jamison point out that when you are in the zone, four conditions are present:

1. Enjoyment—you are having a blast.
2. Focus—you have keen awareness and alertness.
3. Relaxation—you are free from extreme anxiety.
4. Self-trust—you have confidence in your judgment.

None of the above conditions is descriptive of what we are taught about making a living and "working." According to Webster's dictionary, the synonyms for work are "labor, toil, grind." It says nothing about enjoyment, play, fun, and so on. What we have learned in school and in our culture is that work and play are opposites.

My contention here is that profitable trading and investing is much more like play than work. Deep inside, we each know that we perform best when having a good time and not worrying about the outcome, but we have been taught that it is necessary to suffer. I grew up in a very fundamental Protestant atmosphere, where the meaning of the verb *tribulate* was explained every Sunday morning. We were also taught that too much enjoyment was the devil's work and we would pay for that enjoyment over and over again in hell. We now know that *we* are that devil and hell's gatekeeper.

Enjoyment and employment were never considered to be synonyms. Most of the times when traders feel "I should be working harder," they are wrong. They should be working "easier" and making sure that they are taking the "work" out of "trading." If you have been "working hard" at trading or learning to trade, I strongly suggest an opposite approach.

Less enlightened coaches tell us, "No pain—no gain," and we accept it because it fits perfectly with our erroneous learning. What it should say is: "no pain—no gain—you're insane."

Do you know why we are so uptight in America? Because the Puritans came over here and the really fun people stayed behind.

—Roseanne Barr

THE BIG TRAP—THE TWO-OPTION LIMIT

"Win or lose" is a two-option trap. It creates "polar thinking." It places all possible results into a winner or loser class, and there will always be millions more losers than winners. But that doesn't stop us; check out the Lotto players. The newspapers carry stories about the winners but never about the losers. Our effort here is about winning, learning, accomplishing, and taking the stress out of successful trading. Polar thinking does not allow these alternatives. "Winning is not the best thing, it is the only thing." Whenever we put on a trade or make an investment, we immediately monitor the market and/or other people's opinion to see whether we are a winner or a loser. We then become "floor and ceiling" traders: we are happily on the ceiling or sadly on the floor depending upon how we are distorting the new incoming information into their old categories.

Actually, the win/lose scenario is a lose-only situation. So you are champion this year. One day soon, someone will break your record and then where will you be? No one writes about the second best. Sometimes, winning can be even more stressful than losing because the next question is always: "What are you going to do to top this?"

Legendary basketball coach John Wooden of UCLA was so aware of the dangers of polar thinking that he would not allow the use of the word "win." He also would not permit his players to use the word "beat" when talking about the other team. He insisted they use the phrase "outscored the other team." Wooden was well aware of how dangerous polar thinking is to performance and enjoyment. Polar thinking is equally destructive in the stock and commodity markets.

In trading and investing, as in sports, it is always actually *just you against you.* Analysis, buying, selling, profits, losses—all come down simply to the level of performance *you* are able to bring out of yourself. The harsh "win/lose" framework will destroy your potential and your happiness while raising your stress level and your blood pressure and shortening your life, your profits, and your enjoyment of living.

Let's explore in more depth the product of polar thinking. Polar thinking creates a devil that sits and whispers into your left ear or sometimes moves into your brain and decides to live there forever unless you take charge and kick that devil out. Once you do, you can tell him that he is just not welcome there any more.

Trading is a state of being, not doing.

—Bill Williams

MORE ABOUT JOE GREMLIN

There is a critical, judgmental, negative voice in all of us. Part of it is there naturally, but most of it has been learned from our teachers. We use it against ourselves to judge, intimidate, and threaten ourselves. The price we pay for this free loader is our own personal initiative and the success we could have if that part of us could be kept in control or used judiciously. Our personal Joe G takes most of the joy out of living. Our Joe G is born with us, and its job is to keep us out of trouble. In the market, it becomes our risk–reward warden and generally evaluates, from a negative standpoint, every move we make and every thought we think.

Whenever you have a positive, life-enriching thought, Joe G raises its critical head to point out all the things that might go wrong, including a meteorite that just might fall on our heads. Throughout our life, anything that goes wrong or off course is a signal to Joe G to jump up and say, "I told you so," "You shouldn't be trading with that many contracts," "You are going to lose everything that you have ever worked for."

A FEW WORDS ABOUT THE GREMLIN-TAMING PROCESS

Taming your gremlin is a simple (not to be confused with easy) process. It can even be an enjoyable process that takes practice and persistence. Taming your gremlin requires the sort of effort implied by words like "allowing" and "letting," not by words like "trying" and "straining." Three basic processes are involved in taming your gremlin:

1. Simply noticing.
2. Choosing and playing with options.
3. Being in process.

The problem with Joe G's polar thinking is that we have only one option. It is a black-and-white world. "All abortions are bad," "All Indians are lazy," "You can't trust lawyers," and so on. Think what would happen if we had only two choices at a traffic light. (Oops! My own Joe G almost said a red light instead of a traffic light.) What if there were no yellow lights. Every light you approach would bring up anticipation and fear that the light might turn red with no warning and you might be in trouble. That kind of situation is a roadblock to your creativity and your profitability. It is like pointing a pistol at your own head and wondering whether the gun is loaded or not.

No one has the power over you that your gremlin has. To tame him, you must start by *simply noticing*.

To simply notice is to "be-aware"—to pay attention. It is important to notice *how* you are, not *why* you are how you are. Thinking about and simply noticing are two very different activities. Thinking about *removes* you from your present experience. Simply noticing puts you *in contact with* your present experience. Simply noticing is much more exciting and productive than thinking about. Simply noticing is a tool. When you are simply noticing, you are grounded in reality. However, when you focus your awareness on your thoughts, fantasies, ideas, and memories, you are involved in the world of make-believe.

It is often helpful to describe this gremlin and let us share with you our view of our own gremlin. Our goal in this section is for you to glance at how self-hurtful it is for you to entertain this gremlin. Consider the tremendous damage that it does to you every day that you listen to it, because whenever you listen to it, it has control over you.

Gremlin-Free Trading

Highly paid professional athletes are often thought of as getting paid to play children's games. What we often don't see is that to perform at this level, the athletes must play these games *like children*—with a spirit of self-trust, awareness, enthusiasm, belief, imagination, enjoyment, and, most of all, being *completely in the present moment.* Whenever we are completely in the present moment, there isn't time or space for gremlins to act up. In this flowing in the zone, we are completely involved in the process rather than the prize. And this can happen only when we really live in the present. So the first step in taming Joe G is to simply notice him at work. Awareness is your tool. It will allow you to differentiate yourself from your gremlin.

To put this in the here and now, take a moment and just focus on your breathing. Do it now and *just be aware* of what is happening. Most people change their style of breathing as soon as they start noticing the process. You probably started to take deeper breaths. That was not the assignment. You were only to become aware of your breathing, not to change it. Or perhaps you stopped breathing for a moment. What is really going on is a *search* for a *problem to solve.* How am I supposed to be breathing? *You were looking for an old category in which to put this instruction.*

Let's do another exercise. This time, I want you to simply make yourself (or fake it, if you need to) yawn. Become aware of what is happening as you are forcing the yawn. For almost everyone, at a certain point in the faking, the yawn takes on a life of its own and becomes real. That exact point where it takes on a life of its own is the difference between thinking about and allowing. When it is on its own, you are allowing and you can become AWARE.

Trying hard is the opposite of allowing. Let's do one other simple but not easy exercise. The assignment this time is to do something you have already done probably a hundred times today. You certainly know how to do it well, only now let's do it on purpose. Here it is. Swallow five times as quickly as you possibly can. Before you read on, try it now.

What were your results? With most of us it gets more difficult each time and many simply cannot do it five times without pausing for a while. What is happening is our Joe G is not equipped to "allow" and "let go." The only way to swallow correctly is to "let go" and let our mind/body do what it is capable of doing. Think about it.

The final exercise to do right now is to play a simple game of "Now I Am Aware Of." Using only one sense at a time, and going very slowly, simply focus your awareness on one aspect of your surrounding environment after another. Slowly, as thoughts come into your mind (a product of Chaos), simply notice them and let them go. Gently channel your awareness back by returning to the phrase "Now I am aware of. . . . "

Your Joe G will not want you to spend any time at all with this exercise. In fact, if you are reading this and have not done these exercises, that is a sure sign that you are NOT AWARE at this moment.

Joe G doesn't like you to be aware because you might change the environment, and any change means a change in categories. Joe is the KEEPER OF THE CATEGORIES. He knows that clouding your actual experience with preconceived notions will keep you from experiencing the excitement of the current moment, and he is well aware that excitement is a prerequisite for enjoying this life.

Joe G wants you to believe that if you go over and over the facts and factors surrounding the market, a trade, and/or yourself, you will eventually figure your way out of the current dilemma (of losing). He prefers you to "think about" rather than "experience." He knows that when you are experiencing your feelings, your awareness is centered on you rather than on him, and when your awareness is not on him, he has no effect on you.

In our private tutorials, we insist on the participants' experiencing the market and trading while they are attending. Many of them who consistently lose would prefer to just come, listen, take notes, and then work on their trading at home where no one is watching. This is a Catch-22 and doesn't work because they are permitting Joe G to run their trading life. We don't allow that. Often, they will maintain, "I want to learn my own way and at my own pace." Come in Joe, you can be in charge just as you almost always are.

I change not by trying to be something other than I am,
I change by being fully aware of how I am.
—Ancient Buddhist saying

REALITY AND DUALITY

Joe G will insist that your own categories and approach to life are necessary to your well-being. He may even frighten you with catastrophic expectations of a future of losing, reminding you of the nasty consequences of your acts in past situations when you did not listen to him. Taming Joe G depends on your being in reality, not in duality. When you are in reality, which means that you are letting the new incoming information organize itself rather than distorting it by stuffing it into old categories, your energy flows easily and your perceptions are accurate. You feel wholeness and an "in-touchness" with the market and reality.

When, on the other hand, your energy is tied up in internal conflict created by having to know which category to fit the new information in, you don't have much energy left over to experience the reality of the market and enjoy your body or the world around you. In this state of being, you will feel anxious, disgruntled, bottled up, and/or empty. In short, you will not enjoy yourself, the market, or trading. Joe G much prefers that you live in this state of duality.

Having spent a career as a psychologist dealing with the integration of mind/brain/body, I have seen undetected gremlins cause asthma, heart attacks, colitis, headaches, backaches, neuroses, psychoses, and just about any other sort of ailment, including losing in the markets.

A CLOSER LOOK AT GETTING INTO PROCESS: WHY WORDS ARE IMPORTANT

Being in process means paying attention to what is happening now, not what happened a minute ago or what might happen in the next five minutes. As Ram Dass puts it so well, "BEHERENOW."

Often, when doing workshops for traders around the world, we start off by displaying the following on a slide or written on a board:

Opportunity isnowhere

Then we ask the traders to write down that phrase correctly. Over 95 percent write:

OPPORTUNITY IS NO WHERE

Only 5 percent (and often less) write:

OPPORTUNITY IS NOW HERE

The indication is clear. With 95 percent of us, Joe Gremlin is in charge.

No matter which way you read the sign, *you have already made a judgment about the future.* The first way (OPPORTUNITY IS NO WHERE) is exclusive. The second way (OPPORTUNITY IS NOW HERE) is inclusive. If we read the sign the first way, we have already made a judgment about the future. It comes straight from Joe Gremlin, our Critical Adviser. It also puts us automatically into the future and prejudges the future as being a rotten, no-reward land. We have just doubled the odds against our ever winning. The part of us that is in charge (Joe G) is against us, so what chances do we have? Basically, none.

I like the illustration of a videotape recorder. The tape on the left reel is the past and the tape on the right reel is the future.

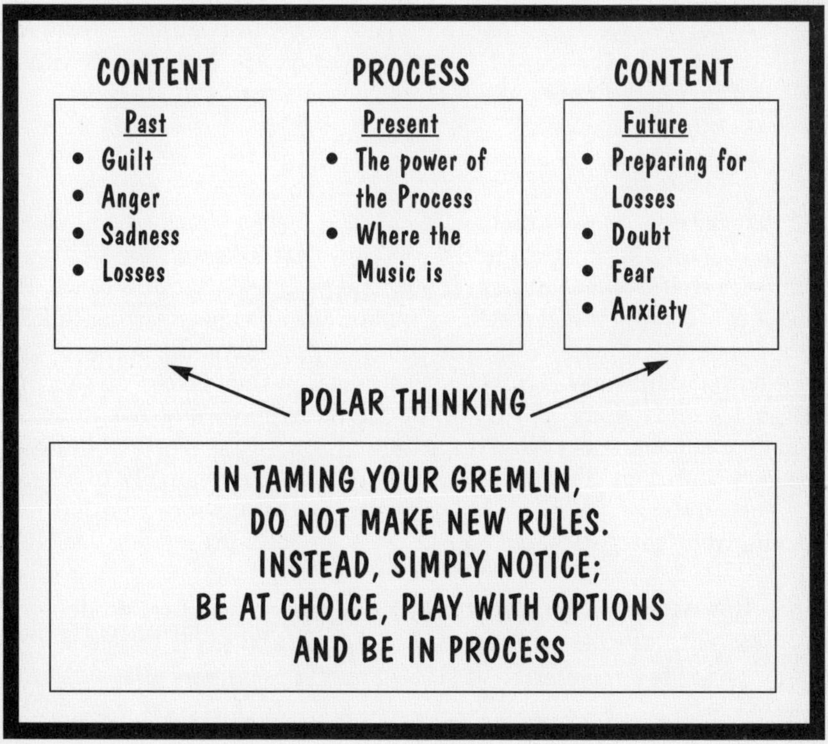

The recording head is the present, and results will always be in the present.

In taming your Joe G, you get a vantage point by using your awareness for grounding yourself. Spotting and grounding your gremlin can often be very challenging. He will try to ask you to believe in the limits that he has set for you. And he knows that if he can get you to believe in those limits, he will always have control over your potential. If you are unaware of Joe G's habits and behavior, he has a decided advantage. You can detect Joe G's work when you begin to hear "You can't" coming from inside your head. Joe G is smart enough to mix into the can'ts some real can'ts like "You can't fly," "You can't grow another three inches taller," "You can't grow younger." Then he will mix in some can'ts that aren't really can'ts for you.

One effective method of dealing with this strategy is to change the word can't into "won't" or "will" or "choose" or "choose not to." Next, you might add the words "until now." For example you might change:

I can't make a profit trading
to
I have chosen not to make a profit in trading
to
Until now I have chosen not to make a profit in trading
to
Now, I choose to make a profit in trading.

As you read these statements, can you feel in your body/mind Joe G's grip loosening just a bit? If you can, that is a wonderfully great sign—a terrific omen! In fact, if you really do feel that difference, the battle is over; it is just a matter of time. Joe G has been trying to keep you in a tunnel of no results, and you have just found the secret of getting out of the tunnel: LET GO. The question then comes up that if I let go I cannot know exactly what might happen, and not knowing would produce anxiety. One definition of anxiety is: the gap between the now and then. The way to eliminate that gap is simply to stay in the here and now. Joe G will always attempt to convince you that preserving your categories and habits is the same as preserving your life.

It is more important that you be able to regulate enjoyment within yourself, regardless of circumstance, than it is for you to be able to modify circumstances. It simply comes in handy more often.

—Richard D. Carson

When you drive your car, you are almost always in the future—where you are going—and that is why you sometimes don't remember passing through a town, although you obviously did it well enough not to have an accident. The reason you don't remember doing it is because you were in the future and not thinking about the present.

Remember how exasperated you get when you are behind people who are driving with fear of having a wreck? They are so careful that they are dangerous. Have you ever gunned the engine so as to quickly get around someone who is being too careful?

What's happening? Their Joe Gremlin is in charge and working overtime, thrusting them into the future with fear of having a wreck. Often, they either do have one or cause someone else to have one. They are not in the zone or the flow, and they become dangerous to those who are.

Your relationship with Joe G is lifelong. Begin now to acknowledge him fully, remembering that acknowledgment and entanglement are not the same.

The message of the 1960s—"turn on, tune in, and drop out"—has changed for the millennium to: "drop into the present, get in the zone and flow."

Whenever your attention and energy leave the present and drop into the fictitious past or future, you might as well "turn out the lights; the party's over," as Don Meredith used to say on Monday Night Football.

A PSYCHOLOGICAL TOOL—WHATEVER YOU FOCUS ON EXPANDS

If you focus on past hurts, losses, and disappointments, they will expand. If you focus on all you are going to do in the future, the future will expand and move further away from the present. However, if you focus on the present, it will expand; your wins will be here, now, in the present. Remember when you purchased your last new car. All of a sudden that particular model and style started meeting you at almost every corner. Did half the population just buy the same car as you? Of course not; you simply started focusing on that model, and your attention received the command to NOTICE that car closely, and so you did. It is that simple; that is the way it works. Whatever you focus on expands. If you focus on process, process expands and is followed by an inevitable expansion in positive results.

Focusing on content or the prize takes you away from process and production. We tell everyone we work with that the most inappropriate question to ask at the end of the trading day is: "Did we make any money?" That is irrelevant! The only relevant question is: "Were we in tune with the market?" You will have some days when you will indeed be in tune with the market and lose money, but, overall, you will be a winner in more ways than just profits.

WEBOMETRY

Webometry, our particular approach to trading, has developed over almost forty years of actively trading in the stock and commodity markets. I was offered well into seven figures for this approach if I would (1) not share it with anyone and (2) quit trading it myself. This offer was made by a world-renowned trader who is in the same financial and trading class as George Soros. I turned the offer down because the price was much too low! Webometry is our summary description of our approach to the market, which we have covered thoroughly in previous chapters. It is taken from the strategy of spiders:

1. You build a nice web surrounding the environment you are now in. After you have completed the web, you go to the middle and simply wait.
2. Once a bug hits the web, you leave the center, get the bug, bring it back home (the center of the web), eat it, rest, relax, and wait for the next bug to hit the web. We do this in trading by placing buy stops above the market, and sell stops below the market, and then just relaxing and letting the market decide which price will hit the web first.
3. An important spider observation at this point: The spider does not care or worry about the bugs that *do not* hit the web. It knows that throughout eons of time and billions of generations of spiders, there have been enough bugs for all the spiders, and it can survive quite well, thank you, on what nature provides for it. As traders, we know that by using this webometry approach the market will provide for us quite well, and we need not worry about the future as long as our web is intact. Whenever you are truly focusing on the process of performance in

the present tense, you are in a state of *BEING* rather than a state of *DOING*. In that state, your mind will *effortlessly* and *automatically* begin to seek out supporting evidence, information, and opportunities to help you win in trading or whatever else you may be involved in.

4. As traders, we have learned that there really is a Holy Grail and it can be expressed in these five simple words: WANT WHAT THE MARKET WANTS! Isn't that great!? We don't have to boss and run the market. We simply have to relax, spin our web, and wait. That is the focus of good spiders and great traders.

There is an old saying: "Think you can or think you can't—either way, you will be right." That saying is true because whatever you focus on expands.

> **I only care about one thing, the present.**
>
> **—Jimmy Johnson, coach of the Miami Dolphins**

THE CYBERNETICS OF TRADING . . . AND THINKING

Cybernetics is a Greek term that means "steersman" or the man who controls a large boat with a small rudder. Today, that term has a scientific and market meaning: "leverage." It means that a smaller object can control and has the power to move a much larger object. For example, a commodity margin of $2,000 can control 50 times that much in bonds. Options create large leverage in the stock markets. This same concept works in our thinking also.

Words are rudders—small objects that control much larger concepts and processes of thinking or analysis. One of these larger objects is you and your potential performance in the markets.

Notice the words that are used in any advertising in a newspaper or on radio or TV. These power words have the effect of taking you into the future and making you believe whatever you are hearing or reading. Advertisers know the power of words, and they choose them with extreme care. They know that you and I will react in predictable ways to these words and they (the advertisers, through their words) thereby control us. They can get us to voluntarily take money out of our pockets and give our money to them. That is the power of leverage.

That being true, it becomes extremely important to examine the words we use to leverage ourselves. This leverage is even more important than the financial leverage we get with commodities and options. Our words to ourselves become habitual and therefore unnoticed and unexamined. We can divide our language into two categories: (1) inclusion and (2) exclusion.

For example, if a family goes to Walt Disney World and you ask the child for his or her reaction, the child will probably say, "It was great." That is the language of inclusion. Ask the parents and they will most likely respond with something like: "It wasn't bad—not as crowded as we expected, and the prices weren't really that bad. All in all, it wasn't a bad day at all." That is the language of exclusion.

Notice how a child describes *what is* while most adults describe *what isn't.* The child is more in touch with reality and is not as habituated as the adults. In our particular culture, the longer we live the more we become habituated to the language of exclusion: "The market didn't treat me all that bad today." The language of exclusion is a sure sign that Joe Gremlin is in charge. Speaking in the language of negatives, Joe G tells us what *isn't* instead of what *is.* He hates to stay in the present. He loves equally the past and the future, and finds ways of talking about what isn't.

Remember when Richard Nixon said, "I'm not a crook." He never said, "I am innocent." Politicians are excellent practitioners of letting their Joe Gremlin run the show. Lately, political campaigns have turned totally to Joe Gremlin tactics. Each candidate talks about what the opponents *are not* instead of talking about what they *are.*

"Joe Gremlin Speak" is also the language we most often use among ourselves. If we like a certain analysis, we say, "That isn't a bad setup." Does that mean it is a good setup? If we feel good, we say, "I can't complain about my health." Does that mean we really do feel good? "Nobody gives you a better deal than we do." Does that mean that you give a good deal? Who knows? What we do know is: that kind of language does not produce results because every exclusionary response is limiting and puts Joe Gremlin in charge, and Joe is not a winner.

When Joe Gremlin speaks, we pay for it in attitude and performance. Joe is cautionary rather than compelling, self-limiting rather than expansive. Joe moves our focus from what is to what isn't.

On the other hand, the language of inclusion is an accelerator when it comes to performing and winning in the market. Remember:

> Our words create our images and
>
> Our images create our emotions and

Our emotions control our perceptions and
Our perceptions control our performance and
Our performance controls our prizes.

So let's get the order straight. When we start down the appropriate path, the results take care of themselves through the cybernetic principle of leverage. The language of inclusion moves from ideas and analysis to trading and profits.

One of the main characteristics of winners is that they can take a bad situation with the odds against them and turn it to their favor. That happens because their underlying structure makes it so. No one wins all the time. If they did, there would be no game, including the game of life.

Losers always have a large, fully developed Joe Gremlin who is usually ruining the show. From these losers, we hear Joe's voice saying, "This always seems to happen to me," "I always get in too late," "The floor always sees and runs my stops." A piece of priceless advice is:

Keep Your *Eye* off the *Prize.*

How many Lotto players have you heard say: "This is the week I am going to win." Don't get me wrong. Winning is great. That's why they invented score cards and P & L statements. But keeping your eye on the prize lets Joe G sneak in and grab the rudder to steer you in the wrong direction. He creates pressure, and pressure makes you stupid. Being in the *zone* is the same thing as being in *process.* And being in process means being in the ever-present *here and now.* Success is learning and improving, more than winning the prize. Life itself is a journey designed to be enjoyed during the *process* rather than only when looking forward to the prize.

To get into the zone, you must be enjoying yourself. The world, the market, you, and I all work through the same underlying natural principles of "give and take," "advance and retreat." When you breathe, you inhale, take whatever oxygen your body needs, and then exhale. When you get into the zone and start to flow, you surge forward. When you get a setback, as we all do, you recover quickly and surge again. This is exactly what a market does, whether it is trending or range-bound. Trending markets surge, then move back, and then begin to surge again. In a range-bound area, the market surges and then turns around and surges in the other direction. The underlying structure of both is: surge–recover–surge.

Surge means focus, awareness, and self-trust during and after the performance. Then Joe Gremlin shows up and wants to share the stage with you. That gives you the opportunity to recover quickly and get on with the next surge. Most of us do the opposite. We let Joe Gremlin run the show and then worry about why we can't win in this game. If that is your problem or even a part of your problem, we will outline a process of gaining control back and trading the market the way you know deep inside that you can. If you didn't realize this, deep inside, you wouldn't have spent all that money on lectures, courses, books, software, and other materials, to try to make it happen. If what you are looking for could be found in the places you have been looking, you would not be reading this book. We are going to make it happen, in the ever-present HERE AND NOW.

This is our game plan for handcuffing Joe and letting the real *you* come out and play. You'll play like a child, with the same intensity and the same enjoyment of winning. The first thing you need is an anchor to keep you in touch with reality.

The Anchor

Neuro Linguistic Programming (NLP) practitioners use what they refer to as anchors. Anchors are rituals that bring oneself back in touch with the present by creating a specific repeating pattern of behavior prior to performing. These "pretask" routines bring the mind and body into focus in present with and emphasize the process that is about to begin. It is said that Houdini, one of the world's most famous performers, had extreme stage fright throughout his entire career. He had a routine that he always went through just before the curtain opened on any performance. He would jump up and down again and again while repeating aloud, "I love my audience, I love my audience." And when the curtain was closed after his performance, the audience always loved him back.

Notice world-class basketball players shooting foul shots. They always repeat the same preliminary routine. Charles Barkley twirls the ball three times and then bounces it on the floor four times. This is his preperformance anchor or trigger. It gets him into the present tense and the alpha brain level.

Some acts clear our mind and place us solidly in the present, fully focused on the job we are about to do. We are all creatures of habit. When you took a shower this morning, I would bet that you dried off exactly the way you did yesterday, last week, and last year. So why not take this powerful force of habit and use it to put Joe Gremlin in his place?

The primary purpose of an anchor ritual is to make it much easier to relax and fall into your "comfort zone," which allows you to focus, put tension aside, and stay in the present. The familiarity makes the zone easy to reach. You have done these rituals many times before, but maybe not on purpose.

In training people to become successful speculators and traders, we also insist that they do what we call the morning pages. This idea came from Julia Cameron, a creativity coach who works with creative artists who have become stuck and lost their creativity. We insist that when trainees get up in the morning, the first thing they must do after going to the bathroom is sit down and write three pages. It doesn't matter how they start; they are simply recording their thinking. If they think, "I don't have anything to write about," they write down "I don't have anything to write about." We have had more positive life-changing feedback from that one exercise than from any others we have ever done in over 40 years of being in the market and working with traders and investors. The reason this ritual gets such astounding results is that it gets Joe Gremlin out of your left hemisphere and lets you drop into your zone and flow more easily. When some people first hear of this required task, they say, "Oh no, I could never do that on a regular basis." In a couple of weeks, they change their tune to "I could never do without this; it has changed my life and I will do it till I die." I personally do it every day, rain or shine, feeling good or not. It clears the deck and lets me free myself of all the negative success-bashing self-talk from Joe. And one of the big features is that it produces a ritual to do each morning before anything else.

> **Repetition brings familiarity, and familiarity is the opposite of the unknown.**
>
> **—Steven Levenkron**

After this ritual (or whatever other ritual feels good to you) is securely in place, you are ready for the next step: *pre*forming your *per*formance.

In this step, you visualize what you are going to do. Jack Nicklaus says that he sees a mental movie before he hits every shot. In his mind, he has never missed a putt. What a great way to get into the zone and flow. This visualizing is a catalyst that gets the energy moving. In the morning pages, we often suggest that you carry on a dialogue with Joe Gremlin: ask him what he wants this day and what it would take to get him out of your way so that you can create results. Often, startlingly impressive truths come from Joe.

Many psychological experiments have been conducted with sports participants—for example, dividing groups into different parts and having one part actually practice a routine like shooting foul shots in basketball. Another group spends the same amount of time "imagining" and visualizing that they are shooting foul shots but are not on the court and do not have a basketball in their hands. After weeks of having both groups spend the same amount of time on their respective activities, the visualizing-only group usually makes the same improvement as the group that was actually doing the exercise. This should impress on you the value of the mental self-talk we engage in all day every day. Just make sure that all your self-talk is inclusive rather than exclusive.

WHAT BIOFEEDBACK IS ALL ABOUT

Basically, we know that our brains produce measurable amounts of electrical current every minute of our lives. These varying currents produce different patterns in the form of waves, and the shape and frequency of these waves depend on what we are thinking about at that moment. For example, your brain wave pattern while in a large winning position is very different from the pattern when you are a significant loser. The real question here is whether the brain wave pattern is the result of the perception of the situation or is the *cause* of the situation. These differences in brain wave patterns can easily be measured and monitored on an oscilloscope.

The brain waves that have been most studied are the alpha brain wave patterns, which are between 7 and 13 cycles per second. This frequency seems to build a context where one feels focused, relaxed, self-confident, and creative. It is more than coincidence that these are the same words used to describe one's feeling while in the zone.

For our trading trainees, we prepared a series of eight audiocassettes specifically designed to teach them how to get into the alpha zone quickly and easily. These are now available to the general public.

This concept is important to understand because this is exactly the way that good visualization works. By visualizing an act in the context of the alpha wave frequency band, your mind actually programs your entire mind/body configuration to drop into the zone and begin the flow. It is quite important to note that we are saying you "drop" into the zone rather than effortfully "climb up" into the zone. Getting into the zone, like good trading, is much more an activity of "letting go" rather than doing something difficult. Letting go produces a TRANCE-ENDING experience. In fact, effort is almost totally counterproductive to getting into the zone. To aid in letting go and dropping into the zone, there are four keys:

1. Forget the prize and focus on the process. See yourself putting on and managing good trades rather than calculating how much profit you are going to make with each trade. Visualize the process.
2. Be very *very* specific. Generalities simply don't work with this part of the mind. For the mind to give orders, the orders must be understandable and extremely specific. Specificity comes from detail, and details should include all the senses. See it happening, feel it happening, hear it happening, smell it happening, and even taste it happening. Details are the fuel of visualization. The more fuel you have, the more power you have and the further you can go on this particular trip.
3. Make it good. Visualize the entire trade progressing perfectly. Remember what Jack Nicklaus said: he never missed a putt in his mind. It takes a bit of courage to see your life and trading as perfection—we usually dismiss them with "just good enough" or "That is just too good to be true." It will be as good as you make it.
4. If something is worth doing at all, it is worth doing over and over again. While what we call the morning pages are designed to be done the first thing in the morning, we repeat the activity at any time of the day when we have a problem or need to get our minds straight. I have often awakened during the night thinking about some problem. After turning and tossing for a while, I get up and write some pages. This has never failed to either find an appropriate solution or dismiss the problem. When Tiger Woods was winning his first Masters Tournament in Augusta, Georgia, you may have noticed that as he was walking down each fairway, he did practice swings. Most likely he was programming his arms and shoulders to remember exactly how his body should move on the next shot.

These steps are like setting a thermostat. If the thermostat is working properly, you need only set it and forget it. The rest happens auto*magically.*

A psychological axiom states that we will see something when we believe it. The steps above will set your belief thermostat to the degree that you may see whatever you desire. The combination of believing and seeing opens up your perceptive mechanisms. The means of developing your wishing become as clear and obvious as the next step when climbing a set of stairs.

> **In the province of the mind, what one believes to be true either is true or becomes true. . . .**
>
> **—John Lilly, Programming and Metaprogramming the Human Biocomputer**

At this point, we have created an anchor, a reference point, and a thermostatic setting for our performance, and we have completed our visualization of the process in rich and varied details that we repeat with enthusiasm. Now is the time to turn the heat up a bit and notch up our performance to another level. In trading and investing in the market, we have identified the five different levels of performance shown in Figure 11–3. The level you are on determines your results in any endeavor.

Each of the levels shown is really a "trancelike state." We are aiming for a "trance-ending" experience. You end the trance you are in by *letting go,* giving up what you think is true about that level. Otherwise, there is no room to let the new level in.

If we sit and struggle for higher performance while living with our two-valued bipolar thinking/philosophy, we get into a vicious circle. Polar thinking leads to procrastination, which leads to further polar thinking, which leads to further procrastination. It becomes a seemingly never-ending merry-go-round ride.

How do you turn it up a notch? Simple. I am sure that you have had this experience while driving down the road in your automobile. You hear a favorite song on the radio. You automatically respond by reaching over and turning up the volume a bit. Your act is responsive, automatic, and pleasing. It is just that easy to do anything we wish to do: we simply respond with no indecision or continual deliberation. In trading, most of us spend endless time rehashing, taking one more look, calling the broker, and wasting other extraneous energy. When

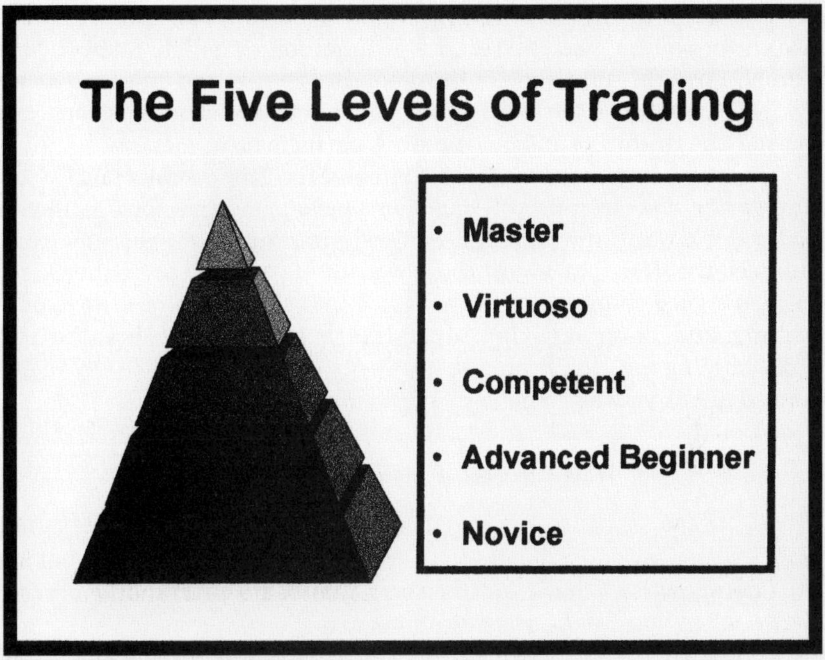

Figure 11–3 The five levels of trading.

we tutor people to become independent speculators, we use a stopwatch. Our goal is to analyze any chart, on any stock or commodity, and know exactly what to do, and when, in *10 seconds or less.* Anything beyond that is "mental masturbation." Letting go of this mental masturbation is what turning it up a notch is all about.

One of my teachers years ago was Fritz Perls, who at that time was living at Esalen Institute in Big Sur, California. He often observed that human beings were the only species on earth with the capacity to interfere with their own growth.

The steps to getting into the zone and beginning the flow are:

1. Anchor.
2. Visualize.
3. Turn up the volume.

There is still one vital step to take. This page is being written on a day when Eddie Johnson of the Houston Rockets won the fourth game in the NBA playoff round against the Utah Jazz. He sank a 27-foot three-pointer with six tenths of a second to go. He immediately jumped straight up, threw both hands in the air, and ran full speed down the court into the waiting arms of his teammates and coach. He enjoyed the reward of his outstanding performance.

You need to pat yourself on the back for good performance. You have gotten Joe Gremlin off your back so you could perform, and you surely don't want him coming back and jumping on you again. Grant yourself the right to enjoy the rewards of your labor. Otherwise, there is a good chance that you will fall into the trance of always performing and never enjoying. Just like breathing, you breathe out while playing and you inhale the rewards of good play. It is OK to get excited about yourself and your performance.

What I do best is share my enthusiasm.
—Bill Gates, Microsoft founder

There just isn't much in this world that beats outstanding performance when you can be your own best fan.

So far, this is all great. But can it be that way all the time? No! Life is never a flat plane. It's a series of hills and valleys, and once you get to the top of any hill the next move has to be down. No matter how high you are on the wave you are surfing, it will come down. So what do you do when you feel that you have "lost it"? How do you find the next surfable wave? The best prescription is to ask yourself a series of questions.

The first question is: EXACTLY WHAT IS GOING ON? Our body/mind has amazingly brilliant techniques for informing us of exactly what is going on, but most of the time we pay no attention. We respond to memories and words rather than the present situation.

Whenever you fall out of the zone, you will notice that you are stationing yourself either in the *future* or in the *past*. Staying in the *here and now* is the biggest gate to entering the zone, and it is impossible to stay in the zone without being in the here and now. Awareness puts Joe G, your critical adviser, into handcuffs and stores him somewhere in the back room.

When you ask yourself, "What am I noticing now?" the content of what you are noticing becomes irrelevant. "I am angry, I am frustrated with my losses" is much less important than the fact that you are taking back, from Joe Gremlin, control over your consciousness.

You are placing yourself back into PROCESS. It is important that the questions you ask yourself be very specific and the answers must be just as specific. "I feel lousy" is a thoughtless answer. What is it that you feel lousy about? Give the answers some color and specificity. Specifics force you into the present tense, into being right here now. This has the effect of sedating Joe G so that you can get back into the game of winning. You must be brutally honest with yourself and cut through senseless and general answers. Simply noticing brings you back into control.

"OK, so I have asked myself these questions and I am noticing that I certainly am not in the zone and I am not having fun. So what do I do? This whole situation is making me feel powerless." You are so right. The primary question is: HOW DO WE REGAIN THIS TEMPORARILY LOST POWER? We look at our options. Remember that the land mine that we want to avoid is the bipolar thinking of Joe Gremlin. Joe knows only two options, but we know our options are unlimited. The very fact that we are noticing the reality of the situation automatically makes a number of new and creative options come to mind. These options would never be noticed by Joe G. Remember that Joe enjoys being a passive victim, and we are looking for action alternatives.

At this stage, the number of options you notice is more important than the content of these options. Don't let Joe convince you that there are only two options: winning or losing. This is not PROCESS. Options always exist. I can continue to write now, or I can go to bed, or I can go for a swim or a walk. There are always options; as long as we are still breathing, we can conjure up at least a couple of options per breath. Joe G wants us to play the same old tunes over and over, and that's why we get stuck like a broken record. Joe likes that old tune and knows it well. We want to be more innovative and discover something new—and we will. Our attitude makes THE DIFFERENCE.

After the generation of new options, the next question is: WHAT CAN I LEARN FROM THESE OPTIONS? This learning becomes a door to more self-trust, and self-trust leads to the alpha brain wave frequency, which enhances our performance and puts us on the flow path again.

The PROCESS of flow–recover flow; flow–fall back–get back–flow; surf the wave–relax–look for another wave, will keep you in the zone and can totally change your profits in the markets and in your life.

What have we accomplished by noticing and generating options? We got Joe G out of the way. What we most need at this point is to regain trust, belief, and confidence in ourselves. One good way to do this is to simply ask: "What am I learning from my options?" The learning process is empowering. We like to use this formula in our tutorials:

$$E + R = W$$

Experience (E) plus Reflection (R) equals Wisdom. Experience is on the x axis, Reflection is on the y axis. By using both, we get a three-dimensional picture of the situation. Wisdom is what allows us to hang in there in adverse circumstances and end up winners rather than whiners.

We have now experienced the zone and flowed inside of it. We have surfed and fallen back, paid attention to what is happening in the present, and created various options. We have reflected on the options to increase our wisdom, and here we sit. What next?

The final question is: WHAT AM I GOING TO DO DIFFERENTLY? This question obviously eliminates some less productive options. Our self-belief is now returning, and we must choose what our next actions will be and how they will be different from the previous ones. It is halftime; the game is certainly not over, but we're behind. What do we do? First, we look at reality (we are losing because . . .). We could try some options, but we know from experience that some of them won't work, so we decide what our best alternatives are. At this point, our morale starts to build and we begin to think that if we do this and then do *this,* we could win at this game. The final question is to pick the best option and THEN DO IT.

Probably the most powerful advertising slogan ever coined is "Just do it!" When you hear those words, you immediately think of Nike. Those three words have created billions of dollars in profit for that company. At this stage, the slogan can be your most powerful ally also. Those words can put Joe G back in the cellar where he belongs.

"All this sounds really OK but I am still skeptical. This could be just another Sunday sermon. How will I really know if it is working or if I am doing this whole thing properly or not?"

That is a good question and it has a simple answer. You will notice that you really feel great! You will feel the power that comes from deep within, and will recognize that it is *your* power, not borrowed or stolen from someone else. You will realize that your life and your potential are like a deep well, and no matter how many times you go there, you know that the next time you try to draw water, it will be plentiful, tasty, fresh, and satisfying.

One final question: What do you think about all this? Are you going to read it and say, "Sounds good," and then place this book on your shelf? Perhaps you may even underline certain passages that strike you as being particularly relevant to your current situation. Well, that just won't do it. You have your Trance-Ending program here, but you must supply the practice. Otherwise, most if not all of what you have learned will be lost and forgotten.

You need to put these principles in practice TODAY. Then, about a month from now, go over your notes and any passages you may have highlighted in this material. Remember how much fun it is to surge–recover–surge again. That's real trading and real living. If you do this, you will find that the best spot on earth is flowing down the zone. MAY YOU LIVE IN THE ZONE AND FLOW FREELY FOREVER.

SUMMARY

As I am writing, I am sitting on my second-story balcony, looking out onto the ocean. I have just finished a relaxing session in my meditation room, which is next to the trading room. This morning, before the market opened, I worked out in my gym in the garage and then took an hour's sail watching a magnificent sunrise over the water. I came in, had a nice breakfast, and began my analysis of how I plan to trade today's markets, which took less than ten minutes. Then I faxed in my trades and am spending most of the day writing. When the market closes this afternoon, I will get my regular massage. Tonight I will take my wife out for a romantic dinner. In a few weeks we are flying our entire staff to Europe for a vacation. The markets made all of this possible.

Ours is one of the best imaginable home-based businesses. Our main occupation is trading our own funds. In addition, we periodically train other people to trade, thus furnishing them with the possibility of a similar lifestyle, a lifestyle that includes freedom from shaky job situations, difficult employers, long commutes, and limited income. There is also freedom from the employer–employee relationship, tough competition, government taxes and regulations, the daily struggle to motivate employees, and the difficulty of finding competent people in today's job market.

You have the freedom to live anywhere in the world. We chose the waterfront for sailing and water sports, but we are near an international hub airport, so we can fly nonstop to almost any place in the world.

You have the freedom to set your own hours and to trade as much or as little as you choose. You report to no one but yourself.

You have freedom from consumer problems, customer relations, complaints, theft, returns, unions, employee benefit plans, stockholders, and—best of all—from boring meetings.

You have total freedom from limits on your income. It takes no more work to buy 100 contracts than to buy one. (It does take a modicum of courage, but actually very little, if you really understand the markets.) You multiply your income by increasing the number of contracts that you trade, not by working harder.

Yes, it is quite true that most people lose money trading and investing. This is not due to the market but to their own individual belief systems. What has worked for them in other areas of life does not work for them in the markets. The two essential ingredients for success in trading are:

1. The right tools.
2. The right attitude (what we call *ATTITOOLS*).

And that is what this material and the Profitunity trading approach is all about. The RIGHT ATTITUDE using the RIGHT TOOLS. In this material, we have shown you precisely the right tools that will allow you to understand the market so that you can join that elite three to five percent of all traders who make money consistently trading the stock and commodity markets.

One of the greatest things about trading and investing is that you never know it all and you can learn every day. I trust that this sharing of our research and information will be of benefit to you. I invite you to join us in our continuing research into the best ways of enjoying this lifestyle and finding out who we really are.

May Everything That You Wish for Be the Least That You Get!

BIBLIOGRAPHY

Abraham, R. H., and Shaw, C. D. *Dynamics: The Geometry of Behavior. Part One—Periodic Behavior; Part Two—Global Behavior.* Santa Cruz, CA: Aerial Press, 1982.

Anderson, P. W., Arrow, K. J., and Pines, D. *The Economy as a Complex Evolving System.* Reading, MA: Addison-Wesley, 1988.

Babcock, B. *Trading Systems.* Homewood, IL: Dow Jones Irwin, 1989.

Bai-Lin, H. *Chaos.* Singapore: World Scientific, 1984.

Bak, P., and Chen, K. "Self-Organized Critically," *Scientific American,* Vol. 264 (January 1991): pp. 34, 35.

Balan, R. *Elliott Wave Principle Applied to the Foreign Exchange Markets.* London: BBS Publications, Ltd., 1989.

Barnsley, M. *Fractals Everywhere.* San Diego, CA: Academic Press, 1988.

Beltrami, E. *Mathematics for Dynamic Modeling.* Boston: Academic Press, 1987.

Beardon, A. F. *Iteration of Rational Functions: Complex Analytic Dynamical Systems,* Springer-Verlag, New York, 1991.

Bernstein, J. *Timing Signals in the Futures Market.* Chicago: Probus Publishing Co., 1991.

Bernstein, P. *Capital Ideas: The Improbable Origins of Modern Wall Street.* New York: Free Press, 1992.

Black, F., and Scholes, M. "The Pricing of Options and Corporate Liabilities," *Journal of Political Economy* (May/June 1973).

Briggs, J., and Peat, F. D. *Turbulent Mirror.* New York: Harper & Row, 1989.

Brock, W., Hsieh, D., and LeBaron, B. *Nonlinear Dynamics, Chaos, and Instability: Statistical Theory and Economic Evidence.* Cambridge, MA: MIT Press, 1991.

Callen, E., Sculley, M., and Shapero, D. "Imitation Theory—The Study of Cooperative Social Phenomena," in *Collective Phenomena and the Application of Physics to Other Fields of Science,* ed. N. Chigier and E. Stern. Fayetteville, NY: Brian Research Publication, 1975.

Callen, E., and Shapero, D. "A Theory of Social Imitation," *Physics Today* (July 1974).

Casadagli, M. "Chaos and Deterministic versus Stochastic Non-Linear Modeling," *Journal of the Royal Statistical Society* 54 (1991).

Chen, B., and Tong, H. "On Consistent Non-parametric Order Determination and Chaos," *Journal of the Royal Statistical Society* 54 (1992).

Chorafas, D. N. *Chaos Theory in the Financial Markets.* Chicago, IL: Probus Publishing Co., 1994.

Colby, R. W., and Meyers, T. A. *The Encyclopedia of Technical Market Indicators.* Homewood, IL: Business One Irwin, 1988.

Cootner, P., ed. *The Random Character of Stock Market Prices.* Cambridge, MA: MIT Press, 1964.

Dalton, J. F., Jones, E. T., and Dalton, R. B. *Mind over Markets.* Chicago: Probus Publishing Co., 1990.

Davies, P. *The Cosmic Blueprint: New Discoveries in the Nature's Creative Ability to Order the Universe.* New York: Cambridge University Press, 1987.

Davis, L. *Handbook of Genetic Algorithms.* New York: Van Nostrand Reinhold, 1991.

Day, R. H. "The Emergence of Chaos from Classical Economic Growth," *Quarterly Journal of Economics* 98 (1983).

Deboeck, G. J. *Trading on the Edge.* New York: John Wiley & Sons, 1994.

Degooijer, J. G. "Testing Non-Linearities in World Stock Market Prices," *Economics Letters* 31 (1989).

DeMark, T. R. *The New Science of Technical Analysis.* New York: John Wiley & Sons, 1994.

DeVaney, R. L. *An Introduction to Chaotic Dynamical Systems.* Menlo Park, CA: Addison-Wesley, 1989.

Douglas, M. *The Disciplined Trader: Developing Winning Attitudes.* New York: Institute of Finance, 1990.

Dreyfuss, H. L., and Dreyfuss, S. E. *Mind over Machine.* New York: Free Press, 1986.

Eckmann, J. P., and Rjuelle, D. *Review of Modern Physics* 57, 3 (1985).

Edmondson, A. C. *A Fuller Explanation.* New York: Springer-Verlag, 1986.

Edwards, R. D., and McGee, J. *Technical Analysis of Stock Trends,* rev. 5th ed. New York: John McGee, Inc.

Ewing, J. H. and Schober, G. *The Area of the Mandelbrot Set,* Numer. Math. 61 (1992).

Falconer, K. J. *The Geometry of Fractal Sets.* New York: Cambridge University Press, 1985.

Farmer, J. D. "Chaotic Attractors of an Infinite-Dimensional Dynamic System," *Physica* 4D (1982): 336–393.

Farmer, J. D., and Sidorowich, J. J. "Exploiting Chaos to Predict the Future and Reduce Noise," *Evolution, Learning and Cognition,* ed. Y. C. Lee. London: World Scientific Press, 1988.

Feder, J. *Fractals.* New York: Plenum Press, 1988.

Fischer, K. L. *The Wall Street Waltz.* Chicago: Contemporary Books, 1987.

Flandarin, P. "On the Spectrum of Fractional Brownian Motions," IEEE *Transactions on Information Theory* 35 (1989).

Fritz, R. *The Path of Least Resistance.* New York: Ballantine Books, 1989.

Frost, A. J., and Prechter, R. *Elliot Wave Principle.* Gainesville, GA: New Classics Library, 1978.

Gallacher, W. *Winner Takes All.* Chicago: Midway Publications, 1983.

Gallway, T. *The Inner Game of Tennis.* New York: Random, 1981.

Gardner, M. "White and Brown Music, Fractal Curves and 1/f Fluctuations," *Scientific American* 238 (1978).

Garfield, C. *Peak Performers.* New York: Avon Books, 1986.

Glass, L., and Mackey, M. C. *From Clocks to Chaos.* Princeton, NJ: Princeton University Press, 1988.

Gleick, J. *Chaos: The Making of a New Science.* New York: Viking Press, 1987.

Graham, B., and Dodd, D. L. *Security Analysis.* New York: McGraw-Hill, 1934.

Henon, M. "A Two-dimensional Mapping with a Strange Attractor," *Communications in Mathematical Physics* 50 (1976).

Hofstadter, D. R. "Mathematical Chaos and Strange Attractors," in *Metamagical Themas.* New York: Bantam Books, 1985.

Jensen, R. V., and Urban, R. "Chaotic Price Behavior in a Non-Linear Cobweb Model," *Economics Letters* 15 (1984).

Jung, C. G. *Cenenary Brochure.* Zurich: Curatorum of C. G. Jung Institute, 1975.

Kasko, B. *Neural Networks and Fuzzy Systems.* Englewood Cliffs, NJ: Prentice-Hall, 1992.

Kaufman, P. J. *The New Commodity Trading Systems and Methods.* New York: John Wiley & Sons, 1987.

Kelsey, D. "The Economics of Chaos and the Chaos of Economics," *Oxford Economic Papers* 40 (1988).

Kilpatrick, A. *Warren Buffett, The Good Guy of Wall Street.* New York: Donald I. Fine, Inc., 1992.

Kindelberger, C. P. *Manias, Panics and Crashes.* New York: Basic Books, 1978.

Korsan, R. J. "Fractals and Time Series Analysis." *Mathematics Journal* 3 (1993).

Koza, J. *Genetic Programing.* Cambridge, MA: MIT Press, 1993.

Laing, R. "Efficient Chaos Or, Things They Never Taught in Business School." *Barrons's,* July 29, 1991, p. 12.

Larrain, M. "Empirical Tests of Chaotic Behavior in a Nonlinear Interest Rate Model." *The Financial Analyst Journal* Vol. 47 (Sept./Oct. 1991): p. 78.

LeBaron, B. "Empirical Evidence for Nonlinearities and Chaos in Economic Time Series: A Summary of Recent Results," University of Wisconsin, Social Systems Research Institute, 9117, 1991.

Lebon, G. *The Crowd.* Delaware: Cherokee Publishing, 1982.

Lei, T. "Similarity Between the Mandelbrot Set and Julia Set," *Communications in Mathematical Physics* 134 (1990): pp. 587–617.

Lewin, R. *Complexity, Life at the Edge of Chaos.* New York: Macmillan, 1992.

Lorenz, H. *Nonlinear Dynamical Economics and Chaotic Motion.* Berlin: Springer-Verlag, 1989.

Mackay, C. *Extraordinary Popular Delusions and the Madness of Crowds.* New York: Crown, 1980.

Makridakis, S. S., Wheelwright, J. J., and McGee, B. E. *Forecasting: Methods and Applications.* New York: John Wiley & Sons, 1983.

Malkiel, B. *A Random Walk Down Wall Street,* 4th ed. New York: W. W. Norton, 1985.

Mandelbrot, B. "Forecasts of Future Prices, Unbiased Markets, and Martingale Models," *Journal of Business* 39 (1966).

Mandelbrot, B. *The Fractal Geometry of Nature.* New York: W. H. Freeman and Co., 1983.

Mandelbrot, B. "The Pareto-Levy Law and the Distribution of Income," *International Economic Review* 1 (1960).

Mandelbrot, B. "The Variation of Certain Speculative Prices," *Journal of Business* 36 (1963).

Mandelbrot, B. "The Variation of Some Other Speculative Prices," *Journal of Business* 39 (1966).

Mandelbrot, B. "When Can Price Be Arbitraged Efficiently? A Limit to the Validity of the Random Walk and Martingale Models," *Review of Economic Statistics* 53 (1971).

Miller, M. H. *Financial Innovations and Market Volatility.* Cambridge, England: Blackwell, 1991.

von Mises, Ludwig. *The Theory of Money and Credit.* Indianapolis: Liberty Classics, 1980.

Moon, F. C. *Chaotic and Fractal Dynamics.* New York: John Wiley & Sons, 1992.

Moon, F. C. *Chaotic Vibrations: An Introduction for Applied Scientists and Engineers.* New York: John Wiley & Sons, 1992.

Moon, F. C., and Li, G. X. "The Fractal Dimension of the Two-Well Potential Strange Attractor," *Physica* 17D (1985): pp. 99–108.

Murphy, J. J. *Technical Analysis of the Futures Markets, A Comprehensive Guide to Trading Methods and Applications.* New York: Institute of Finance, 1986.

Naisbitt, J. *Megatrends.* New York: Warner Books, 1982.

Naisbitt, J., and Aburndene, P. *Megetrends 2000.* New York: Avon Books, 1990.

Neil, H. *The Art of Contrary Thinking.* Caldwell, ID: Caxton Printers, 1980.

Pacelli, A. P. *The Speculator's Edge.* New York: John Wiley & Sons, 1989.

Palgrave, F. T. *The Golden Treasury of the Best Poems.* New York: New American Library, 1961.

Pardo, R. *Design, Testing and Optimization of Trading Systems.* New York: John Wiley & Sons, 1992.

Parker, T. S. and Chua, L. O. *Practical Numberical Algorithm for Chaotic Systems,* Springer Verlag, 1989.

Peters, E. *Chaos and Order in the Capital Markets: A New View of Cycles, Prices and Market Volatility.* New York: John Wiley & Sons, 1991.

Peters, E. "A Chaotic Attractor for the S&P 500," *Financial Analysis Journal* (March/April 1991).

Peters, E. *Fractal Market Analysis.* New York: John Wiley & Sons, 1994.

Peters, E. "Fractal Structures in the Capital Markets," *Financial Analyst Journal* (July-August, 1989).

Plummer, T. *Forecasting Financial Markets: Technical Analysis and the Dynamics of Price.* New York: John Wiley & Sons, 1991.

Plummer, T. *The Psychology of Technical Analysis.* Chicago, IL: Probus Publishing Co., 1993.

Priestly, M. B. *Nonlinear and Nonstationary Time Series Analysis.* New York: Academic Press, 1988.

Prigogine, I., and Nicolis, G. *Exploring Complexity.* New York: W. H. Freeman and Co., 1989.

Prigogine, I., and Stengers, I. *Order Out of Chaos.* New York: Bantam Books, 1984.

Rosser, J. B., Jr. *From Catastrophe to Chaos: A General Theory of Economic Discontinuities.* Boston: Kluwer Academic Publishers, 1991.

Ruelle, D. *Chaotic Evolution and Strange Attractors.* Cambridge, England: Cambridge University Press, 1991.

Scheinkman, J. A., and LeBaron, B. "Nonlinear Dynamics and Stock Returns," *Journal of Business* 62 (1989).

Schiller, R. J. *Market Volatility.* Cambridge, MA: MIT Press, 1990.

Schroeder, M. *Fractals, Chaos, Power Laws.* New York: W. H. Freeman, 1991.

Schwager, J. *A Complete Guide to the Futures Markets.* New York: John Wiley & Sons, 1984.

Schwager, J. D. *Market Wizards.* New York: New York Institute of Finance, 1989.

Shannon, C. E., and Weaver, W. *The Mathematical Theory of Communication.* Urbana: University of Illinois, 1963.

Shaw, R. *The Dripping Faucet as a Model Chaotic System.* Santa Cruz, CA: Aerial Press, 1984.

Shiller, R. J. *Market Volatility.* Cambridge, MA: MIT Press, 1989.

Smith, A. *Powers of the Mind.* New York: Random House, 1975.

Steidlmayer, P. J., and Koy, K. *Markets and Market Logic.* Chicago: Porcupine Press, 1986.

Stetson, H. T. *Sunspots and Their Effects.* New York: McGraw-Hill, 1937.
Stewart, I. *Does God Play Dice? The Mathematics of Chaos.* Cambridge, MA: Blackwell, 1989.
Thompson, J. M. T., and Stewart, H. B. *Nonlinear Dynamics and Chaos.* New York: John Wiley & Sons, 1986.
Thurlow, B. *Rediscovering the Wheel: Contrary Thinking & Investment Strategy.* Burlington, VT: Fraser Publishing Co., 1981.
Tobias, A. *The Only Investment Guide You'll Ever Need,* rev. ed. Toronto: Bantam Books, 1986.
Tong, H. *Nonlinear Time Series: A Dynamical Systems Approach.* New York: Oxford Science Publications, 1990.
Vaga, T. "The Coherent Market Hypothesis." *Financial Analysts Journal* (Nov/Dec 1990).
Vaga, T. *Profiting from Chaos.* New York: McGraw-Hill, 1994.
Waldrop, M. M. *Complexity, The Emerging Science at the Edge of Order and Chaos.* New York: Simon & Schuster, 1992.
Wallach, P. "Wavelet Theory." *Scientific American* (January 1991).
Weiner, N. *Collected Works,* Vol. 1, ed. P. Masani. Cambridge, MA: MIT Press, 1976.
Wiggins, S. *Introduction to Applied Nonlinear Dynamical Systems and Chaos.* New York: Springer-Verlag, 1990.
William, F. E. *Technical Analysis of Stocks, Options & Futures: Advanced Trading Systems and Techniques.* Chicago: Probus Publishing Co., 1988.
Williams, B. M. *Trading Chaos: Applying Expert Techniques to Maximize Your Profits.* New York: John Wiley & Sons, 1994.
Zeidenberg, M. *Neural Network Models in Artificial Intelligence.* New York: Ellis Horwood, 1990.
Zipf, G. K. *Human Behavior and the Principle of Least Effort.* Reading, MA: Addison-Wesley, 1949.
Zweig, M. *Winning on Wall Street.* New York: Warner Books, 1990.

ABOUT THE AUTHOR

Bill M. Williams is the president and founder of the Profitunity Trading Group and has been successfully trading since 1959. His main occupation is trading his own funds. He is also a consultant to foreign banks, producers, hedgers, and large traders worldwide.

His research over the past four decades has been on the cutting edge of applying advanced physics, mathematics, and psychological research to profitable trading. He has held workshops and seminars for over 25,000 traders and has privately trained over 700 people who are now full-time private and/or professional traders. He has published numerous articles, has been featured on the front page of several of this country's largest newspapers, and has appeared regularly on national TV.

He is the original developer of the Market Facilitation Index (MFI), which is now standard on many analytical computer programs worldwide, and is the discoverer of the fractal of the Elliott Wave. He is the first trader to develop a practical and profitable use of the new Science of Chaos and is well-known for his original 10-second complete analysis of any chart on any time frame.

His most recent innovation is a stand-alone computer program that includes all the material, indicators, and signals contained in this book. You may download a free, fully functioning version of this software from his Web site at:

www.profitunity.com

The software can be a great tool in further understanding the material in the book. He has also produced a home study course, including manuals, study guides, audio and video tapes, and computer learning disks, to help traders and investors at any level maximize their profits.

He has received worldwide acclaim for his ability to turn losing and inconsistent traders into consistently profitable professionals. He still gives a limited number of private tutorials.

For more information, contact:

PROFITUNITY TRADING GROUP

Bill M. Williams, PhD
2300 Pilgrim Estates Drive
Texas City, Texas 77590–3750 U.S.A.
Tel. (409) 945-8880 Fax (409) 945-8887
E-mail: *ptg*@phoenix.net WebSite: *www.profitunity.com*

INDEX